Clinical Interventions with Gang Adolescents and Their Families

Clinical Interventions with Gang Adolescents and Their Families

Curtis W. Branch

WestviewPress

A Division of HarperCollins*Publishers*

Published in 1997 in the United States of America by Westview Press, 5500 Central Avenue, Boulder, Colorado 80301-2877, and in the United Kingdom by Westview Press, 12 Hid's Copse Road, Cumnor Hill, Oxford OX2 9JJ

Library of Congress Cataloging-in-Publication Data
Branch, Curtis W.
   Clinical interventions with gang adolescents and their families /
Curtis W. Branch.
      p.   cm.
   Includes bibliographical references and index.
   ISBN 0-8133-2903-5 (hc).—ISBN 0-8133-2904-3 (pbk.)
   1. Gang members—Mental health.   2. Juvenile delinquency—
Prevention.   3. Gang members—Mental health services.   4. Gang
members—Psychology.   5. Gang members—Rehabilitation.   6. Gang
members—Family relationships.   I. Title.
RJ506.J88B73   1997
616.89′00835—dc21   96-53461
                                                                                              CIP

The paper used in this publication meets the requirements of the American National Standard for Permanence of Paper for Printed Library Materials Z39.48-1984.

10   9   8   7   6   5   4   3   2   1

Contents

Part 1
Theory and Foundations

Part 2
Clinical Assessment

Part 3
Interventions

Tables, Figures, and Boxes

Tables

Figures

Boxes

Preface

There I sat in the quiet of my Denver private practice office, bathed in the warm sunshine of an autumn afternoon, surrounded by artifacts and gifts that had been given to me over the years, and becoming more and more consumed by the self-doubts and unspoken fears about what the afternoon would bring. I was scheduled to see my first *gangstas* as clients that day, a pair of siblings who were scheduled to be released from the local juvenile hall the following week. The referral had been arranged by a probation worker whom I had taught at the local college. I had a high level of respect for the probation officer, and I suppose he thought of me with high regard. After all, he had selected me to see these two gang adolescents over all of the other adolescent and child therapists in the neighborhood. Just as I was basking in my own grandiosity, reality struck me. Wham! The *gangstas* would be here that afternoon. Did I really know what to do with them? What would I do if they were really oppositional and threatened to shoot me? What if they did not like me and yelled racial epithets at me? I had a lot to think about and little time in which to do it.

The two appointments were scheduled for four and five o'clock, one hour per *gangsta*. That should be enough time for a clinical screening, I thought. By one o'clock everything started to unravel. The courier who was supposed to deliver a complete referral package on the clients at noon had not arrived. The probation officer who referred the cases was not in his office. What should I do? Worry and panic? I had no appointments for the afternoon but the two *gangstas*. Two o'clock came and went. Three o'clock came and went. Still, the courier did not arrive. Then it was four o'clock. Time for the first appointment. My worry quotient increased exponentially.

What would he be like? Would he be a big, burly football type who would delight in trying to intimidate me? What would I say to him? The probation officer had warned me that "Junior" was a tough, streetwise kid. I waited. No Junior. Finally, after twenty-five minutes, I decided he would not show up. Perhaps he had impulsively given in to some irrational urge on his way to the office without an escort. I worried even more, but still no client showed. In a twisted way I was privately relieved that he was a no-show. What an awful thing to think, but it was true. Time continued to pass, until it was 4:50.

My second appointment was with Junior's sibling, Gene, who had not been described to me in any detailed way. He was due at five o'clock, also traveling to my office without the benefit of an escort. It now became curious and frightening to me that the probation officer had only described Gene as being fifteen years old and a high school dropout. A full description of Gene's history was to be included in the referral report that never arrived.

Ring! Ring! The office intercom buzzed and the secretary announced, "Dr. B., your five o'clock appointment is here. I'm leaving now. Be sure you turn off all of the lights when you leave. Good night." Gene was downstairs. Had he frightened the secretary into leaving promptly at five? What would he be like? What would I say to him? Oh well, it was too late to worry about that now.

As I slowly descended the stairs, my stomach seemed to sink into an abyss of uncertainty and pain. How did I get into doing this? I wondered. Too late for that now! My pace slowed and my gait wavered. Each step drew me closer to dealing with a real gang banger. I did not like the way all of this made me feel. But it was too late to turn back. I tried hard to open my mind, but as I turned the corner and entered the waiting room I spontaneously closed my eyes. When I recovered from this brief moment of distancing myself, reality struck. Wham! My inner voice yelled, *It is a girl. . . . Gene is really Jean. . . . He is really a she!* How did I get confused about this? My startle reaction must have been so great that it shook the peaks of Aspen. Obviously, Jean could see that I was surprised. She simply smiled, an embarrassing sort of smile that accepted my apology for all of the unfounded assumptions I had made, even though I never overtly voiced any of them. They must have shone brighter than the midday sun.

This was the unceremonious beginning of my clinical work with gang-affiliated youth. I had to work hard with myself and with many of my assumptions, which turned out to be unfounded. Somehow, I managed. Jean and I had a significant and enjoyable therapist-client relationship for two years. In one of our last sessions, she reflected on how "strange and goofy" I acted during our first meeting. She undoubtedly was recollecting the same events that I have just reported.

Several things about my meeting Jean illustrate the state of my own ignorance and reliance on unsubstantiated assumptions. First, I agreed to see a client without having a detailed discussion with the referring party. I barely knew Jean's name. The probation officer insists that he told me beforehand that Jean was the younger sister of Junior. He may have, but I did not hear it. In retrospect, I think my assumption was that the most active and disruptive gang members were necessarily males. In addition, the poor planning of getting a referral report only hours before seeing a client is simply unacceptable behavior in a therapist. In this case, the courier went to the wrong ad-

dress with a document that was of dire importance and the report was returned to the sender. Finally, the prereferral conversations that I had with
the probation officer accented my tendency to focus on the "really pathological" client to the exclusion of the apparently less disturbed sibling. I learned
a lot that day. Many of the lessons of that experience have stayed with me
over the subsequent ten years in which I have seen many gang adolescents
and their families as clients.

Many of the unconfirmed assumptions that I made in the early days of my
work grew out of folk wisdom about gang members and their families. The
images of out-of-control inner-city ethnic minority youngsters as the most
likely candidates for gang membership are ideas that have now been purged
from my mental template of who joins gangs. It is true that more adolescents of color are arrested for gang-related offenses, but this may be a function of who gets targeted for arrest rather than an absolute statement about
gang membership.

My work with gang adolescents and their families has taught me a lot
about the quest for interpersonal relatedness and the extent to which some
people will go to accomplish that objective. In the early days of the Family
Intervention Project (FIP), I remember working with a couple of mothers
who had completed the program. They returned to subsequent sessions as
"junior staff" to try to be of assistance to other families. Their desire and attempts to help were greatly appreciated, but it became very clear that they
were returning also to get some of their needs met. A similar pattern of trying to be relational was at the core of one client's behavior. Wilbert would
call my office during hours he knew I was on duty at the local psychiatric
hospital. Each time he did so, he attempted to engage the secretary in a protracted conversation about small and incidental matters such as the weather
or what time the local football team was playing on Sunday. The secretary
reported that he never was "grossly inappropriate," just always very needy.
Yet another example of attempting to be relational is the young man who
had a special interest in the type of clothing I wore. He would often start out
by commenting on the "threads" I was wearing. Luke frequently noted that
my socks didn't match my suit or necktie.

Luke   Yo doc', what about them shoes. We gotta get you some better
shoes.
Me   You don't like my shoes?
Luke   They look like something a gramps would wear. Not a doctor.

*   *   *

Luke   Hey man, that's a fly necktie.
Me   I'm glad you like it.

Luke   It looks like you been listening to me. When you gonna buy another
ride [car]? I saw a bad ride down on Broadway . . . a 240Z. That's what
you need. . . . Check it out.

In addition to serving the purpose of trying to facilitate relatedness, these
types of conversations also prevented Luke from working on his "issues."
Occasionally, I would point those dynamics out to him. Invariably, his response was to belittle my observation or to laugh.

Individual clients have taught me a lot about the human spirit and the desire to be wanted and to love, but families of gang adolescents have been an
even more powerful teacher. I have been struck by how willing families have
been to participate in the FIP. I interpret such behavior as an eagerness to
reestablish their family unit as a place where all its members can be positively
rewarded. It has been very moving for me to observe hard-core gang members struggle with the impact of the passionate plea of a grandmother. One
of the most memorable experiences for me was when a hard-core gang
member and his mother got into a shouting match across the room. The
gangsta accused his mother of having chased the father from their home.
The mother denied that she had behaved in such a manner. They both were
crying, obviously moved to this point in part by the therapeutic impact of
watching other families work and come closer together, for the day if not for
a more sustained period of time. All of these experiences run counter to the
folk images of gang adolescents. The primary task facing the clinician working with gang-affiliated families, I think, is to help the family find enough
strength to start healing its wounds while it helps its member who is "in
trouble." Much of this can be accomplished by using the resources that are
already present but have become tarnished because the family has come to
see the world through someone else's eyes.

The author gratefully acknowledges the contributions of Dr. John
Campbell, Dr. James Tucker, Ms. Yolanda Gotier, Dr. Kathy Wade-
Campbell, Ms. Marian Lawrence, and Mr. Karim Abdullah in developing the
Family Intervention Project.

Curtis W. Branch

Clinical Interventions with Gang Adolescents and Their Families

Introduction

Research on adolescent gangs originates with the seminal work of Thrasher (1927), who systematically studied 1,303 gangs in Chicago over a number of years. Thrasher identifies gang members as juvenile delinquents, an association subsequently repeated so strongly and so frequently that delinquency now is implicitly incorporated in the definition of gangs. Indeed, the terms *gang* and *delinquency* are often used interchangeably. A recent, more balanced definition of gangs stresses the organization and functions of such units rather than their informal street origins:

> A gang is an organized social system that is both quasi-private (not fully open to the public) and quasi-secretive (much of the information concerning its business remains confined within the group) and one whose size and goals have necessitated that social interaction be governed by a leadership structure that has defined roles; where the authority associated with these roles has been legitimized to the extent that social codes are operational to regulate the behavior of both the leadership and rank and file; that plans and provides not only for the social and economic services of its members, but also for its own maintenance as an organization; that pursues such goals irrespective of whether the action is legal or not; and lacks a bureaucracy (i.e. an administrative staff that is hierarchically organized and separate from leadership). (Jankowski, 1991, p. 29)

Note that Jankowski includes antisocial and delinquent behavior. Departing from earlier definitions, however, he implies that an element of volition and decision making draws individual recruits to the gang. This suggests that a variety of economic, personal, and social reasons explain why and how youngsters make the decision to join a gang, the often-repeated stereotype of adolescent gangs populated exclusively with Thrasher's (1927) urban juvenile delinquents—frequently presumed to be adolescents of color—must be recognized as too simplistic. Recent evidence also suggests that adolescent gangs are becoming a more pronounced phenomenon in contemporary U.S. society. Their proliferation in suburban and middle-class communities reveals that adolescent gangs are not specific to any class, race, or ethnic group. (Other examples of nonstereotypical adolescent gangs, although not usually considered under the rubric of gangs, are politicized white youth groups such as skinheads and the Aryan Nation.)

This expansion of gangs throughout U.S. culture makes them a pervasive issue. Yet, gang proliferation seems to defy explanation. Perhaps this is due to U.S. society's limited understanding of the functions, organization, and dynamics of gangs. Historically, research on gangs was focused almost exclusively on ethnographic approaches, outlining characteristics of gang members but neglecting the dynamics of gangs and the inner psychological life of gang members. A disturbing trend in the past five years has been the automatic association of gangs with crime and violence and a new stereotype identifying gang members as not merely juvenile delinquents, but violent criminals. Because the conjunction of gangs, crime, and violence is so clearly articulated in the literature, the combination has begun to be accepted as given.

Although some gang members do engage in violent acts, a distinction must be made between gang violence and violence committed by gang members acting on their own behest. Acts of violence that are planned and executed by gangs as a unit include drive-by shootings, looting neighborhood stores, and fighting with rival gangs. Implicit in this type of activity is a high level of organization and a methodical approach to the commitment of the acts, two characteristics of gangs. At the other end of the continuum are violent behaviors committed by individual gang members on their own. According to Jankoswki (1991), this distinction is important for a number of reasons:

1. It helps differentiate acts of violence that are the result of individual decisions from those that come about as the result of group think.
2. It has implications for statistical reporting of violence and crimes committed by gangs.
3. It potentially shows that gang members have a life, replete with individualized conflicts, separate and apart from membership in the gang.
4. It also helps quantify and contextualize violence among gang members.

In addition, the distinction helps in identifying those gang members likely to behave violently without benefit of the gang presence as a stage.

Despite the spread of adolescent gangs and increasing public concerns about this pattern, very little attention has been given to the topic of providing mental health services to gang members. This book is intended to fill part of that void. It is an introductory text for mental health clinicians providing services to gang members and their families. To acquaint clinicians with the general issues of gang membership and how they may impact adolescents' mental health, I also address issues associated with providing diagnostic and psychotherapeutic services to gang members and their families.

Gang members pose special challenges for clinicians who work with them. Standard clinical assessments and interventions have not been shown to be effective, or appropriate, for use with individual gang members, and misconceptions about group dynamics have resulted in ineffective assessments and interventions at the level of the group. Additionally, psychological theories that offer potential for understanding the thinking and behavior of gang members have not been utilized in a systematic manner, and developmental theories that hold great utility for better understanding some of the "how" and "why" questions associated with gang membership have been overlooked.

Much of the challenge that gang members present to clinicians has to do with a lack of exposure to the issues on the part of clinicians. Social attributions to the term "gang" are overwhelmingly negative, making it difficult for outsiders to see gang members as anything other than out-of-control sociopaths. Indeed, as already noted, in many places gangs are viewed as being synonymous with violence and crime. Clinicians who work with gang members must look beyond this oversimplification to unravel the relationships between many factors in these clients' lives. The task can be difficult. The assumption that gangs, violence, and crime coexist in a linear and predictable relationship can interfere with clinicians being able to fully understand gang members. Thinking that crime, violence, and gangs are necessarily correlated may also contaminate referrals, leaving a clinician to undo the erroneous assumptions of the referring party. The dearth of literature on providing mental health services to gang members makes it difficult for clinicians to become acquainted with the relevant issues as they would with other types of cases. Although a sizable literature exists on conduct disorders and antisocial personality types, these two diagnostic categories do not fully capture the complexity of gang membership. Nor does this material offer much help to conceptualize the dynamics of joining a gang, the struggles about continuing in a gang, or the conflicts associated with divided loyalties (i.e., family of origin versus the gang) that many new gang members experience. Likewise, the absence of a clinical literature dealing with the issues of clinicians' attitudes regarding working with potentially violent adolescents outside of the boundaries of a juvenile detention hall or psychiatric hospital is a challenge for clinicians called on to provide services to gang members.

Current assessment and intervention strategies have not been shown to be effective for working with gang-affiliated adolescents, although a small but growing literature addresses violent adolescents. Goldstein and Huff's (1993) *Gang Intervention Handbook* is an example of that literature. The authors provide a variety of approaches for working with adjudicated violent adolescents. The descriptions of the approaches are crisp and impressive but generally do not answer the question of whether the approaches work with gang members. Implicit in most of the chapters of the book is the idea that the violence component of gang membership presents the greatest need for intervention. There is little discussion of other dimensions of gang life (i.e., affective disruptions, impaired decision making, a lack of a sense of autonomy, emotional blunting, and so on).

Another issue that remains unsettled is what is "really" the purpose of clinical interventions with gang adolescents? To convince them to leave the gang? To reshape them into prosocial beings? To provide them with new internal barometers (i.e., insight) so they can consider altering their thinking and behavior? The answer(s) vary according to who is doing the treatment and under what circumstances. What seems consistent across all settings is the desire for gang adolescents to change so they become a less disruptive and volatile factor in communities. The current mental health approaches have not sufficed to accomplish that goal at the level of individual gang members. Due to ineffective assessment and intervention strategies, a similar ineffectiveness also exists at the level of group (i.e., gangs) change.

Misconceptions about gangs and their dynamics have been responsible for the failure to develop effective assessment and intervention strategies. Much of the incomplete information on gangs seems to be related to media portrayals—the lack of understanding of ethnic and cultural components of some gangs is a prime example. In some neighborhoods, gangs have existed as a part of the social fiber of the community for generations, with a coexistence of gang and nongang factions. A lack of knowledge of the historical precedence for gangs in such neighborhoods causes them to be interpreted as overwhelmingly negative factors that must be destroyed. Yet, these gangs may serve important social functions for the community or they may become the objects of projection, a convenient group for the community to loathe. Interventions based on incomplete or erroneous information usually advocate suppression, as opposed to other strategies that might capitalize on the presence of gangs as an approach to community organization. Community-oriented clinicians are rarely called on to assess the psychological importance of gangs to neighborhoods or the perceived social value of the gangs.

Another way of thinking about gangs and what they contribute—positive and negative—is through developmental theory as articulated in psychology and psychiatry. This approach is more than merely measuring an adolescent against social and emotional developmental growth charts, but includes subjecting multiple contexts (i.e., home and family, school, peer group, and gang) to formal appraisal. Thus, a clinician would gather information from all of these sources to make an evaluation about the level of evolution of the system and how it relates to the particular gang member. For example, it would be vital to know where a family unit is in its own developmental process before deciding that it is or is not capable of providing an adolescent with what he or she needs.

Most of the research on gangs and their members' reactions to the activities of the gang are ethnographic in nature, void of replicability and subject to rather limited interpretations. In most accounts of gang members retelling their adventures in the areas of individual violence and gang-oriented clashes with others, the gang members are depicted as cold, callous, and calculating individuals who are not overtly expressive of any emotions, even in the face of losing friends in turf battles. These recapitulations almost always take place in the context of the gang, thereby creating an artificial stage on which the gang members are expected to express their "feelings." What usually gets expressed is a stoic detachment in which the gang member minimizes any sense of emotional attachment to fallen comrades, even those who are also family members. In the clinical tradition, such detachment would be explored in great detail and undoubtedly be seen as a mask for a deeper and more complex internal state.

A clinically oriented explanation for the lack of emotional expressivity in gang members in the face of violence is the idea that they have become traumatized from repeated exposure to violent acts. The traumatization causes them to defend against expressing feelings. In some cases, it has been suggested, they have no reaction that can be articulated and measured in terms meaningful to others. Still another explanation of their limited responses is that many gang members are very reactive to acts of violence but do not show it overtly. Instead, they internalize their feelings and seek other venues to displace and project them. All of this is clinical inference based on standard clinical wisdom. To date, there is virtually no psychological research testing these or related hypotheses about the inner psychological life of gang members or their responses to violence. The unchallenged assumption remains that gang members have a history of exposure to intensive violence significantly different from that of the general population of youngsters, an assumption that may or may not be true. The developmental course of individual gang members prior to affiliating with the gang undoubtedly holds many answers for understanding the inner psychological lives of these youngsters and should be explored before any generalizations regarding gang members are made.

To better understand the antecedents leading to the here-and-now functioning of several gang-affiliated youngsters and to provide them with effective clinical services, a psychoeducational model, the Family Intervention Project (FIP), was developed. As the youngsters had not always been gang members, the FIP examines pregang socialization to seek clues for an individual's decision to join a gang and perhaps even an explanation of the adolescent's behavior within the gang culture. Whatever early socialization the youngster received is assumed to be the foundation on which gang acceptance and behavior is superimposed. Thus, the emphasis in the program is equally on gang-affiliated youths and their families of origin.

The FIP has become a combined educational and therapeutic activity to help families effectively deal with teenagers who currently are at risk for or participating in antisocial behavior. At the core of the program is a belief that since families are the original agents of socialization, they are the most logical agents to exert an impact on wayward children and adolescents. This program also presupposes that the psychological energies inherent in families can be harnessed to aid a family in improving its quality of functioning. Sadly, many gang-affiliated youths do not have any members of their family of origin available to them, but the FIP model can be adapted to accommodate these youths without sacrificing the intensity of the experience.

In this book, I present the FIP as a prototype of an intervention designed to assess the strengths and weaknesses of families that have produced a gang-affiliated youngster. The book is divided into three sections. Part 1 is concerned with historical and theoretical foundations to assist in providing a clear conceptualization of gangs. In Chapter 1, I review the history of gangs and introduce psychological constructs that appear to have some utility for understanding the developmental dynamics of gang membership. Traditional psychological concepts such as moral development, need for affiliation, and intimacy are discussed as relevant topics for understanding the social and emotional development of gang members. In the second chapter, I explore the developmental aspects of gang membership. The part ends with Chapter 3, a discussion of the roles of race and ethnicity in the lives of gang members and gangs. I use a developmental focus for discussing how gang members evolve as racial and ethnic beings. Part 2 is devoted to clinical assessments of gang members and their families. Chapter 4 is on affective assessments. In Chapter 5, I review approaches for conducting behavioral assessments. Conduct disorder as a diagnostic category is presented and reviewed for its appropriateness as a descriptor of gang members. Chapter 6 is devoted to clinical assessment of cognitive processes as they occur among gang members and their family members. I offer examples of cognitive processing errors and how they lead to faulty conclusions and cycles of miscommunication. Chapter 7 covers family asssessment procedures, utilizing the approaches developed in Chapters 4 to 6. Chapter 8 is on developmental assessment procedures. Part 3 is concerned with conducting clinical interventions with gang adolescents and their families. In Chapter 9, I offer practical suggestions to consider when planning clinical interventions for gang adolescents and their family members. I present the FIP in Chapter 10 as a protypical structured approach to assessing gang-affiliated families, and I discuss the rationale and exercises included in the eight-hour intensive multiple-family therapy exercises. In the last chapter, I review research concerning the efficacy of the FIP and other clinical intervention and assessment models. Appendices contain clinical case material and examples of recommended psychological instruments discussed in the text.

Part 1
Theory and Foundations

1

Since the Days of Knights: Historical and Psychological Overview of Gangs

Delinquent gangs have been documented in European societies since the Middle Ages as serving various functions depending on their membership and the sociopolitical climate in which they existed. Recent scholarly work highlights the functions and demographics of gangs prior to the nineteenth century (Covey, Menard, & Franzese, 1992). One of the most exciting findings concerns the elements in operational definitions of gangs that seem to be constant across historical eras (i.e., Europe in the Middle Ages and in the sixteenth and seventeenth centuries; colonial America) and places (i.e., Australia, England, Germany, Asia).

Gangs almost always are collections of individuals whose behavior in the group places them outside the prevailing mores of their society. But some gangs have served socially condoned functions or even carried out desired social activities avoided by ostensibly more upstanding members of communities. According to Covey, Menard, and Franzese (1992), youth groups in medieval France, Germany, and Switzerland often

> viewed their role as being the guardians of social morality; they performed social control functions and had the moral support of the community. . . . One practice of these groups was the charivari. Charivaris were moblike demonstrations usually directed toward deaths, scolds, cuckolds, and upcoming marriages between mismatched couples. The principal motive of charivaris was to disrupt the community and harass the victims until they paid a bribe to quiet the commotion. (p. 91)

According to Shorter (1977) charivaris consist of religious, political, and economic protests. This relationship between gang members and their parent community is described by Jankowski (1991) as being a *social contract* between the gang and community. He suggests that it is precisely these

9

kinds of arrangements that allow gangs and communities to coexist—as long as each party stays in its place. When either side violates the implicit boundaries of the relationship (i.e., gang members harass a politician's family; police arrest cooperative informants), chaos ensues and usually the gang becomes agitated and unruly.

There is also much evidence of juvenile gangs during the seventeenth and eighteenth centuries in England (Capp, 1977; Fyvel, 1963; Whitfield, 1982) and colonial America (Fox, 1985; Sanders, 1970), and writers who have focused on the history of delinquent gangs agree that they flourished in great numbers in the nineteenth century. Jankowski (1991) provides an interesting account of the proliferation of gangs, some juvenile and some not, on the U.S. frontier during the nineteenth century. He draws parallels between the relationship between *gangstas,* or gang members, and researchers now and then: "Interestingly, a problem researchers face today also presented itself to the researchers of the nineteenth century outlaws—namely, accessibility to (and the cooperation of) the outlaws themselves. Outlaws, after all, had little reason to cooperate with the researcher" (p. 2). Despite the problem of access, researchers have noted enough of the activities of nineteenth-century gangs to develop a historical literature on which modern researchers can draw.

Asbury (1927) documents the proliferation of gangs in New York and Chicago. He traces their appearance back to the early 1800s. Thrasher (1927) investigates the structure and lives of gangs in Chicago in work that to this day is foundational for much theoretical thinking about gangs and juvenile delinquency. Both researchers conclude that gangs are often a vehicle by which socially marginalized individuals participate in the life of the community, reaping economic benefits and causing others to note their presence in the process. Some writers, capitalizing on this notion, suggest that early in the twentieth century juvenile gangs became a way for recently immigrated youth to gain economic and political careers. Describing some of the gangs that originated in New York City (i.e., Nineteenth Street Gang, Short Boys) Covey, Menard, and Franzese (1992) note, "These gangs were often affiliated with saloons and political parties. The gangs would drive the competition from the neighborhood and help ensure that elections had the 'correct' outcome by using strong-arm tactics. In return, gangs either were paid or were guaranteed protection from public officials, including police. These juvenile gangs were often led by adults" (p. 93).

Because these juvenile gangs were ethnically homogeneous, a pattern that continues to this day, some researchers (Covey, Menard, & Franzese, 1992; Incardi, 1978); conclude that the concentration of recently immigrated Italians, Jews, and Irish in New York City promoted the rise of ethnic juvenile gangs, a sentiment also noted in Jankowski (1991).

These interesting historical observations reinforce the idea that juvenile gangs have been around for centuries. They do not, however, provide much insight into gangs in the United States since 1945. Covey, Menard, and Franzese (1992) provide a good chronology of events associated with the rise and stabilization of juvenile gangs in U.S. society since World War II. Several points they and other scholars make about the history of gangs in post–World War II United States merit reiteration and amplification.

Gangs have existed in a variety of ethnic communities with varying degrees of intensity at different points in history. The research of Thrasher (1927) is generally regarded as the core of behavioral science understanding of gangs and related phenomena. Thrasher asserts that gangs are composed of marginalized boys who are poor, very likely to be residents of a slum, and transient. Until very recently, these observations have been considered the canon and have gone unchallenged. In expanding on Thrasher's findings, some contemporary theorists now include girls in gangs, accept the idea that gangs are fairly permanent fixtures in some communities, and note that gang participation is not limited to marginalized individuals. Indeed, some gang members are star athletes in high schools and even leaders in organized mainstream political activities. In the next section, I look briefly at the modern development of gangs in the United States and explore how their members can be characterized psychologically.

From Ghetto Life to Political Activism: 1920s–1990s

Covey, Menard, and Franzese (1992) suggest that during the 1920s and 1930s juvenile gangs were populated mostly with children of recent immigrants. They also note that ethnicity came to be a defining feature of gangs, a pattern that continues to this day. Examples of ethnic gangs include Taylor's (1990) documentation of the Sugar House Gang, formed to protect Jewish merchants in Detroit, and the Mexican immigrants in southern California who gave rise to barrios. The aggregation of Mexican Americans in barrios also came to have a perceived protective function, making them safe from predators from the larger community.

Despite gangs being assumed to be vehicles for overcoming economic poverty, there is very little documentation of gang life during the Great Depression. In U.S. history, World War II and the postwar involvements overshadow all other events of the 1940s. Gangs were a reality during this period, but there is very little scholarly writing about them. Two examples in the gang literature of the 1940s are the Zoot Suiters in Latino communities and the resurgence of gangs in New York City. Vigil (1990) shows a connection between the Zoot Suit riots of the 1940s and a solidification of gangs in Latino communities of southern California. Implicit in his argument is the idea that the more political and philosophical pressure placed on young Latino males, the more resistive and creative they became: They not only resisted efforts to make them comply in manner of dress, but they also found acceptance in their communities. Thus, they were inoculated against a hostile larger environment, much as the barrio had protected individuals in the 1920s. But in being embraced by the barrio in which they lived, the gang members also created cognitive dissonance for other residents. Much of the behavior of the gang was not condoned by community residents, but the gang itself as a collective entity was accepted as a reality, perhaps with a sort of ambivalence. Horowitz (1990) reports a continuation of these mixed feelings in modern-day barrios.

New York City gangs made a resurgence, in the literature if not in reality, during the 1940s. Bernard (1949), Dumpson (1949), and Robison, Cohen, & Sachs (1946) write about Harlem gangs. They note in different ways that these gangs were composed of a single ethnic group and frequently predisposed to behaving violently toward nonmembers. Only a small portion of the members, however, were involved in delinquency (Robison, Cohen, & Sachs, 1946). Unique manners of dress distinguished the gangs from each other. Writers in the 1940s began to note that youth gangs in New York City were often tied to adult organizations, much as in the 1920s. Other social problems thought to be facilitative of gangs are also noted by researchers in the 1940s.

Wattenberg and Balistrieri (1950) introduce a theoretical dissonance into the theories current by the 1950s. They suggest that gang members tend to come from homes that are poorly supervised but conclude that broken homes alone did not lead to gang involvement. Many of the most popular images of gangs that have found a place in history are products of the 1950s (Covey, Menard, & Franzese, 1992), a period in U.S. history that can be characterized as a transition between the postwar era and the civil rights era. Some describe this period as being a calm before the storm. Perhaps the most noteworthy activities concerning gangs during this decade involve the migration of several East Coast gangs to the Midwest. Hagedorn and Macon (1988) describe it as the period of expansion of the Blackstone Rangers and the Latin Kings. One other significant chain of events noted by scholars in this area is the infiltration of gang culture into the penal system.

The exact nature of gang activity during the 1960s is the object of some debate. Somewhere in the debate, gangs come to be a synonym for juvenile delinquency. The result of that association is that the general public cannot perceive gangs as anything other than disruptive units devoted exclusively to delinquency. Such is not the case, however, with gangs whose members came to see themselves as social and political activists, performing political activities (i.e., voter registration drives, economic boycotts of merchants accused of being unfair to customers) even while they occasionally engaged in antisocial activities. Images of gangs as lawless citizens, created to a large extent by the popular media, have become so entrenched that other facets of gangs' programs never reach the public's attention.

Enhanced feelings of ethnic and racial pride in the Black community in United States may have inadvertently spawned ganglike organizations. Frequently, such groups start as self-help groups, but they occasionally disintegrate into racially driven groups, antagonistic toward anyone other than their own members, reminiscent of the Harlem gangs of the 1940s. Vigil (1990) describes a related pattern in the barrios of southern California. He notes that the Vietnam War drew many positive role models away from the barrio. The result was an indirect reinforcement of the development of barrio gangs.

In summarizing the 1960s and its impact on gang culture, Covey, Menard, and Franzese (1992) note the connection between gangs and social and political activism:

> In the 1960s, some politicians and social activists thought that gang energies and resources could be channeled into activism and constructive social change. Gangs such as the "Vice Lords," the "Black Panthers," the "Young Lords," and the "Black Liberation Army," provided politically conscious alternatives to traditional gang activity. The degree of these gangs' commitment to civil rights objectives varied, and the gangs ranged from tacit support to active militancy in the degree to which they supported the goals of the civil rights movement. (p. 101)

Since 1970, adolescent gangs have been the object of much attention in both the scholarly literature and the popular media. The nature of this attention has varied, ranging from denouncing disruption of communities to glamorizing the lives of *gangstas* to targeting gang-initiated youth violence as an issue of epidemic proportions in U.S. society, as illustrated in the determination of the Centers for Disease Control that violence is a public health threat. Among the advancements in the area of theory building and attempts to understand adolescent gangs is Campbell's (1984) work in the 1970s and 1980s on gangs. She introduces the idea that girl gangs—on the order and magnitude of boy gangs—do in fact exist. Historically, girls were discussed as auxiliaries to male gangs. Campbell raises issues relative to female socialization and how those issues impact the behaviors that girls emit as part of gangs and the public's perceptions and reactions to the idea of violent females. Female socialization issues and dilemmas among girl *gangstas* are portrayed in the recent film *Mi Vida Loca* (Callender, Henkel, & Anders, 1993), the saga of a group of young Latinas who attempt to balance gender, culture, and gang issues.

Social and Demographic Factors

The economic strains on U.S. society are frequently identified as contributing factors to the rise of violence and proliferation of gangs during the 1970s. Economic gain theory has been noted as the major causative factor driving the behavior of gangs. The flourishing of the drug trade in many major urban centers is also cited as evidence to support the economic gain hypothesis. The theme of economics found expression in the works of many writers during the 1970s and is still applied to gangs across ethnic and racial boundaries. Increases in the frequency with which gangs are identified with selling drugs is discussed as being associated with the wholesale availability of firearms, thereby making empirical investigations of gangs far more dangerous than in years gone by. Other social and demographic changes in U.S. society during the 1970s directly influenced the proliferation of gangs, most notably urban renewal, school safety programs, and an emerging pattern of gang members being drug users as well as vendors.

Huff (1993) notes that with urban renewal the historical idea of gang turf has taken on new meaning. He reports that the creation of superhighways and the wholesale availability of cars make gangs much more mobile than they used to be. Cleveland and Detroit, two prototypic midwestern cities, are cited as examples of how gangs have become dislodged from their communities of origin but still exercise a sense of entitlement over them, enhanced by superhighways and cars. Within a matter of minutes, Huff reports, gang members are able to reach any part of the metropolitan area. Mobility has also been reported to be a factor encouraging gang movement from the West Coast to the East Coast. This migration not only influences the West Coast concentration of gangs (i.e., south central Los Angeles) but also has implications for towns like Topeka, Kansas; Carbondale, Illinois; and Grand Island, Nebraska, places where gangs can set up with minimum resistance from the community and local police department.

Another pattern of gang mobility—perhaps transplantation would be a better descriptor—is reported by Mydans (1990b) in the *New York Times*. He documents the surfacing of gangs once believed to be the province of urban neighborhoods in affluent, mostly white suburbs of New York City.

In the same way that gangs started to change their places of residence in the 1990s, there was also a shift in many of their programs noted in the news media and to a lesser degree in the social science literature. The Board of Alders election in Chicago in 1994 drew several openly proclaimed gang members as candidates. At least two of the candidates garnered enough votes to be included in the runoff. Similar public image changes are reported for New York City gangs, some of which embarked on collaborative entrepreneurial programs with major corporations (Gonzalez, in press).

The popular media have probably played as important a role in creating U.S. images of and knowledge of gangs as any other institution. During the early 1990s, talk shows devoted to youth violence routinely featured gang members and an often-contentious audience. Such widespread publicity serves not only to heighten the country's consciousness but also as a forum for glamorizing the gangster lifestyle, so much so that many school districts have found it necessary to institute gang education and school safety programs. Gangs nonetheless exist in large numbers in school communities (Branch & Rennick, 1995; Horowitz, 1990; Monti, 1994) and often use them as recruitment grounds for new members.

Clearly, today's gangs have a long history. The various ways in which gangs have functioned throughout history, as reported by the scholars cited in this chapter, suggest that gangs have been well-formulated groups with both internal and external regulatory mechanisms. They are more than loosely constructed collections of marginalized individuals. The fact that gangs in some geographical locations of the United States are found to be multigenerational also evidences stability in communities despite the qualitative differences in membership that occur with each new generation.

The brief historical overview presented in this chapter suggests that gangs have a mixed history, at times being antisocial but at other times behaving in prosocial ways. Do gangs also serve to meet the psychological needs of their members, especially the marginalized and disenfranchised of the community? On the one hand, individuals who find active roles in gangs are rarely, if ever, accepted in the larger community without major reservations. Conversely, the fact that gangs are allowed to exist in communities suggests that the communities are willing to tolerate even antisocial groups as long as clear boundaries delineate the limit of their behavior. Jankowski (1991) suggests that it is this sort of social contract that allows gangs to thrive and refine their internal functioning mechanisms. The reality that gangs have existed across different historical eras shows further that there are some social functions that are met by having such individuals exist in communities.

A major issue addressed by gang researchers is what conditions facilitate the transformation of individuals from adolescent gang members to adult community members, perhaps even socially acceptable members of the community. In the 1940s and 1950s, some researchers suggested that gang members simply matured chronologically and phased themselves out of the gang after becoming married and assuming an adult role in the community. That this explanation is perhaps an oversimplification is evidenced in recent years by the number of chronological adults who actively participate in community gangs while simultaneously maintaining a dual status within the respectable adult world.

What Is a Gang?

The definitional dilemma relative to gangs is considerable. Various definitions have been offered over time, invariably reflecting the particular interests of those generating the definition. Thrasher (1927) conceptualized of a gang as

> an interstitial group, originally found spontaneously and then integrated through conflict. It is characterized by the following types of behavior: meeting face to face, milling, movement through space as a unit, conflict, and planning. The result of this collective behavior is the development of tradition, unreflective internal structure, *esprit de corps,* solidarity, morale, group awareness, and attachment to a local territory (Thrasher, 1927, cited in Jankowski, 1991, p. 3).

Thrasher's words have formed the foundation of many subsequent definitions, each stressing different element of the gang's existence. A few examples of the range of definitions are presented in Box 1.1.

Despite the divergence of opinions about what actually constitutes a gang, there is agreement on some of the critical dimensions of a gang, for example that it is a collectivity and has membership requirements, an implicit ability

---

BOX 1.1   Various Definitions of Gangs

Miller (1981): A youth gang is a self-formed association of peers, bound together by mutual interests, with identifiable leadership, well-developed lines of authority, and other organizational features, who act in concert to achieve a specific purpose, which generally includes the conduct of illegal activity and control over a particular territory, facility, or type of enterprise.

Huff (1993): Youth gang—A collectivity consisting primarily of adolescents and young adults who (a) interact frequently with one another; (b) are frequently and deliberately involved in illegal activities; (c) share a common collective identity that is usually, but not always, expressed through a gang name; and (d) typically express that identity by adopting certain symbols or claiming control over certain "turf" (persons, places, things, or economic markets).

   Organized crime gang—A collectivity consisting primarily of adults who (a) interact frequently with one another; (b) are frequently and deliberately involved in illegal activities directed toward economic gain, primarily through the provision of illegal goods and services; and (c) generally have better defined leadership and organizational structure than is found in a youth gang.

Fagan (1996): Research conducted by Fagan during the 1980s identified two types of gangs: party gangs that were mainly involved in drinking and drugs as well as drug sales and social gangs that used drugs and committed numerous petty crimes. He also found other gang types (delinquent gangs, young organizations) that resembled the territorial and corporate gangs described by Taylor (1990).

to remain loyal, and an organizational structure. These variables have signifi-cance for understanding gang members' psychological development and their capacity for tolerating abstract ideas in their quest to find acceptance and affirmation.

Each of the definitions presented in Box 1.1, as well as Jankowski's (1991) definition offered in the Introduction, note that a gang is a collection of in-dividuals bound by a commitment to an ideal. This demand characteristic of a gang suggests that individuals who join gangs and function as active mem-bers are required to be able to relate to others in an ongoing relationship that must be assumed to be rewarding to all parties involved. It also high-lights the idea that gangs are forums in which individuals may be required to set aside their individual needs for the larger goals of the group. Inherent in this logic is the idea that extremely individualistic, egocentric, and narcissis-tic persons may not function well as part of a gang, as their needs for con-stant affirmation and reinforcement would be likely to cause ongoing con-flicts within the organizational structure. It may even be true that their extreme needs for being the center of attention may preclude them from being accepted into the gang family.

The capacity for belonging to a group has its developmental roots in early personality development in which the young child learns social negotiation skills and flexibility in relationships with others, particularly peers. It is likely that this same type of acceptance of others is tested by the gang as members are required to deal with the strengths and weaknesses of their fellow gang members. Not only are they required to deal with these traits in an intellec-tual way, but they are often confronted with them on a practical level in face-to-face conflicts with each other. In many nongang settings, including fami-lies of origin, situations of conflict are dealt with by simply walking away, dismissing the person with whom the conflict occurs or in extreme cases act-ing aggressively against the offending party. All of these options continue to be available to the gang member but with new conditions and constraints added. Walking away from an interpersonal conflict with another gang mem-ber may not be a good choice. The conflict itself may be a contrived situa-tion in which the gang is attempting to test the member to see if he or she has "heart." Not dealing with the conflict in a way that is condoned by the group may not be in the member's best interest. Likewise, dismissing a con-flict or a level of neediness that another gang member may express can be risky for a new member. In some situations, the dismissal of the needs and concerns of others also may not be a realistic option, because the needy party may assume that fellow *gangstas* will always be there for them. That may or may not be true. As conflicts arise between gang members, new be-havioral responses may have to be developed, even in situations analogous to conflicts experienced outside of the gang. The difficulty for many gang members is not knowing what exactly is at stake or how they should respond

BOX 1.2   The Case of Jason

Jason, a 19-year-old African American male who has been a gang banger since he was fifteen, reports a change of heart about continuing in the gang. Recently, he and his girlfriend of 2 years had a baby. The arrival of the infant created some stressors in their relationship. Jason has been abusive of the girlfriend and occasionally been in court on domestic violence charges. A major source of relationship tension has been that members of his old gang frequently make demands on his time. Several gang associates have recently been incarcerated in the county jail. Jason reports that they have been calling him at home, requesting that he come to visit them or that he contact estranged family members for them.

There are several features about the calls that are disturbing, or at least annoying, to Jason, including:

They always want to talk about the ole days. . . . That's over now, I'm not into gang banging anymore.
A lot of the stuff they ask for they can do for themselves.
I don't have time to do that stuff.
It's like they make up reasons to be calling and shit.

Note that even though Jason claims to have quit the gang, his fellow gang members continue to see him as a central figure in their lives and their gang network. It appears that they want something from him (i.e., attention, validation) that he is reluctant to give.

---

to the conflict. The case of Jason and the repeated requests for validation that he received from incarcerated fellow *gangstas* illustrate this point (see Box 1.2).

All of the definitions offered in Box 1.1 suggest that there are explicit membership requirements for all gangs. It is interesting to note that membership and initiation requirements vary from acts of antisocial behavior with others as the victim (i.e., to participate in a drive-by shooting, physically assault a member of a rival gang, respond to a challenge from a member of one's own gang, and so forth) to being the victim of a hazing type of initiation or gang rape. The level of risk associated with the initiation is intended to test the level of courage of the new recruit. Perhaps more important than the initiation ritual itself is the idea that new members are expected to subscribe to the goals and ideals of the gang. Gangs have multiple and creative ways of testing the level of commitment of followers.

Implicit in the membership requirements of gangs is the capacity to meet the requirements of the group and to live up to the expectations of others, even when those expectations are not explicitly articulated. One of the areas that is often problematic for new members is that they do not fully understand all of the nuances of gang membership. Many gangs have explicit codes of behavior but encourage the new recruit to think clearly and logically (i.e., "use your head"). The novice member often uses "common sense" that fails to find approval among the other gang members. This conflict seems to be related to residual pregang socialization that interferes with functioning as a good gang member. Attending school, maintaining close relationships with family members, and valuing religion are examples of sources of conflict that gang members report (Branch & Rennick, 1995).

The capacity to remain loyal to the ideals of the gang is an area that poses special problems for new members. Much of the conflict is related to not knowing the totality of the things for which the gang stands. Perhaps more basic than standing for specific ideals is the question of whether gang members have the ability to be committed and faithful, even in the absence of concrete markers. In accepting new members into their ranks, older gang members sometimes erroneously assume the recruits have that ability despite there being no evidence, other than their own naive or idealistic assessments of the individual, to support such a belief.

All of the foregoing issues illustrate common features that the multiple definitions of gangs highlight. Substantiating that one can rise to the challenge of each of these demand characteristics is the task of the new member. Failures at that task result in new recruits being pushed out of the gang, other gang members having to take action to save face (i.e., mask the fact that they made a bad choice), or rejected members needing to find ways of reducing the dissonance of not being good enough for the gang.

For those who want to understand gang behavior, it is necessary to have a good operational definition of a gang, one that eliminates ambiguity and at the same time offers a valid analysis of the psychological capabilities of the individual described as a good gang member. The definitions presented in Box 1.1 present a small cross-section of the variety in use. Jankowski's (1991) definition (presented in the Introduction) is both inclusive and detailed. From his definition one is able to infer psychological qualities about the organization and the individuals who profess membership in it, including the individual's capacity to function within a set of well-articulated limits. This psychological trait is an important one, perhaps inherently excluding individuals whose levels of sociopathy and disorganization are so great that they cannot function in settings structured by others. The level of organization of the gang is also significant. Jankowski's definition suggests that gangs must be able to plan and implement a program of action—they are not a loosely structured collection of socially marginal individuals characterized by impulsive, nonreflective behaviors. Lastly, Jankowski presents the idea of gangs being both private and public simultaneously. The external presentation is not the full story. The "life" (i.e., philosophy) of the gang becomes internalized by its members, often eluding outsiders who try to "understand" the allegiance that members have for the organization. All of these qualities of the organization require a certain level of *goodness of fit* on the part of the gang member if there is to be a lasting match. On an individual psychological level these qualities can be described by the characteristics of *need for affiliation, ego-virtue fidelity,* capacity for *delay of gratification,* and willingness to *sacrifice personal goals for superordinate goals.*

Developmental Factors

An individual's developmental status on the psychological attributes just discussed can provide a good clinical picture of readiness for gang participation. A pervasive problem with understanding the developmental status of adolescents is to relate the milestones to the context in which the adolescent has been socialized. This difficulty has been addressed by attempts to generate culturally sensitive developmental measurements. Although that approach is laudatory, it fails to overcome the need to make evaluative assessments of adolescents whose life experiences may not have matched those reflected in the developmental schedules applied to them.

The following discussion is not intended to address this large and very important topic but rather to introduce the idea of developmental factors and explore how they figure in understanding the dynamics of adolescents and gang membership. Issues related to specific developmental milestones and the question of cultural variation will be addressed in later chapters. This section is designed to provide an understanding of gangs' demands in the areas of social functioning (i.e., affiliation, fidelity, and so forth). The information will be used as a foundation for examining an adolescent's capacity to respond to the social demands of gang membership. Collectively, these thoughts provide the clinician with a set of tools that can be used to assess the goodness of fit between the gang and the individual adolescent.

Psychological Affiliation

The need for affiliation—an individuals' longing to connect to others but to retain their own sense of self—is a very basic human condition. The concept occupies a central position in psychoanalytic and other developmental theories. Maslow (1954) introduces the idea in his theory of human development by indicating the need for human affiliation as one of the most basic conditions that must be met if an organism is to survive. Spitz (1945) also highlights the primacy of human attachment in his early work with infants. More recent variations on this theme occur in the attachment theories of Bowlby (1969) and Ainsworth (1979). Collectively, these theories support the idea that early relationships and infants' capacity for tolerating physical and emotional closeness are prognostic of their later ability to nurture relationships with others but at the same time maintain boundaries between themselves and others. The critical idea in this line of reasoning is that relationships are important. It is through relationships that individuals learn about themselves and others.

Developmentally, the earliest expressions of need for affiliation occur when the infant first attaches to the primary caregiver. Later, the infant splits away and becomes an autonomous being. Despite splitting away from the caregiver, the infant still retains a need to be with others. This condition is satisfied by transient social engagements with parents, siblings, and eventually friends. Extremely low levels of affiliation in infants correlate with isolation and shyness in adolescence. These individuals do desire affiliation, but it is not very important to them and they do not assertively act to have the need met.

In the case of adolescents in gangs, the need to be with others is very strong. As part of the psychological developmental process, adolescents slowly separate from their family of origin and move toward the peer group as a source of affirmation. This process is not as dramatic or categorical as many would believe. Instead, it takes place slowly over a number of years and selectively across domains. Steinberg and Silverburg (1986) show that as adolescents move toward autonomy they gradually replace dependence on parents and family with dependence on the peer group. Other researchers have echoed this same finding but with the qualifier that the dependence on peers is more related to "adolescent issues" (i.e., dating, manner of dress, and so forth) (Hill & Holmbeck, 1986; Kandel & Lesser, 1969; Offer, 1969). Psychologically, the demands of gang membership are such that members are expected to merge themselves with the group. This surrender is paramount if the individual is to be considered part of the group, but it can be problematic if he or she has never really affiliated with or attached to others. The show of affiliation can range from the cosmetic, such as wearing the colors of the gang and knowing a few gang hand signs, to a much deeper commitment, such as a major philosophical immersion in gang ideology.

The need for affiliation must be as pronounced in the adolescent's life as the capacity for it if membership in a gang is likely to materialize. An urge to join a gang can arise for a variety of reasons, including part of the process of individuating from parents, acquiescing in peer pressure in early and mid-adolescence, part of the internal exploration for an answer to the "Who am I?" question, and in response to feelings of existential detachment.

In thinking about the quest for affiliation and affirmation, adolescents often look to older adolescents who they assume are knowledgeable about social issues and how to navigate the maze of complex issues confronting them.

Ego-Virtue Fidelity

Markstrom-Adams (1994) identifies ego-virtue fidelity as the capacity to be faithful and committed to another or to a set of ideals. According to her, adolescents must develop the ability to evaluate the many philosophical and social options available and make choices between them (i.e., evidence fidelity) to successfully negotiate the developmental tasks of adolescence.

Initial commitments—presumed evidence of fidelity—in the forms of attachments to caregivers, beliefs consistent with those of parents, and behaviors that reflect the value system of parents and family, weaken after early adolescence. In the process of negotiating new types of relationships, adolescents ideally become tolerant of perspectives other than their own. In so doing, they develop the capacity to be steadfast in their commitments.

Membership in gangs requires a high level of fidelity. Most gangs explicitly demand that members "stick together." One way of demonstrating togetherness is to defend the honor of the group, in word and deed. These two behavioral imperatives are usually interpreted to mean acting aggressively if necessary. At extreme levels, fidelity to the gang and all of its symbols has found expression among gang members who have, on order, shot or physically attacked individuals who were wearing the colors of an opposing gang. In such instances, the fidelity was to one's own colors, with a belief that the opponent's colors posed a real threat. Another illustration of fidelity to an extreme can be found in an anecdote a colleague recently shared with me (Fagan, 1996). Two gang members, from different gangs, had been recruited by the football program of a school contending for a national title. Supposedly, neither young man knew that the other was a "*gangsta* at heart." In the locker room at halftime during a nationally televised game, the two gang members became hostile toward one another, not because their team was trailing in the game but in response to the agitation each experienced at noticing the other wearing a "dew rag" in a color associated with his rival gang. The sense of fidelity that each young man felt toward his respective gang made it difficult, if not impossible, for them to also make a strong commitment to the football team and its goal of winning a national championship.

Capacity for Delay of Gratification

It appears that the decision to join a gang is willful and deliberate. The decision also appears to be linked to seeking to have a need, or several needs, met. Identifying the exact nature of the needs that compel young people to join gangs has been problematic for researchers and law enforcement officers. When asked about their motivation for joining gangs, members often make obligatory-sounding statements about finding someplace they can feel valued or using the gang as a venue for acquiring things (i.e., cars, electronic gadgets, and so forth). Whatever their reasons for joining, they expect that the gang will provide them with something that they did not have in their pregang status. Two interesting facets of gang members' behavior in this regard are how long they are willing to wait to attain the "things" assumed to be associated with gang membership and how well they are able to suppress their desires for the rewards of gang membership while they wait. These patterns of behavior are related to the question of delay of gratification, or willingness to wait for reinforcement. In social science, delay of gratification is usually measured by a subject's ability to postpone immediate reward with a small prize in favor of a later reward with a significantly larger prize.

Delay of gratification is a concept with a rich tradition in psychology. Most of the seminal early work was performed by Walter Mischel and his colleagues (Mischel & Baker, 1970; Moore, Mischel, & Zeiss, 1976). They focus primarily on children's and adolescent's knowledge of self-control strategies and the development of waiting behavior. Mitsutomi (1994) proposes that delay of gratification should be reconceptualized and reclassified based on "types of failure to wait." J. McWhirter, B. McWhirter, A. McWhirter, and E. McWhirter (1994) note that delay of gratification, a capacity to exercise control, is critical in helping children overcome problems in their social, family, and school environments; students' high- versus low-risk status in this area has major implications for the likelihood of successful interventions.

The exact nature of delay of gratification capacity is not understood. It is suggested that the skill is related to cognitive and self-regulation competence (Shoda, Mischel, & Peake, 1990; Wasserman, 1987), ego-control and ego-resiliency (Fender & Block, 1989), and attentional deficit (Schweitzer & Sulzer, 1995).

It appears that there is a developmental trend in delay of gratification capacity, originating in the preschool years and becoming more pronounced with the passage of time (Rotenberg & Mayer, 1990; Shoda, Mischel, & Peake, 1990). The age progression is exacerbated by intelligence and personality traits. Fender and Block (1989) show that delay of gratification capacity in a group of middle adolescents is correlated with personality ratings for boys and girls:

> Subjects who exhibited the most delay of gratification tended to be independently described as responsible, productive, ethically consistent, interested in intellectual matters, and overly controlled. They tended not to be described as unable to delay gratification, rebellious, unpredictable, self indulgent, or hostile. Delay behavior in both sexes was also correlated positively with IQ. (p. 1041)

Delay of gratification appears to be a cross-cultural phenomenon. Rotenberg and Mayer (1990), using a racially mixed sample, find the same pattern of age and cognitive level of differentiation as in the early studies that were completed with racially homogeneous subject pools. Group differences are found when Black subjects are compared to other racial groups. Black children and adolescents appear to have greater difficulty with delaying gratification than equivalent samples of Whites. The age differentials still seem to exist, however. Older Black subjects have greater facility in the area of delay of gratification in responding to environmental stimuli than their younger Black cohorts. Unfortunately, unlike the work of Fender & Block (1989), much of the cross-cultural research supporting these patterns is not controlled for differences that may be attributable to variability in intelligence. Other variables identified as affecting delay of gratification capacity include gender (Witt, 1990a; 1990b), locus of control (Witt, 1990a), and psychiatric status (Newman, Kosson, & Patterson, 1992).

Witt (1990b) reports that in a group of 133 undergraduates delay of gratification tended to moderate the relationship between satisfaction with the university and social responsibility. He also notes (Witt, 1990a) that results of analyses of sex differences and interactions between locus of control and delay of gratification in predicting organizational satisfaction and commitment suggest that the relationships are more complicated than originally thought. Linear locus of control and delay of gratification relationships are not found.

Newman, Kosson, and Patterson (1992) indicate that in a group of psychopathic and nonpsychopathic White inmates provided with repeated opportunities to select an immediate response with uncertain reward or a delayed response with a higher rate of reward under one of three incentive conditions, outcomes are related to the trait anxiety (of the subject) and incentive conditions. The researchers conclude, "Self-control in low anxious psychopaths is somewhat impaired under various conditions involving a combination of monetary rewards and punishments" (p. 630).

The findings from the delay of gratification literature have direct and profound implications for working with gang adolescents. An age trend is observable in normative samples of children and adolescents as well as among adjudicated emotionally disturbed children and adolescents. Gender differences in capacity to delay gratification are not as simplistic as once thought. The concept of delay of gratification is verified cross-culturally. Racial differences that exist seem to still follow the universal age trend. The capacity for delaying gratification is the result of several factors (i.e., age, gender, intelligence, salience of reward, personality traits), not merely a main effect of environment. These findings suggest that the skill may be observed in different ways in gang members. To make a clear and accurate assessment of gang members' capacity to delay gratification, it is necessary to gain a thorough understanding of the environment in which they function as well as of their constitutional factors.

The clinical literature reports that ethnic minority children are less able to delay the need for gratification than are their White counterparts, often preferring a small, more transient reward to waiting for a larger, more intrinsically rewarding prize. Can the same logic be applied to gang members and their inability to work through the system and acquire material things slowly but in a less risky fashion?

How can the pattern of apparent lack of delay of gratification among adolescents of color be explained? By a history of limited opportunities in which they are adequately rewarded after a long and protracted effort? Autonomic arousal suppression problems? Or unmeasured biases in the experiments themselves? Discussion of impaired delay of gratification capacity should not focus exclusively on adolescents of color but should be extended to include Whites who may be marginalized in the communities in which they live. These groups collectively form a group of individuals who are deficient in their ability to "wait," a deficiency that could be a partial explanation for impulsive and otherwise spontaneous behavior on the part of gang members.

Whatever their reasons for joining gangs, most gang members obviously cannot get all of their needs met continuously and immediately. To do so would require that they be in a constant battle with the communities in which they live. If their objective is the acquisition of economic capital, they are constantly at risk for arrest by the police. The reality is that most gang members are able to plot their courses of action and hold in abeyance urges to go for the big prizes without a reasonable amount of planning and assurance that their approach will succeed. Otherwise they would be out of business quickly.

Impulsive non-gratification-delaying individuals do not seem to fit into most gangs without jeopardizing the safety and program of the gang. This seems to suggest that substance abusing and attention deficit–disordered individuals with hyperactivity are poor prospects for being good gang members.

Personal Goals Versus Superordinate Goals

A true test of the commitment of a gang member is willingness to put a personal agenda aside in the interest of the gang's objectives. It appears that such a level of self-denial is not easily accomplished by many adolescents, particularly those with a high level of narcissism.

One of the first studies documenting suppression of personal goals for the well-being of the group is a classic experiment by Sherif and Sherif (1947). They demonstrate that a group of boys at summer camp are willing to suspend their personal interests and work for a larger collective prize if the stakes are high enough. The boys' choice is one that often confronts gangs. The true test of a gang's strength often rests on how willing members are to forego their personal agendas, which may be at odds with the gang's, in the interest of working for a "higher calling," devotion to the gang.

Developmentally arrested individuals who are unable or unwilling to delay personal agendas weaken the gang's sovereign control over its members. They also pose a problem for the leaders of the gang and their ability to legislate what will be done when and by whom. The ultimate authority of the group can be seriously challenged by gang members who also have personal agendas that conflict with the program of the gang.

A commitment to the goals of the larger group at the expense of one's personal agenda is seen as a form of sacrifice and commitment that extends beyond the capacity of some gang members. To override the tendency of some gang members to lapse into "what about me" attitudes, gangs often stress the spirit of community and sharing. In some ways this is not unlike team-building exercises used in workplaces. The idea seems to be that all parties involved in the group, in this case the gang, are expected to claim partial ownership of the task to be completed. "I" and "mine" are replaced with "we" and "our." This requirement of self-denial becomes problematic when the individual gang member is unable psychologically to suppress the need for self-gratification in the service of pleasing a collection of individuals. Jankowski (1991) uses the term *defiant individualism* to describe many of the gang members he studied. He notes that because of their high level of individualism it frequently became problematic for them to "get with the program." Instead, they often found themselves struggling over choices about whose will should be done, their own or that of the group.

Gang members' abilities to acquiesce in the superordinate goals of the gang also raise questions about their ability to trust others, especially others with whom they may not have had a lengthy relationship. Frequently, they are unable to identify the issue by that label, but they are very aware of their misgivings about taking directions from someone they do not know. Neophytes are often told that such blind allegiance is a good thing. From the gang's perspective it is, but eventually it comes to be problematic for many seasoned members. Needless to say, the beginning of questioning the gang's activities and one's commitment to superordinate group goals is often the origin of a decline in the member's investment in the gang.

Summary

In this chapter, I have discussed a few dimensions of personal psychological functioning that can be demonstrated to have implications for whether or not a person will make a good gang member, consistent with Jankowski's (1991) definition of a gang. It would be naive to assume that the goodness of fit between gangs and members is related only to the developmental status of members. The stage of evolution and psychological qualities of the gang also add significantly to the relationship. In the next chapter, I examine developmental aspects of gang membership. Individual developmental issues are compared to organizational issues.

2

Developmental Aspects of Gang Membership

Over the years, there have been a variety of theories advanced to explain the origins and dynamics of adolescent gangs. Goldstein (1993) notes that even the definitions of gangs have varied with time and place, in response to political and economic conditions as expressed by police and private citizen concerns. Because of the absence of a consistent definition, the literature has been plagued with the mixing and matching of incongruent concepts. The most common pattern has been to equate adolescent gangs with violence, juvenile delinquency, and antisocial behavior. Although these features are often a part of the gang scene, it would be overly simplistic and reductionistic to claim that they explain the totality of gang life.

The preoccupation with the disruptive and violent aspects of gangs seems to be related to the fact that these are the features of gang life most often reported by the media and most likely to provoke public concern and even outrage. Other dimensions to gang life have escaped media and scholarly exploration. These aspects include, for example, the blind allegiance that many members develop toward the gang, even in the face of personal danger and the risk of death—allegiance that could potentially compromise the rest of their lives. Likewise, young people who spend their adolescence within the constricted confines of a gang may limit their opportunities for the exploratory behavior psychologically appropriate for adolescence. They instead find themselves in a state of foreclosure from which they may spend the rest of their lives attempting to escape. Unfortunately, many never succeed. Confusion among scholars concerning what to study and how to approach it has contributed to a limited understanding of gangs and their roles in the lives of some adolescents.

Most of the early research on adolescent gangs was sociological, focused primarily on describing the conditions that gave rise to gangs and highlighting social and economic conditions as the major causes. Goldstein (1993) provides a detailed overview of the early theories of adolescent gangs (concerned mostly with the aggression and violence dimensions of gang life). In summarizing the history of the delinquency theory of gangs, he observes:

> Early interest in delinquent gangs on the part of social scientists was largely descriptive. What gangs were and the societal/familial conditions that were their antecedents and concomitants were the focus of concern. Little emerged during this time in the way of formal gang theory, that is, conceptualizations of the structural and dynamic variables underlying gang formation, organization, and especially, the delinquent behavior which characterized a substantial amount of gang functioning. These theoretical lacunae began to be filled in the 1950s, and the majority of the theory development was sociological in nature. It focused primarily on seeking to explain the development behavior of individual youth gangs and groups of gangs. Some of the more prominent theories developed during this period were: strain theory, subcultural theory, control theory, labeling theory, and radical theory. (pp. 257–258)

In the area of criminal justice, there has been a comparable development of interest in adolescent gangs, with an expected emphasis on crime. Since the 1960s, researchers have been very active in describing the law enforcement efforts that have been waged to contain the illegal behaviors of gangs, most notably drugs sales and homicide. Major contributors to this research tradition are Huff (1990) and Spergel (1967). These authors offer valuable insights into the severity of the problem of violence and antisocial behavior among young people, gang members in particular, but they provide little insight into the psychological evolution or dynamics of gang-affiliated youths.

Jankowski (1991), a sociologist, claims that there has been no comprehensive theory of adolescent gangs. He attributes this to a historic pattern of equating gangs with delinquency and violence. He offers another interpretation, suggesting that gangs are social organizations that can be described as meeting economic needs of individuals and communities. Technically, this might be characterized as *economic gain theory*. Jankowski also points out that researchers should take care to distinguish between gangs acting collectively and gang members acting on their own behest.

Theories of Gangs

Balk (1995) groups theories explaining youth gangs in three categories: strain theory, cultural deviance theory, and dysfunctional family theory. The first, *strain theory*, suggests that youths in an impoverished underclass strive to solve the problem of their economic oppression. Finding no doors opening on the world of economic advancement, the youths strain to overcome obstacles preventing attainment of their economic aspirations (p. 479). The gang provides an opportunity for youths to move out of the state of economic disenfranchisement. Once youths join a gang, they exhibit little or no regard for the legality of the gang's revenue-producing activities. Selling drugs and other commodites, stealing cars, and prostitution are activities often pursued by gangs. Evidence of this theoretical orientation is found in Jankowski (1991) and Knox (1991).

Cultural deviance theory attributes participation in adolescent gangs to an environment that encourages cultural defiance and sociopathy, traits that are validated and find expression within the gang. Proponents of this viewpoint often subscribe to the position that many gang members are conduct disordered or highly marginalized in their larger communities. These theorists contend that it is only within the context of the gang that its members are able to function with few or no reprisals for their behavior.

According to the *dysfunctional family theory* (Bing, 1991; Bloch & Morales, 1981; Niederhoffer, 1958), the negative impact of psychologically impoverished families drives youngsters to join gangs. Knox (1991) notes that many gang members claim that the gang is "like a family." A similar observation is also made by Jankowski (1991). Inherent in this theoretical notion is the idea that gang members are seeking relief from less-than-satisfying relationships in their family of origin by joining the gang, irrespective of what the gang may require of them to remain in good standing.

A hitherto-unnamed theory of adolescent gangs is one of *psychological affiliation*. According to this theory, many adolescents who join gangs do so in a quest to have their needs for affiliation and social validation met, even if it means running afoul of the law and placing themselves in situations of great danger. A sprinkling of evidence supports this position in the writings of gang researchers who note that many gang members report that they join in an attempt to find a sense of belonging and purpose (Branch, 1995; Campbell, 1984; Goldstein, 1993; Hagedorn & Macon, 1988; Jankowski, 1991; Knox, 1991; Moore, 1978). The participation in antisocial activities may be secondary to the fulfillment of a more basic need, that of finding psychological validation. This dynamic holds true even for flagrantly conduct-disordered individuals with limited capacity for connectedness to others. In their case, the gang serves as a forum for fleeting, perhaps shallow, relationships of a short-term duration.

It is apparent that no single theory of gangs adequately explains the origin of gangs and the psychological dynamics that bring members to the gang and keep them connected. It is quite possible that the images that adolescents have of gangs and gang lifestyles are radically different from those held by adult outsiders, especially researchers. Just as there are multiple theories intended to explain the purpose and dynamics of adolescent gangs, there are also many attempts to answer the questions of why adolescents are motivated to join gangs and how they achieve membership. In the next section, I focus on levels and types of membership.

Membership Issues

Gangs exist for a variety of reasons (i.e., mutual protection in a tough neighborhood, a part of the U.S. acculturation process, economic gain, sociopaths attempting to normalize their state of marginality, and so forth). Some researchers have attempted to show that gangs themselves provide a measure of psychological socialization, but these positive aspects of gangs have often been obscured by the public's preoccupation with the negative dimensions of adolescent gangs. Indeed, merely mentioning the words "adolescent gangs" can conjure up images of out-of-control drug-crazed adolescents, even in the absence of details to confirm that these features accurately portray any particular gang. Before setting out on a detailed discussion of types of gangs and levels of membership, the two primary topics of this section, I discuss distinctive features of gang membership.

Gangs, like other social organizations, have components to their membership that distinguish them from rivals. These characteristics are essential elements for interviewing gang members about the nature and extent of their participation in a gang.

Membership. Who are the members of gangs? Most organizations, gangs included, have fairly explicit statements about who may join and who may not. In creating a psychological profile of a gang, it is vital to know the makeup of the group. Is the gang composed of same-sex individuals of a narrow, three- or four-year age span or is the gang a co-ed collective covering the span of the teen years and beyond? Most gangs are segregated by gender. Girls have formed their own gangs, often in response to being excluded from gangs led by boys. There has been a considerable amount of debate in the literature as to whether or not female gangs are the equivalent of male gangs. Ann Campbell (1984) highlights females and the social dilemmas facing girls in gangs that are not inherently among the issues that male gang members face.

Leadership. In addition to understanding who actually composes the membership of a gang, it is also important to know something about the leadership of the gang. Is the leadership drawn from among the rank and file or provided by a more distant older gang member, perhaps known only to the individual gang members by reputation and not as a result of personal interaction?

Insignia. A feature of many gangs is a distinctive style of dress or grooming that sets members apart from other adolescents who are also attempting to distance themselves from their parents and other adults. Johnson (1994) devotes a significant amount of his research to identifying the distinctive styles in which some gang members have chosen to dress as a way to make themselves unique. This topic has become a major point of emphasis for law enforcement officials as a way to help parents determine whether their youngsters are at risk for joining a gang or already participating in organized gang activity. The issue is raised here not as a definitive diagnostic tool but only to indicate that gangs, like other organizations, have distinctive styles of dress or emblematic insignia. For socially condoned organizations, membership often takes the form of a membership card, having one's name included on a roster, or even having one's name engraved at some site available for public examination. Gangs are like other social organizations in this respect. In addition, they often provide their members with insignia that confirms their continuing membership in the organization.

Initiation.   Numerous studies have discovered distinct gender differences in initiation rites. It is well documented that girl gangs conduct a variety of initiation rituals that place the initiate at risk, a break with traditional initiation rituals of male gangs. For example, a few years ago, a national network reported that as part of an initiation ritual female gang members in San Antonio, Texas, had sexual intercourse with a man thought to be HIV positive. This story caused a furor and subsequent recanting by several of the young women interviewed. In several other cities, including Denver, New York, and Chicago, girls report that part of their initiation ritual is to subject themselves to gang rape or physical attack by a group of girls. This procedure is radically different from what most male gangs require. Indeed, for groups composed of boys, initiation usually involves acting aggressively against some other member of the community, another gang member, or one's family of origin. An initiation that places the member in the victim role is often explicitly articulated to girls at the time they are recruited to join the gang.

A lesson that seems to grow out of these initiation rituals is the value of aggression and destruction in the scheme of the organization. Groups that tend to make initiations something bizarre and unusual, that is, outside of the usual program of the gang, should be viewed very differently from organizations for which initiation is simply a continuation of the daily business of the organization.

Recruitment.   Preceding actual initiation into a gang, most gang members are actively recruited by established members of the group. Three methods of recruitment are reported by Jankowski (1991). The first is *invitation.* Gang members seek to replenish their numbers with individuals whom they perceive as being like them or who will reflect positively on the image of the group. Young people report being approached to join a gang because of their social status in the community; their ability to defend themselves physically; or their ability to be persuasive in situations that require intricate social skills, such as negotiation and social problem solving.

A second method of recruitment for gangs that has been highlighted in the literature is *coercion*. This tactic is reserved primarily for individuals who reject the gang's initial overtures toward them. Typically, individuals who respond negatively to the gang's invitation are threatened through a younger sibling or some other family situation about whom they feel some sense of vulnerability. The message is made clear that if they do not join the gang "family" something unpleasant may happen to a member of their other family. This kind of dilemma often begins the dichotomous thinking experienced by young recruits regarding their family of origin and their new "gang family."

The third method of recruitment involves those who spontaneously seek out the gang and *request membership*. Reasons underlying such behavior include a desire to improve one's social status among peers, seeking safety in the neighborhood, and attempting to escape the influence of parents and family of origin. Not surprising, this type of affiliation is reported by youngsters who subsequently find themselves requesting or being referred for social service intervention.

Across the three types of recruitment tactics of the gang, the decision to join the gang ultimately rests with the new gang member. Even when the gang uses coercive tactics with an individual, the potential recruit must decide that the pressure and implied risks are severe enough that he or she will give in to the gang's overtures.

Continuing in Good Standing. What constitutes being a gang member in good standing is an area that has been the subject of much debate among scholars and social program planners. It is not entirely clear when a new recruit's status in the gang changes and hard-core gang membership begins. It follows general logic that once a person joins a gang it is a lifetime commitment. One might also believe, however, that as an individual ages the frequency and intensity of his or her participation in flagrantly antisocial behavior would decrease dramatically. Such has not been shown to be the case with gangs. In fact, there is no empirical research evidence documenting developmental changes in levels of participation in gang membership that can be directly related to age. There is, however, anecdotal evidence of gang members in their mid-twenties reporting that they eventually taper off in the frequency and intensity of their participation. Reasons articulated as explaining such behavior include the death of many "homies," "partners" being confined to prison, starting a family, and recognition of the dangers associated with much of their high-risk behavior.

Another question associated with being a gang member in good standing is whether an individual acquires inactive status with infrequent participation in gang-banging behavior or a lack of active involvement with new recruits. It is also suggested that there are differential criteria in male and female gangs for continuance in good standing. A recent set of interviews (Patel, 1994) with a group of female gang members in New York City reveals that they significantly altered the level and frequency of their participation in gang activities after having a baby. Despite their not being physically present for gang battles or initiations, they saw themselves as supportive of the objectives of the gang and participating by offering counsel and emotional support to young female gang members, particularly those who find themselves impregnated or alone with young children.

The Gang's Program.　 Gang activities seem to generate the most disagreements between scholars of adolescent gangs and members of service agencies who interact with gang members. Adolescent gang activities cover a broad spectrum of organizational tasks and vary widely between gangs. At one extreme are gangs organized in tough neighborhoods to provide collegial and affiliation opportunities for members and to ensure their safety within the confines of the community. A very different type of gang may be organized around criminal activity, sometimes with involvement in politically motivated crimes.

Age and Gender Factors

An examination of the reasons for joining a gang can yield important insights into the level of psychological sophistication and maturation of individuals who subsequently will be active members. Most of the present-day literature suggests that gangs are, for the most part, organized along gender lines. There is more variance of opinion as to whether or not gangs are composed of individuals of a narrowly defined age group or whether there is an allowance for individuals spread over a larger age span.

The psychological literature shows a clear developmental phenomenon relative to how adolescents surround themselves with individuals of similar age and interests. This linear progression has been interpreted by some theorists to suggest that pressure for conformity decreases as individuals get older, simply because they have surrounded themselves with individuals perceived to be like themselves. Within gang structures, it is interesting to note whether the gang affiliation is critical to the perception of closeness to others. It is also critical to note that individuals who are separated by more years (i.e., eight, nine, or ten years) are assumed to have less in common in psychological interests and ability to be affectively connected to each other than individuals who are closer in chronological age. In thinking about the cohesiveness that could potentially exist in a group, it is important to note whether or not the group is the result of a clustering of individuals around a few years in age or across a wide spread of years. In the case of a wide age span, say, with a gang composed of individuals in early adolescence as well as late adolescence and maybe even early adulthood, several questions relative to the roles that individual members of a gang are allowed to play should follow. Do the older members assume the leadership roles? Are the chronologically younger members also the most recent recruits?

In some instances, the membership requirements for a gang are not explicit as to age. Many young people report an absence of age restrictions but very explicit requirements as to physical abilities and psychological capabilities. The absence of explicit age requirements raises the possibility that many very young adolescents who are recruited into gangs may be too young to fully comprehend the extent of their decision to join the gang or the implicit demands that will be made on them by the gang. Perhaps more important than chronological age, a degree of social maturation and worldliness may be desired in new recruits. In some situations, it turns out that new recruits to the gang are not nearly as sophisticated or capable of responding to the demand characteristics of the gang as both they and more senior gang members may have assumed.

Age is not the only factor for judging the inclusiveness or exclusivity of an adolescent gang. Dimensions used to segregate other groups should also be considered, in particular, sexuality. Recently, in New York City, a well-known and very large gang established a chapter on Christopher Street in the heart of the city's gay community. This fact prompted statements of puzzlement and even disbelief on the part of the many otherwise well-informed and progressive-thinking theorists, raising the question of whether this gang accepts members who were not rigidly heterosexual in their orientation. This response, of course, speaks more to the theorists and researchers' assumptions than to gang members' tolerance or sexual orientation.

There is almost no research on variation in sexuality in adolescent gang members. Is it reasonable to assume that gang members assume that their new recruits are heterosexual? Or that the sexual orientation of the new recruit is inconsequential? More research in this area may prove that the assumption of the cardinal importance of a heterosexual identity among adolescent gang members is perhaps more an artifact of the thinking and reasoning of the researchers than the reality of life for a group of adolescents struggling to discover who they are and where they fit in.

Branch and Rennick (1995) observe that in an urban setting there is a significant concentration of gang members represented in the general populace of a public high school. The students who voluntarily identify themselves as gang members are not significantly different from the norm for the school in attendance, participation in extracurricular activities, or frequency with which they report depressive symptomatology. Girls are represented in the gang subsample, but only approximately one fourth as often as the boys. Gang members are found disproportionately in special education classes.

Leadership

Leadership is another dimension of gangs that can be used to analyze the level of development and nature of the gang. Frequently, young people joining gangs lack direct access to the leaders and simply march to orders provided indirectly from an absent or perhaps even fantasy leader. I suggest that the quality (direct versus indirect) of the leadership and the availability of the leaders to individual gang members evidence the level of development of the group. A series of studies (Vigil, 1988) conducted in southern California indicate that among several gangs the leaders are removed from the day-to-day activities of the group, spending most of their time giving directions and negotiating new programs for the organization. These researchers found that leaders of adolescent gangs tend to not attend school as regularly as other members of the gang. Researchers believe that leaders of the gang are busy conducting the business of the gang and are therefore unavailable to attend school on a regular basis or as often as other gang members.

The Gang's Program

Finally, the gang's *structured program* is a very useful prognostic and diagnostic sign of the developmental level of the gang. It is not clear whether or not gang members see their gangs as organizations within the structure of the communities in which they live or as peripheral attempts to assert themselves and garner some measure of respect in the larger community. How the organization's program of action is created and the content of that program are both valuable ways of assessing the *developmental perspective* of the gang. For example, gangs in which the members are content to focus all of their activity on an antagonistic relationship with the larger community should be seen as being less well articulated in a sense of autonomy and purpose. I suggest that if in fact gangs are only reacting to others and not setting their own agenda— if they are not independent and autonomous of the behavior of others—they are in an early state of evolution and *individuation* from others.

A useful way to think of gangs and their developmental states is provided by Bronfenbrenner's (1979) ecological systems approach. Using the ecological systems identified by Bronfenbrenner, one can determine the focal point of the action of a gang and the nature of its action. Gangs that are neighborhood bound and have no larger political agenda are likely to function exclusively in micro- or mesosystemic relationships. In Figure 2.1, the

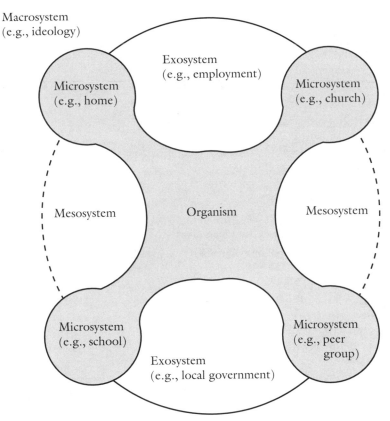

FIGURE 2.1   *The ecology of human development.* SOURCE: Adolescent Development
by Garbarino, James, © *1985. Reprinted by permission of Prentice-Hall, Inc., Upper
Saddle River, NJ.*

Bronfenbrenner system nomenclature has been expanded to show how
gangs can limit themselves to one or two systems based on the extent and
nature of their programs. The organizations that are most limited are probably structurally and sociologically less well developed than organizations that
expand activities to the macrosystemic level with the intent of making profound social changes that will primarily benefit members.

Levels of Gang Membership: A Taxonomy

Several attempts have been made to classify levels of gang membership (Boys
and Girls Club of America, 1993; Goldstein, 1991; Johnson, 1994).

TABLE 2.1   Levels of Gang Involvement
_____
Level I: Fantasy Identification with Gang
1. Knows about gangs primarily from newspapers, newscasts, and the movies.
2. May know about "real" gangs.
3. May know gang members but does not associate.
4. May like, respect, or admire a gang, a gang member, or the gang lifestyle.
5. Sees gang members "living out a fantasy."

Level II: At Risk of Gang Involvement
1. Has personal knowledge of gangs and gang members.
2. Casually and occasionally associates with gang members.
3. Lives in or near gang areas (turfs).
4. May like or admire gangs or gang members as individuals.
5. May like or admire the gang's lifestyle but not fully participate.

Level III: Wanna-Be/Associate Gang Member
1. Personally knows and admires gang members.
2. Regularly associates with gang members.
3. Considers gangs and related activity as normal, acceptable, or admirable.
4. Finds many things in common with gang members.
5. Is mentally prepared to join a gang.

Level IV: Gang Member
1. Is officially a gang member.
2. Associates almost exclusively with gang members to the exclusion of family and former friends.
3. Participates in gang crimes and other related activities.
4. Has substantially rejected the authority or value system of family and society.
5. Is not yet considered hard core by fellow gang members or others.

Level V: Hard-Core Gang Member
1. Is totally committed to the gang and gang lifestyle.
2. Totally rejects anyone or any value system other than the gang.
3. Is considered hard core by self, other gang members, and authorities.
4. Will commit any act with the approval or a demand from the gang.
5. Does not accept any authority other than the gang.
6. Has fully submerged personal goals for the collective goals of the gang.
_____
SOURCE: Boys and Girls Club of America, 1993. Reprinted by permission.

Common to all of these schemas are various levels of membership, each characterized by different affective, behavioral, and cognitive postures on the part of the gang member. The classification schema developed by the Boys and Girls Club of America is highlighted for presentation here because of its inclusion of preidentification status and varying degrees of affiliation, including active membership as well as early fantasy identification (see Table 2.1).

The Level I criteria listed in Table 2.1 are cognitive in nature. Individuals classified at this level have information about gangs and may have a positive regard for gang life. Missing from the criteria, however, is any statement of how the individual came to internalize the information. Notice that news media are identified as the sources of data, but the role of community networks or the grapevine in passing information about gang life is omitted.

Level II involvement criteria are extensions of Level I requirements. Criterion 1, "Has personal knowledge of gangs and gang members," suggests that the subject has directly experienced some element of gang life. This is a direct progression from the first criterion of Level I, which only required the subject to "know about" gangs from secondary sources such as newscasts and movies. The attributions that are made to gang life in Level II are through the filters of the child's own life. Representations of the benefits of gang life are likely to be significantly distorted, based on the context in which they are generated. This level of recruit is a prime candidate for describing the appeal of the gang to be its appearance of being "like family."

The second item in Level II involvement ("Casually and occasionally associates with gang members"), a behavioral indicator, is very similar to Criterion 3 ("Lives in or near gang areas"). Individual social experiences with gang members are likely to be used to negate parental warnings about the evils of gangs. Frequently young people think about advice and warnings in a personalized way. If their limited experiences do not fit the big picture presented to them by an adult, then the adult advice is seen as being irrelevant or "wrong." This movement from the generalized and abstract to personalized specifics of self is not unique to adolescents but reflects a pervasive cognitive style that makes it difficult to extrapolate from globals to self. The pattern becomes even more pronounced in adolescents when the issue of perceived invincibility is added. Death, police arrests, and tangible losses are almost always thought of as things that happen to others but not to oneself. In many ways, Criterion 3 is out of the control of youngsters, since they for the most part live where their parents locate the family. The final two criteria for Level II require an ability to observe and make decisions about the attractiveness of the gang lifestyle.

Level III, wanna-be, or associate membership, is a significant quantitative shift from Level II. The youngster is now transforming potential admiration of gang members and their lifestyles into a definitive and discernibly positive mind-set that is expressed through gang-affirming behaviors. It is not certain how this process occurs, but it is reasonable to assume that the frequency and intensity of exposure are contributing factors. Criterion 3, "Considers gangs and related activity as normal, acceptable, or admirable," strongly suggests that there has been sufficient exposure to gang life that it now represents the norm. Statistically, the frequency with which gang-like behaviors are watched by wanna-bes is so great that individuals moving toward a gang find it hard to be dismissive of gangs in their environment. The seeds of normalizing gang behavior have been planted, and the wanna-be's mind is providing a fertile ground for germination. It is almost as if the new recruit comes to see the world through new eyes, not his or her own, and with new meanings attached to what is seen. This change is cognitive in nature but has implications for affective fluctuations. For most individuals, significant shifts in views of one's social environment and the people in it are expressed through parallel shifts in mood and affective states. Frequently, there is a feeling of loss when deciding to abandon the "old ways." Melancholia and depression are common affective states experienced as an individual starts to move away from the old self in search of a new identity. Sometimes, anger and rage may also punctuate the moving away phase of an identity change. Also typical are expressions of despair and disappointment at having remained in the old identity for so long. At the other end of the affective continuum are euphoric states that occur when a seeking individual gains a glimpse of what he or she anticipates becoming. It is very common for the new identity to be elevated to a lofty status. This type of bipolarity of affective presentation is common in identity transformation cycles.

Despite the alternating affective states, radical shifts in verbalized opinions about gang members and gang life, Level III is still characteristic of individuals about to change. The transformation, however, is not complete, and the wanna-be is in a habitual state of *liminality*, complete with feelings of ambivalence and uncertainty about the major change of identity that is imminent.

The final criterion for Level III, "Is mentally prepared to join a gang," further attests to the cognitive and inner psychological processes that are so important at this stage. Finding commonalities with gang members (Criterion 4) also suggests that the wanna-be is capable of making a representational comparison between self and others. This may range from a restatement of obvious demographic characteristics ("we all live in the hood") and an exaggeration of their importance ("that means we all be brothers and gotta hang together") to more detailed analyses. The problem inherent in many such analyses, however, is that they are often fraught with errors of logic, misinterpretations, and inferential leaps that far outdistance the information on which they are based. Where drugs or illicit substances are a part of the logic and decision making, the distortions and faulty conclusions are likely to be even more extreme.

Between Levels III and IV, an initiation, real or symbolic, occurs. The classification scheme in the table does not clearly note this all-important transformation. It does indicate as Criterion 1 of Level IV that the individual is now officially a gang member. But initiation and the apparent affective, behavioral, and cognitive expressions associated with it are critical. Initiation represents the culmination of the identity transformation, typically concretized by the change of one's name. Of course, it goes without saying that what one is called is of immense psychological importance. Names for gang members are based on behaviors they may have exhibited during the trial membership period or in direct mockery of the family of origin socialization the member is attempting to leave. In some ethnically closed gangs, names of members reflect ethnic pride or political aspirations that are fantasized to be met by group membership.

Because the level of membership progression in the table is concerned with movement toward hard-core membership, the table does not address the question of what happens to individuals who are not initiated into the group. Three reasons why recruits may not be accepted into gangs have been highlighted by researchers (Branch, in press; Jankowski, 1991; Monti, 1994):

1. They fail the initiation tests.
2. They are deemed "fakes" by the group and considered unworthy of membership even if they pass the initiation tests.
3. They are no longer available for active affiliation. This situation usually occurs as a result of the family moving away from the community or sending the at-risk youth to live with relatives in another part of the country.

To date there have been no systematic studies of individuals who fail to be initiated into gangs.

Assuming that the initiation requirements are successfully negotiated without any change of heart by the recruit, a wanna-be progresses to the status of gang member. Criteria 1 through 4 in Level IV are focused on behavioral and cognitive dimensions. Being officially recognized as a gang member suggests that a successful initiation occurred. It also suggests a level of acceptance on both the part of the gang and of the new member. No provisions are made in this schema for trial membership. It is well known, however, that the early days of a recruit's membership are considered tentative (Jankowski, 1991). New members are often subjected to tests of loyalty (i.e., contrived conflicts with members, being forced to choose between the new family and the old family). Jankowski reports that during his brief membership in gangs he was often tested to see if he was a police informant.

Participation in gang crimes is the ultimate statement of commitment to the gang, evidencing a rejection of both societal and familial authority. The assumption appears to be that behavioral expressions are good and sufficient statements that the recruit is commited to the gang. Missing from this formulation are the cognitive and affective fluctuations that may be directly attributable to an individual's responses to changes of identity status. Despite the fact that Level IV members associate almost exclusively with other gang members, they continue to hang on to residues of former relationships with family and friends. Psychological bonds created in former relationships dictate strengths and weakness the gang member expresses in gang relationships. Individuals with a history of difficulty with boundaries are likely to show the same or similar propensities in the gang. It appears that the gang simply provides a forum for the expression of individual personality dynamics. New personalities are rarely, if ever, the direct result of gang membership. Stable and unrelenting personality traits may explain most internal gang conflicts. Individual members often have traits they are unwilling to put in abeyance in the service of the gang's goals. The end result is frequently conflicts between gang members with uncomplementary personalities.

No studies of the premorbid personality functioning of gang members are available. Some theorists and interventionists suggest that gang-predisposed youths can be identified as troubled youngsters as early as elementary school (Monti, 1994). More research is needed to confirm certain diagnostic labels as early predictors of those who later become hard-core gang members. Of course, no continuity between early childhood and adolescent behavioral problems and gang membership can be assumed. Such a link will not always be true, as evidenced by the conversion of many reasonably well-adjusted, achievement-oriented, even middle-class, children to gangs when they reach adolescence. Perhaps, then, inquiry should focus on the developmental trajectory of children with early personality and behavioral problems. Are they more susceptible to later affiliation with delinquent gangs than their nonadjudicated counterparts?

The classification scheme in Table 2.1 identifies Level V gang members as hard core. The criteria for this level of membership suggest a complete severance of ties with everyone and everything except the collective will and goals of the gang. Primary among the criteria for this level is total commitment to the gang and its lifestyle. Of course, this level of commitment can only be substantiated by self-report from the gang member and thus is at risk for distortion or exaggeration. In the absence of objective verification of Criterion 1, it is difficult to prove that an individual is a hard-core gang member. There are, however, other criteria associated with this level of gang membership. Among them is the requirement that the gang member "Totally rejects anyone or any value system, other than the gang." Applying this standard requires that the evaluator make an inferential leap from observed behaviors, concrete and verbal, of a gang member to his or her value system. Since value systems are abstract in nature, one can only speculate that the behaviors emitted by gang members reflect their values. This is an inferential leap that is often made but rarely examined for appropriateness. A small body of literature indicates the emitted behaviors of many gang members are not consistent with their internal values system (Branch, 1995; Branch & Rennick, 1995). A third criterion for Level V membership requires confirmation that an individual "is considered hard core by self, other gang members, and authorities." Again, the issue is how a gang member is perceived by others, probably on the basis of observed behaviors. The same can be said of Criteria 4 and 5. In both cases, observations of the gang member are used to formulate global and definitive opinions about him or her. "Has fully submerged personal goals for the collective goals of the gang," the final criterion, is a behaviorally based standard that does not account for the possibility of the member's expressed behavior being an incomplete representation or situation-specific manifestation of the true self.

Overall, the Level V membership criteria in Table 2.1 are behaviorally oriented, diametrically opposed to the Level I criteria, which are exclusively cognitive in orientation. These criteria are useful as a preliminary way for classifying gang members. They provide a simplified overview of the developmental shifts that are likely to occur in the lives of young people as they move from outsider to wanna-be to hard-core gang member. Assumptions inherent in the model suggest that the evolutionary process is linear and unencumbered. The potential role of sociocultural factors and life developmental processes is not considered. The Boys and Girls Club classification system in the table is not unlike others in that it is explicit in the recognition of varying levels of membership. Each level of membership is unique. To better understand the developmental course of gang membership, it is useful to juxtapose the developmental stages of gang membership against normal developmental processes in adolescence, focusing on the areas of affect, behavior, and cognition. The next chapter will provide this overlay with an examination of race and ethnicity as life developmental issues from the perspectives of how these issues are reflected in the lives of gangs and the personal lives of gang members. The application of developmental theory to the lives of gang members and implications for interventions will be discussed in Parts II and III of this book.

3

Race and Ethnicity

Historically, race and ethnicity have been dimensions along which gangs are classified by researchers. A multitude of studies categorize homicides and arrest records by racial designation assigned to a gang (Baker, 1988; Bobrowski, 1988; Curry & Spergel, 1988; Miller, 1989; Short & Strodbeck, 1965; Spergel, 1984, 1990). The emphasis of the racial and ethnic compartmentalizing has almost invariably been on African American and Latino groupings. Despite the limited attention given to White U.S. gangs, Covey, Menard, and Franzese (1992) show that such gangs are increasingly becoming a part of the social fiber of the United States. There are, of course, gangs in neighborhoods populated by recent immigrants, and these tend to be discussed in the literature as, for example, Asian American or Chinese American or by reference to their country of origin (i.e., Jamaican). The racial and ethnic designations used to date provide little insight into the inner workings of the groups in question; the current research situation probably reveals more about the researchers and their acceptance of the status quo than about gangs.

There are some racially mixed gangs, but they are rare. Most researchers note the racial homogeneity of adolescent gangs but never stop to ponder the host of issues that are related to that reality. For example, do gangs make conscious efforts to keep themselves racially pure or does this happen by a process of natural selection? Covey, Menard, and Franzese (1992) note

> In a racially and ethnically divided society, the existence of gangs organized along racial and ethnic lines may be inevitable. Gangs appear to evolve out of primary friendship groups, and to the extent that segregation in our neighborhoods and schools leads to racially and ethnically homogeneous friendship groups, we may also expect it to lead to racially and ethnically homogeneous gangs. (pp. 72–73)

Or, on the other hand, do adolescents congregate with others who are racially and ethnically like themselves as a natural selection process? Several writers who subscribe to the idea that gangs are an outgrowth of underclass bonding suggest that gangs are a natural by-product of life in ghettos and barrios. This position implies that gangs come to be formed of ethnically and racially homogeneous groupings inadvertently. In this chapter, I examine the role of race and ethnicity in gangs, on an institutional level and in the lives of individual gang members. Ethnicity, as a variable I deem to have greater explanatory value than race, relative to social growth and development, will be used as the basis for organizing data highlight differences between gangs in different communities. Finally, the question of ethnic identity as a preventative or risk factor for gang membership will be addressed.

Race Versus Ethnicity

The distinction between racial and ethnic groupings has caused much confusion in the behavioral and social sciences. Some authors use the words interchangeably, whereas others make very clear distinctions between race and ethnicity. Race is a concept derived from genetic distinctions with results in phenotypic characteristics (i.e., skin color, hair texture, and so on). It is an idea rooted in historical precedents. At different points in history, there have been various reasons to classify individuals by race for religious, political, and social purposes. The result has been that these social constructions have become so reified that racial categories are at times treated as if they are absolute, real, and sacred. Racial labels are usually created and then applied to individuals. It has been a rare case indeed where individuals are allowed to choose their racial category. More often than not, racial designations are either/or propositions. That there is no place for biracial or other categories is evidenced in the United States by such individuals being recognized by the U.S. Bureau of the Census only by an ill-defined group of "other." Racial categories tend to be global, incorporating people who have nothing in common except a series of physical characteristics, assumed similar genetic makeup, and the attending social responses to their racial category.

Ethnicity, as conceptualized here, is generally more narrowly defined and somewhat more restrictive than race. An ethnic group can be thought of as a group of people with a common historical heritage, originating in the same place and sharing cultural expressions such as manner of dress, art, music, food, and literature. In U.S. society, ethnic identification often serves the purpose of bonding individuals who function fully in U.S. life despite maintaining clear ties to other places. Such a spiritual and philosophical connection manifests itself most visibly in how groups identify themselves ethnically, such as African American.

Race and Ethnicity in Gangs

How do race and ethnicity figure into the programs and lives of gangs? In light of the history of racial conflicts in U.S. society, one might expect race and ethnicity to be factors that drive the programs of gangs involved in violent and disruptive behaviors. Empirical evidence to support this line of reasoning, however, is scant. There does exist a large literature of anecdotes and single cases that suggest that many episodes of gang violence are racially motivated. Establishing an accurate baseline for such a statistic is difficult, if not impossible, for two reasons. First, the way in which many jurisdictions report crimes that appear to be racially motivated makes it difficult to establish that an act was indeed committed as a group decision or action versus the individualistic conduct of persons who may be affiliated with a gang. Another reason preventing the development of baseline data is the problem of reporting itself. Many incidents of violence are not reported to the police but rather are simply seen as acts one associates with life in particular neighborhoods. This is especially true in neighborhoods populated by people of color. There has been a tradition of categorizing gangs by ethnicity and race when discussing the rates and types of crimes committed. Such categorizing offers very little for understanding the dynamics of gangs. In fact, continuing to sort homicide and other crime data by ethnicity and race fosters stereotypes such as the often-held view that gangs are the exclusive domain of poor inner-city neighborhoods populated by people of color. All parts of this assumption (i.e., gangs exist exclusively in poor neighborhoods, gang members are exclusively members of ethnic minority groups, and so on) are being seriously challenged in recent research on gangs. Here, I examine first the economic deprivation hypothesis from the perspective race and ethnicity perspective.

Until very recently, the *economic deprivation hypothesis* accounted for a major portion of gang research. Assumptions associated with it include the ideas that gang youth are marginalized by the larger society because of their lack of economic power. In an attempt to gain a greater share of the economic pie of U.S. society, poor adolescents organize themselves into gangs that often engage in illegal activities for the purpose of making money. This reasoning has been so prevalent that it has almost been elevated to the status of being a canon, above reproach or suspicion. It has also been applied almost exclusively to people of color, frequently under the assumption that gangs are part of underclass life of the United States. Economic gain as the primary catalyst for the establishment and evolution of gangs is central to the works of Duster (1987), Fagan (1989), Hagedorn and Macon (1988), Huff (1989), Jankowski (1991), Spergel (1990), and Wilson (1987). In each work, the focus has been on people of color but is described as focusing on the underclass. Are there no Whites in the U.S. underclass?

Hagedorn and Macon's (1988) study of gangs in Milwaukee has been the object of much debate. The authors suggest that the gangs in their study are a new phenomenon evolving from the growing African American underclass. Despite the economic thrust of the gangs, poverty is a major causative factor. The authors also insist that gangs evolved from break-dancing and street-corner groups, which they consider by-products of intergroup conflict. The media is specifically identified as a contributor to the perception of racial tensions in the city, thereby intensifying the conflicts between groups. Miller (1989) disagrees with Hagedorn and Macon's association between unemployment and the prevalence of gangs. He uses Boston as a case in point. Despite its low unemployment rate among African American residents, Miller notes, Boston still has a ghetto and serious gang problems. In his criticism of the Milwaukee study, Miller emphatically rejects the idea of getting rid of the underclass as an approach to getting rid of gangs.

A similar assault on the association of gangs with poor neighborhoods and people of color is offered by Monti (1994). He provides extensive data that show that gangs are also a fact of life in many suburban neighborhoods, among students who are enrolled in school, and among White as well as Black youngsters. I have also reported on a group of suburban students, of multiple racial and ethnic groups, who do not match the stereotype of gang members as being poor ethnic minority group inner-city residents (Branch and Rennick, 1996).

Mydans (1990b) adds to this literature concerning White youths and their tendency to affiliate with gangs. He reports that White suburban youths are joining established gangs most often identified with African American youth. Such a pattern of affiliation is interpreted as representing a romantic adventure for the White youths.

All of the foregoing literature suggests that gangs are homogeneous in nature, but it fails to even recognize the existence of gangs among White youths. Indeed, there has been some lively debate about the existence of gangs, as conventionally defined, in White neighborhoods, except in the case of recent immigrants. Covey, Menard, and Franzese (1992) suggest that one instance in which race does figure heavily in the life of the gang is in the case of skinheads, White groups with racist supremacist values at their core. The connections between skinheads and the neo-Nazi movement have been plentiful. Reports of violence committed by these groups usually highlight the fact that the victims are people of color, recent immigrants, or gay men or lesbians. Much of the skinheads' program of activity is anti-Semitic in nature. Are they then an example of a gang with an explicit racial or ethnic criterion for membership and for which racism is a pronounced item of business? Many current gang theorists have answered these questions in the negative. There is very little interest in skinheads as a gang in recent scholarly writings. Moore (1993) and Hamm (1993) are exceptions. They provide detailed and informative works on skinheads as an example of a gang in which the concept of race reigns supreme in determining who can join and the program of what is the gang.

Hamm (1993) suggests that the recent surge of skinhead activity in several large U.S. cities is cause for concern. He notes, however, that there are some significant differences between street gangs and neo-Nazi skinheads. Part of his argument is predicated on his observation that "scholars have found that gangs are largely an immigrant, adolescent, underclass phenomenon, but they have not found racism to be an organizing principle for gang membership. In those instances where racism has been discovered by gang researchers, it has usually been cited as an excuse for juvenile delinquency" (p. 62). Other distinguishing features of gangs that Hamm reports not to be relevant to neo-Nazi skinheads include (a) gangs often have a positive relationship with their communities, and (b) gang violence seems to be attributable to external tangible causes (i.e., turf battles, use and distribution of drugs, ethnic and cultural differences between neighborhoods, poverty and social disorganization, and so on). According to Hamm, "The evidence on the Neo-Nazi Skinheads stands in instructive contrast to this body of criminology. For the skinheads, violence is their signature trademark because *violence is part of their subcultural style*. . . . The skinheads seem to use violence for the explicit purpose of promoting political change by instilling fear in innocent people" (p. 62).

Hamm's (1993) account of the origin and rise to prominence of the skinheads highlights the intensity with which this group responds to issues of race and racism. Moore thinks that there are two factions in the group, nonracists and racists, and it is the latter group that has proved to be most volatile and disruptive in communities: "While they were originally in America a minor distraction on the punk scene, they have grown into a dangerous, far more politically engaged source of hate, thought and crime in America" (p. 3).

Despite his complaint that skinheads were not mentioned once in Huff's (1990) *Gangs in America*, Hamm (1993) himself does not find skinheads conforming to the classic criminological definition of a street gang. Rather, he believes their origin—international rather than domestic—and apparent singleness of purpose, predicated on race, makes them "something with a wider agenda that is potentially more dangerous to society, and certainly more elusive to academic gang scholars [than street gangs]. Because of their overt racism, political violence, and links to homologous international subculture of Neo-Nazism, the skinheads constitute what can best be described as a terrorist youth subculture" (p. 65).

On another level, gangs have remained racially homogeneous in composition but apparently more flexible in their business dealings. This raises an interesting point concerning the business orientation of the group not being limited by its racial politics. Are gangs likely to limit their business dealings to individuals of their own racial and ethnic groups? It is also interesting to note that the voluminous literature detailing the business dealings of gangs has never addressed the question of gang clientele in any detailed or systematic way. To do so would reveal some valuable information about the implicit social contracts between gang members and the larger communities in which they function. Studying the clientele would also illuminate the issue of how exclusive gangs are in limiting their interactions along racial and ethnic lines.

Race and ethnic categories are dimensions that gangs use in identifying their victims. The example of neo-Nazi skinheads who choose victims exclusively on the basis of race is an obvious case. There are more subtle situations where the variance of race and ethnicity of victims according to the type of crime committed offers valuable information about how race and ethnicity figure into the life of the gang. Unfortunately, research on gang crimes has not achieved sufficient level of specificity in reporting. Racial designation of victims does occur with Asian gangs that operate in the United States, however. Their victims are almost exclusively other Asians. A variety of interpretations have been offered to explain this preying on members of the same group, including internalized feelings of self-hatred, justifying an attack on others who resemble oneself, choosing targets who are most convenient and least likely to retaliate, displacement of feelings of rage and anger, and a combination of the above.

Impacts of Race and Ethnicity for Individual Gang Members

Race and ethnicity are powerful social issues in U.S. society. Researchers demonstrate this fact with their obsessive categorizing of gangs racially and ethnically. Such classifications are convenient but of questionable heuristic value. Grouping gangs racially and ethnically does not provide any information about the microsystems or inner psychological life of gang members and their families, the purpose of this book. Logically, it is reasonable to believe that one can make conclusions about the lives of individual gang members. The idea here is that a good grasp of the organizational dynamics of gangs provides a blueprint that can be used to understand individual members. This type of logic is prevalent among researchers, but it is fraught with problems. Among other things, it is reductionistic. It assumes that whatever the gang's script and dynamics, they are sufficient to explain the multitude of variations that exist among gang members. It would be just as naive and simplistic to think all of the individual dynamics and histories that exist within the collective membership of a gang could be identified and understood. We can, however, shift our thinking from an organizational level to a personal level. To do that in the context of the present discussion requires restating the issue of concern. The question becomes, How do race and ethnicity figure in the lives of gang members?

Wang (1994) provides one of the few empirical studies of adolescent gang members focused on their inner psychological life. He compares gang and nongang high school students along measures of self-esteem, racial attitudes, and self-professed role models. The sample was dichotomized along racial lines, seventy-eight Caucasians and seventy-seven African Americans. Concerning the issues of self-esteem and ethnic attitudes, Wang proposed two hypotheses for testing: Gang members would have lower levels of self-esteem than nongang members, and gang members would evidence higher levels of ethnocentrism. The Self Esteem Scale and the Racial Attitude Adjective Checklist (RAAC) were administered as parts of a larger battery.

Both positive and negative feelings of self-esteem were measured by the twenty-five–item Self Esteem Scale. The result was three scores: positive self-esteem, negative self-esteem, and overall self-esteem (positive minus negative score). On the RAAC, designed to measure racial attitudes toward one's own and other racial groups, students were assigned a positive, a negative, and an overall score.

In summarizing the self-esteem scores, Wang (1994) observes, "Gang members had significantly lower levels of overall self-esteem than did nongang students, $F(1,119)=20.44$, $Ms_e=.41$" (p. 284). No other relationships are found to be statistically significant. He also notes that the absence of a main effect for Race suggests that African Americans do not have lower levels of self-esteem, as measured by the test, than their Caucasian counterparts. Other analyses of the data confirm that among Caucasian students, gang members have higher positive self-esteem than non–gang members. No positive self-esteem differences are found in the African American subsample. A significant difference in negative self-esteem is found in the Caucasian and African American subgroups, however. In both subsamples, the tendency for the gang members to have higher negative self-esteem scores is significant at the .05 level.

When racial attitudes are examined through a 2 (Race of Subject) × 2 (Race of Target) × 2 (Condition: Gang versus Nongang) ANOVA, Wang (1994) finds "a highly significant interaction between Race of Subject and Race of Target, $F(1,151)=29.18$, $MS_e=1017.63$" (p. 285). A consistent pattern is found: Among both groups, greater negative stereotyping is directed toward the out-group than to their own racial group.

Wang (1994) interprets his findings as supporting Tajfel's (1981) *social identity theory*. Reduced to its most elementary form, Tajfel's theory suggests that social identity, which is formed as a function of group membership, comprises three components: motivational, cognitive, and sociocultural. The motivational component is based on the premise that individuals attempt to form positive evaluations of themselves. Thus, people are motivated to identify with groups in ways that enhance rather than detract from their personal self-esteem (Wang, 1994, p. 280). The racial attitudes finding in Wang's study shows consistently that all groups of students are more negative toward the out-group than to their own group. Thus, Wang's hypothesis is not supported. He was somewhat surprised at this result and the documentation in the literature that gang members tend to report more racial tensions in their neighborhoods than non–gang members. The gangs participating in Wang's study are racially homogeneous, but their response was similar to nongang youngsters of both races. This pattern of similarity of social views matches a finding reported by Branch and Rennick (1995) in a study of gang and nongang youths compared on measures of social values and attitudes.

Racial and Ethnic Variations in Gang Members (and Gangs)

Race and ethnicity have been prime dimensions by which gangs have been categorized for purposes of tracking crimes and for indexing the incidence of drug use. Wang (1994) reports that gang members tend to have rather fixed and extreme racial attitudes. There is very little else in the literature that documents the positions that gangs and gang members take on issues of race and ethnicity. Researchers frequently make inferences about where gang members stand on these issues based on the collective behavior of the group. Typical examples include the following scenarios:

1. An incident that appears to be racialistic in motivation occurs in a community. Gang members respond after much media hype and publicity concerning the incident. The gang, most likely homogeneous in its racial and ethnic composition, is identified as being racist in its behavior.

2. A gang is implicated in an incident that occurs in a racially or ethnically identifiable neighborhood. The targeted victim is characteristic of the neighborhood. If the gang is of a different racial or ethnic makeup, the incident is likely to be classified as a racially or ethnically driven incident when in fact it may not be. It may be that the incongruence between perpetrator and victim was coincidental. The media are unlikely to explore this possibility, but instead prefer the more sensationalized interpretation of race or ethnicity being a contributing factor in the conflict.

These two examples demonstrate the simplistic ways in which attributions, often erroneous, are made to gangs and their members. Such reductionistic approaches add to the stereotypic ways in which gang members are perceived by the general public. These attitudes make it difficult for human service professionals (i.e., counselors, social workers, and so on) to view gang members objectively or fairly.

In the next portion of this chapter, I examine ways in which different racially or ethnically identified gangs conduct themselves psychologically, exclusive of criminal behavior, in their communities of origin and in the larger society. Ethnic and racial variations on four issues will be articulated, not from a traditional cross-cultural comparative approach but merely to show how there are differences across groups. These substantive differences in how gangs relate to their reference communities strongly suggest that some original socialization effects are still apparent in the lives of gang members, despite their insisting otherwise. African American, Asian, Latino, and White are the classifications I use here to describe gangs.

Relationship to the Community of Origin

One explanation for why young people join gangs is to meet their affiliation needs. They seek out gangs, according to the affiliation theorists, as a way of moving away from their family of origin and a larger community that they perceive to be unsupportive and hostile. But even while moving away from their family, many gang members continue to maintain a very active role in their reference ethnic communities, perhaps because they internalize some of the values of the family they are attempting to leave. Blos (1979) describes this adolescent movement away from family as a *second individuation*. He proposes that it is a revisiting of earlier attempts at separation that occurred in infancy and toddlerhood, but this time the effort is more complete and occurs on a more abstract and psychological level.

Although gang members may be responding to their internal drive to be "unlike" their parents and siblings, they never break out of the cycle as profoundly as they claim. The fact of the matter is that many young people who choose to affiliate with gangs are symbolically joining a smaller select community within their community of origin (racial or ethnic). Such a gang derives its sense of purpose and direction from lessons learned in the ethnic community. The literature on adolescent gangs and members' sense of ethnic and racial rootedness is amazingly clear on this point.

By far the greatest amount of attention to ethnic and racial allegiance in the gang community has been generated on Latinos. Covey, Menard, and Franzese (1992) note, "Hispanic gangs have existed in this country since the turn of the century, and may have become a way of life for some Hispanics" (p. 57). They also imply that the gang affiliation noted in many barrios may be designed for purposes of psychological protection from an outside community that is considered hostile. Inherent in this line of reasoning is the idea that many Latino gang members have been individually reduced to a status of marginality. The gang becomes the vehicle for altering that undesirable state. Because of the prevalence of gangs in many economically poor neighborhoods in southern California, gangs in many cases have become institutionalized in the social fabric of the Hispanic barrio subculture (Vigil, 1983).

The precise relationship of Latino gangs to the larger society has been the source of much debate. Some theorists have supported the notions surrounding Vigil's (1983) idea of "multiple marginality" as a major causative factor in gang membership. Harris (1988) contends that for Latinos who experience high levels of difficulty in school, family problems, economic poverty, few opportunities to improve themselves economically, and general discrimination by the society in which they live, the gang comes to be viewed as "the answer." An opposing view of marginal status as a major contributor to gang affiliation is articulated by Horowitz and Schwartz (1974) and Horowitz (1982). They note that Latino gang members in Chicago are skillful at assuming socially desirable roles. In summarizing the two sides of this debate, Covey, Menard, and Franzese (1992) observe

> One possible reason for the differences between different Hispanic groups (e.g., Mexican Americans as opposed to Cubans and Puerto Ricans) are being highlighted here, and that marginality is a more important explanation for gang membership among Mexican Americans because their marginality is more pronounced than that of other groups. (p. 58)

Latino gangs have been characterized by some authors as being longer lived and more inextricably linked to the neighborhoods—the barrio—than is the case with other ethnic gangs. The longevity of some gangs, particularly in southern California, makes them multigenerational. A by-product of this longevity is that the gangs become a factor in the life of the barrio with which all residents of the barrio must deal. Horowitz (1987) discusses the relationship between adults in the Latino community and the acts of violence perpetuated by gangs. She notes that many nongang individuals in the barrio tolerate gang violence not because they condone it but because they perceive the acts of violence as necessary for a young man to establish himself in the larger social order and to express his honor.

The overreaching issue for many Latino gang members is a sense of identity. The gang provides them with multiple opportunities to assert themselves within the context of the barrio and its relationship to the larger community. Vigil (1988) indicates that the concepts of barrio and family are synonymous for many Latino gangs. Many ideas that have their origin in the ethnic community (i.e., La Raza) are reinforced by the gang. Paramount in the gang's ideology is the idea of commitment and pride in self, even when it leads to conflicts with outsiders. This emphasis on Latino identity issues is exemplified in the names that are chosen by the groups, often combining an intense sense of personal pride and a calling to a political and economic struggle with the larger community.

It should also be noted that in research about race and ethnic identity among gang members it is not only the gang members' attitudes that are at issue. The attitudes that researchers have about issues related to race also enter into the literature, sometimes in very pronounced ways.

Research concerning racial and ethnic issues as they find expression in African American gangs is limited. Huff (1990) provides some information concerning African American gangs and their modes of operation in the cities of Cleveland and Columbus, Ohio. He notes that as geographical boundaries for ethnically identified neighborhoods shift likewise there is a shift in the location of African American gangs. Improved roadways and public transportation increase the likelihood of gangs operating throughout the Cleveland and Columbus metropolitan areas and decrease their presence and activities in neighborhoods that might otherwise be identified as African American. Beyond this observation about the ecology of African American communities, Huff offers few comments relative to race and ethnicity as issues that find expression in the program of African American gangs.

The one other important study relative to African American gangs and their psychological presentations was authored by Hagedorn and Macon (1988). Their study of gangs in Milwaukee is seen by many as being one of the most exhaustive relative to African American gangs located outside of the major cities of the East and West Coasts. Hagedorn and Macon relate much of the gang activity in Milwaukee to membership in the economic underclass. In fact, they go so far as to suggest that by eliminating the underclass, one could expect that there would be an equivalent decline, if not elimination, of active membership in gangs in the African American community. Their analysis, however, does not speak to the issues of race and ethnicity in the lives of gang members or the program of gangs except secondarily to their state of economic deprivation. Unlike their Latino counterparts, African American gangs are not noted by researchers to be firmly committed to issues of identity resolution or even the issues of their community of residence.

Since 1990, there has been much discussion of traditional African initiation rites of passage and realignment with the African heritage as intervention strategies for eliminating gangs in the African American community. Despite animated discussion of this political and spiritual reconnection of otherwise marginalized African American youths, to date there has been little published literature attesting to the efficacy of these programs.

Of all of the racially and ethnically identified adolescent gangs, the least information is available from Asian American gangs about inner workings and thinking. The one piece of information that appears frequently in the literature is the fact that such gangs prey almost exclusively on other members of the Asian American community. These gangs are suspected of being affiliated with high levels of organized crime in selling drugs. Individual gangs are composed almost exclusively of individuals originating from the same Asian country. It is not clear why the gangs are motivated for within-community crime activity. Other important but unanswered questions about Asian American gangs operating in the United States include how members make use of the gang to move into the larger society, other than through economic improvement.

Covey, Menard, and Franzese (1992) provide a brief compendium of Asian American gangs. They note that the most information is available on Chinese American gangs, which date back to the early 1900s. But in their analysis and summary of the programmatic dimensions of Asian American gangs, they fail to comment on how race and ethnicity figure in the daily activities of these gangs except as helping to target who may be the potential victims of their violent acts. The authors summarize the role of race and ethnicity in contemporary Asian American gangs as follows:

> Asian American gangs appear to most closely resemble the gangs in their cultures of origin. Unlike African American, Hispanic and white ethnic gangs, Asian American gangs appear to be highly organized and pragmatic. Profit is the principle motive and violence is typically avoided except as a last resort. Asian American and Hispanic gangs share one important characteristic, the linguistic barrier that exists between them and the host culture, a barrier less evident for African American and most contemporary white ethnic gangs. (p. 72)

No other details concerning the complexity of racial and ethnic issues in fostering or impeding the psychological acculturation and assimilation of Asian American youngsters who participate in gangs are offered by these authors.

Whether gangs even exist in White communities is the subject of considerable debate. In some analyses, individual researchers are quick to note that skinheads differ from other adolescent gangs in their political agenda and their singleness of purpose of changing the world politically through violent acts. Despite clear structural and behavioral programmatic differences between themselves and other gangs, neo-Nazi groupings of youngsters who call themselves skinheads do very much qualify for consideration under the label of adolescent gangs. They differ from other gangs in race and ethnicity being paramount in their membership requirements. These gangs are open to Whites only. Racial and ethnic matters also figure prominently in the program of neo-Nazi skinhead groups in that their victims are primarily people of color but occasionally White individuals who are gay men or lesbians. Very little else is known about race and ethnicity as variables in the life of neo-Nazi skinhead groups except that they are committed to White supremacy and the annihilation of people of color. The clear evidence that race figures prominently in the selection of victims for these groups is to be expected in light of the fact that race is such a cardinal dimension in their philosophy.

The Gang as a Connector to the Larger Society

The overwhelming emphasis in research on the relationship between gangs and society has been from the perspective of the impact of law enforcement agencies and the criminal justice system on gangs. Discussion here is concerned with how gangs in their normal course of existence are impacted by connections and brief encounters with the "outside world." The usual approach is to consider how ethnic minority gang members relate to the larger society. That is now being expanded to include White and middle-class youths, who are increasingly participants in gangs (Mydans, 1990b), and their exposure to life in communities populated by people of color.

Mydans (1990b) notes that many middle-class and White suburban youths are affiliating with gangs. He finds a variety of reasons explaining this phenomenon, which defies the "usual socioeconomic explanations for the growth of gangs in inner cities," including "a misguided sense of romance about gangs, pursuit of the easy money of drugs, and self-defense against the spread of established hard-core gangs" (p. A7). Evidence corroborating Mydans's ideas is found in other newspaper accounts reporting episodic involvement in gangs among middle-class White youth (Dao, 1990; Siegel, 1990) and television documentaries on gangs that have highlighted this new trend in membership to include White youth. (Neo-Nazi skinheads are classified here as a gang.)

By far the greatest emphasis in this area in the literature has been on how gangs and their members respond to law enforcement efforts to suppress them. Examples can be observed in the intensification of the federal government "get tough on gangs" position and antigang legislation. Some researchers suggest that much of this effort is a misplacement of energy and resources (Fagan, 1996; Randolph, 1996). These authors contend that instead of attempting to crush gangs and decrease their appeal to young people, more emphasis should be directed to eliminating the social conditions and beliefs that cause youngsters to be drawn to gangs. Social alienation, dysfunctional families, and faulty thinking are identified as causative factors. More will be said about these points later.

Much of what African American and Latino adolescents experience in the context of the gang is a painful connection to the larger world through the law enforcement and criminal justice systems. This pattern is well documented in the literature. Other issues have not received much attention:

How gang members react to the larger society's reactions to them and the pregang socialization of gang members. It has come as a surprise to many poor youths that in addition to the obvious disregard the larger society feels for them, evidenced in part by poor-quality local schools and the absence of opportunities for economic growth and development, there is also a staggering societal indifference to the plight of the economically poor. The popular literature contains many accounts of gang members who react with disbelief when confronted with the reality that the larger community blames them for their economic deprivation and lack of opportunities for significant change. McCall's (1994) popular novel, *Make Me Wanna Holler,* is a good example. Other evidence of the demonization of gang members can be seen almost weekly on television talk shows on which gang members desperately try to defend their chosen path of antisocial behavior as a way of changing their life situation. Many talk show hosts unfortunately do little to shift public attention to the larger picture of gang life, including pregang functioning and members' earlier periods of reasonably prosocial development. It is indeed a rare talk show host or popular media reporter who tries to create an atmosphere of empathy in which an audience can imagine the unrelenting deprivation, anguish, and helplessness experienced by many youth who later come to affiliate with gangs. Unfortunately, many of the popular, often glamorized presentations of dilemmas of gang youths fail to address the emotional anguish that young people experience before and after making the decision to engage in a lifestyle that is often tempered with violence and illegal acts.

Gangs have in themselves blocked opportunities for some adolescents of color. Gangs limit the style and type of participation gang members can have with their indigenous communities. Being a gang member often gives an adolescent *out-group* status in his or her own neighborhood. Joining a gang also interferes with an adolescent's likelihood of participating in the larger society in a positive way.

On the other side of the continuum is the experience of White youths who participate in non-White adolescent gangs and what this does to provide them with an exposure to what life is like "on the other side." I suggest that the interaction many middle-class youths have with the legal and criminal justice system secondary to their gang involvement is a foreign experience for them and their families. In some ways, they briefly encounter what many people of color describe as being a part of their normal routine. I base this statement on the well-documented fact that most juvenile offenders in the United States who reach the criminal justice system for adjudication are indeed adolescents of color. I do not suggest that adolescents of color are more likely to engage in crime than are their White counterparts, but only that adolescents of color are much more likely to wind up in the criminal justice system.

In addition to the novel experience of interacting with the criminal justice system, many White youths who affiliate with gangs find themselves in the unusual position of being outcasts in their own community. This new experience of being socially marginalized may provide them with an opportunity to experience what many adolescents of color report experiencing on a daily basis. Instead of being part of the power structure in the macrosystem, White adolescents who participate in gangs become a minority in the majority culture, although they never assume the identities attributed to ethnic minority youth. Mydans (1990b) thinks that many White youths who participate in gangs are doing so out of a sense of *social alienation*. Joining a gang is their way of romanticizing life as they perceive it to exist for ethnic minority adolescents.

Recently, members of several African American gangs have attempted to redefine the purpose and program of their organizations. In 1995, during elections for the Chicago Board of Alders, to the surprise of many, several adolescent gangs organized themselves politically and ran candidates in the election. To the even greater surprise and dismay of some, the gang alumni garnered enough votes in the primary election to be included in the runoff. Public responses to the gang members' participation in the election was intense, ranging from outrage to disbelief. This participation in the organized political process is evidence that as some gang members have grown older they have come to recognize the potential benefits that can be derived for them and their fellow gang members by participating in socially condoned activities such as organized politics.

A similar pattern of change in the programmatic activities of a gang is occurring in New York City. The Zulu Nation is engaged in an effort to politicize and reorganize the collective thinking of the group through constructive activities such as participating with local banks in the creation of entrepreneurial programs. In the Latino community in the metropolitan New York area similar efforts have been reported. Some individuals think that this type of opportunity provides a conduit to the larger society for many gang members, a connection that is vital when their gang careers are over.

Information on Asian gangs and their relationship with the larger community in the United States has been very limited in the literature. Most of what has been reported concerns their connections to organized crime and their efforts to penetrate the economic bases of Asian American communities, primarily in large cities such as New York, San Francisco, and Los Angeles. It is interesting to note that public attitudes about gangs are very different when applied to individuals of Asian ancestry as opposed to African American and Latino adolescents. Much of this differential seems to be related to larger societal images of these ethnic groups.

The Gang as a Vehicle for Resolution of Identity Issues

The cardinal developmental issue of adolescence concerns identity. Most theorists suggest that in adolescence individuals receive multiple messages about who they are or can be. Information from a variety of sources helps adolescents in their quest to answer the ultimate question of "Who am I?" The development of competence in a tangible domain is often seen as a powerful adjunct to individuals during the period of adolescence. Some young people are able to develop an interest and sense of competence in athletics; others may excel in academic matters; and still others pride themselves on their sociability and their skills at making and sustaining friendships. The issue of identity among adolescents includes personal and group identity.

Latino gangs are much more pronounced in having ethnic identity as a part of their group's program than other ethnic gangs. Much of the activity of Latino gangs is affiliated with the barrio and *familia*. This seems to help in Latino adolescents' quest for a solid sense of identity, personal and group.

I do not suggest that ethnic identity is a simplistic notion that gives rise to an absolute sense of other areas of an individual's life. Rather, the development of a firm sense of ethnic identity enables individuals to experience other dimensions of themselves and the world around them with a higher level of comfort and resolve. For example, in many communities of color there are very clearly defined gender roles. Individuals who behave inconsistently with those roles frequently find themselves in conflict with the community. Recent examples are young women who have opted to pursue employment and careers in work areas that have been traditionally populated by men, such as heavy equipment operation, commercial aviation, and public safety (i.e., law enforcement and fire fighting). These women are likely to experience some conflict with their primary reference groups such as family and ethnic community. If the issues are successfully resolved at the microsystemic level, the young woman will have a renewed sense of confidence even though she may become more marginalized by her larger reference group. The same can be said of adolescents who use the gang as a place to figure out their strengths and their weaknesses.

It is interesting to note that despite the importance of identity issues during adolescence, there has been very limited psychological research on the issue of ethnic identity development and how it fits with the quest for a more *global identity*. There is a body of literature about ethnic identity as an issue in adolescence, but this research has been conducted without regard for the larger issue of identity. The work of Phinney (1991, 1992; Phinney & Allipura, 1990; Phinney & Tarver, 1988) is a good example of the range of work that has been done on the issue of adolescents and ethnic identity. My own recent work (Branch, 1995) raises the question of ethnic identity as a generic developmental task of adolescents and how the issue finds expression in the lives of adolescent gang members; my findings confirm some of the observations noted by Wang (1994).

Participation in Gang Life as Fulfillment of a Social Script

For many adolescents of color, participation in a street gang has been a social script that others have created for them. This is well documented and relates especially to Latino families who may have been members of gangs for several generations (Vigil, 1983). Some of the fathers and uncles of the current generation of active gang members, however, point out that gangs as they knew them in their youth were not nearly so violent as they have come to be in the present generation. This observation is usually associated with the wholesale availability of firearms and assumed extreme level of substance abuse among gang members. For many adolescents who are members of families that recently immigrated to the United States, participation in gangs has been a condoned activity that provides much-needed economic revenue to aid the family in its quest for financial stability. For yet another group of adolescents of color, participation in gangs may simply represent the fulfillment of a social script that has been created by others.

In several inner-city communities, young people have commented that it is expected that an individual will join a gang as a method of protection from other residents of the community who are already members of gangs. Participation in a gang may be a rite of passage to manhood in some ethnic cultural groups. Young men see it as their moral, if not community, obligation to affiliate with a gang once they have become members of "the community" in the United States. In some situations, participation in adolescent gangs is a prelude to involvement in organized political activity. Jankowski (1991) reports a similar occurrence in some communities in Boston. Organized political clubs, often ethnically identifiable, use street gangs as the recruitment setting for participation in their social and political clubs.

Vigil (1983) also suggests that for many Latino youth, a family history of gang involvement seems to increase the likelihood that a young person will participate in gangs in adolescence. This issue of multigeneration participation versus first-time participation in gangs is one that seems to have significant ethnic group differences. Latino and African American youths whose families have been in this country for less than two generations perhaps are at greater risk for easy identification because of the accessibility of juvenile court and school records. Caution should be used in making sweeping generalizations that Latino and African American youths are at greater risk because of family histories. It may be that this is a function of whose histories are available for review. For recent immigrants from Asia, there is the distinct possibility that although there may be a history of family involvement in gangs, it is not clear that gangs in the indigenous homeland are structurally or psychologically the equivalent of gangs that recent immigrants may find as a form for expression of themselves and their quest for economic gains in a short period of time.

All of these pieces of information suggest that there are striking similarities and differences that contribute to the ethnic identity others create for adolescents, individuals' internalization of these identities, and how these internalizations find behavioral expression in contemporary society. The larger question, it seems, is whether ethnic identification and socioeconomic status in tandem significantly increase the likelihood that a youth will affiliate with a gang.

Ethnicity—Protective or Risk Factor?

The essential question is whether ethnic group membership increases the likelihood that a young person will affiliate with a gang. A simplistic response to this question is that ethnic minority youths are at greater risk for gang membership. This response is usually based on the statistic that more adolescents of color than Whites are processed in law enforcement agencies. This numerical differential should not be taken as confirmation of an equivalent difference in rate of gang participation but as a difference in the rate of arrests for gang-related offenses. Adolescents of color, irrespective of gang membership, are also more likely to be detained and arrested for offenses than their White counterparts. Collectively, these factors suggest that residents in poor neighborhoods are at greater risk, demographically if not psychologically. Perhaps a closer analysis of the risk versus protective nature of ethnic group membership can be achieved by approaching the issue from another perspective.

It is not ethnicity per se that determines the margin of risk for gang membership, but rather the associations that are made to a group (i.e., residence in poor neighborhoods, acquiescing in stereotypical behavioral scripts, high probability of being targeted by law enforcement officers, and so on). In some situations, gangs are an integral part of the social fiber of neighborhoods. Therefore, they are a fact of life with which young people must deal. In other neighborhoods, gangs are an exotic anomaly. Young people who join gangs in those neighborhoods may do so simply because the experience is so different and novel compared to options in the neighborhood. In this case, it appears that gang affiliation may occur as a thrill-seeking experience or an overidentification with the stereotypical "minority experience."

Vigil (1983) believes that in many Latino communities in the Southwest, the best predictor of a young person's risk for joining a gang is a family history of active gang membership. Despite receiving clear messages against gang membership, many young people give in to the implicit pressure and choose to become active members.

When one's sense of ethnic identity is defined as a reaction to the larger society, the risk for using ethnic identity explorations and achievements in the context of political activism increases dramatically. This all suggests that young people who see their ethnic group as being a large distance from the real seat of power are likely to turn to the gang as a way to lessen the distance. The gang becomes a vehicle for the achievement and resolution of ethnic identity even when it entails open and continual conflict with the larger community. In such situations, ethnic identity, narrowly defined, seems to increase the likelihood that in the searching phase, adolescents are at risk for turning to gangs for resolutions to questions regarding their place in the world and their ethnic identity.

A similar analysis can be made for White youngsters who join gangs as a political statement about their dissatisfaction with what they perceive to be the imbalance of power and preference in the communities surrounding them and across the United States. Specifically, many neo-Nazi skinheads report that they have been drawn to the calling of White power and White supremacy as a way to turn back affirmative action and social justice changes that have occurred since 1985. In this situation of individuals feeling disenfranchised and projecting their sense of rage and frustration onto the outgroup—in this case people of color—racial identity instead of ethnicity dramatically increases the likelihood of a young person affiliating with a gang. In both of these situations, gang affiliation becomes a way to relieve the angst and internal dissonance caused by psychological processes and interpretations of the larger world. Young people who have not been in the United States very long may find in gangs and their glamorous marketing a quick transition to the good life.

The situation for recent Asian immigrants is one of complexity and deserves careful analysis. As indicated earlier, most of the writing about Asian immigrants who participate in gangs has been done from the perspective of involvement in illegal activity and extortion practice in the Asian American community. It appears that for many of these young people participation in gangs is the fulfillment of a social script written and supplied to them by other members of the Asian American community, most notably, participants in high-level organized crime. In this context, it appears that ethnic identity as matching the stereotypic image increases the likelihood that others expect a young man to join and actively participate in a gang. This is not to say that the expectation is one that is appropriate—simply that it is very real.

It is widely believed that there is a high level of correlation between political consciousness and political activity among individuals with a sharply differentiated level of ethnic identity achievement. The reasoning behind this complex association is that the high levels of political consciousness and activism are facilitative of individuals resolving the question of ethnic identity achievement. For some of these individuals, ethnic identity achievement (i.e., a strong sense of who they are ethnically) suggests that they should be oppositional to the macrosystemic blueprint of the United States. Many of these individuals interpret the macrosystemic blueprint as saying that ethnically identified individuals, particularly people of color, are devalued in the larger scheme of things and provided very few legitimate opportunities for advancement. In defiance of that implicit script, many young people use the gang as a forum to express their discontent and displeasure.

In early developmental phases, ethnic identity can be a risk factor for associating with collectives such as street gangs and other subversive organizations in the attempt to resolve one's sense of personal identity. Individuals who feel socially marginalized are likely to try a variety of approaches to resolve their identity crisis. One common strategy is to affiliate with individuals whom they perceive to be like themselves.

Ethnicity and race, bases on which individuals compare themselves to others, are often chosen as variables to help adolescents organize their world. In some situations, individuals who feel marginalized and disconnected from the larger community join a gang as a way of eliminating their feelings of isolation. It also seems that the other extreme—full participation in appropriate and healthy expressions of ethnic identity—would be facilitative of young people being able to resist the appeal of gangs. Unfortunately, the literature concerning this last point is in a very early developmental stage; I know of no published studies that directly address the issue of ethnicity as a protective factor. There is, however, a belief that gang intervention programs should use cultural identification as a key component in their programs. This is especially true of recently started programs in the African American community.

Part 2
Clinical Assessment

Part 2
Clinical Assessment
The Mental Status Examination

4

The Mental Status Examination

The mental status examination is designed to assess the present mental functioning of the identified client, the gang member. Such assessments can be derived from direct observation of clients as well as from queries about ideations. Behavior during the interview session itself can be diagnostic of clients' functioning in other settings. In assessing the mental status of gang-affiliated youths, it is important that clinicians intersperse questions and reflections about gang activity with discussion of more ordinary daily activities in which the gang member may also participate. Because the affiliation with the gang is such a critical component in the member's sense of identity, however, this affiliation itself should be considered as a valuable source of information about the member's developmental status and general psychological functioning.

In completing the mental status examination, clinicians should keep the focus on the present. Critical information about past events and anticipated activities can, however, be gleaned from carefully crafted questions. Past and future perspectives can be indicators of clients' ability to shift points of reference. An emerging body of research suggests that many gang members, and other young people who frequently engage in violent behavior, have a limited vision of the future (Doucette-Gates, in press). They believe there is no future for them and they should live a life of reckless abandon today because tomorrow they will be dead. Asking gang members about the future not only yields clues about their ability to project and plan but also offers opportunities for clinicians to observe clients' ability to think of themselves as individuals with the capacity to change with age. Do they assume that they will always remain in their current psychological state? Or do they hold open the possibility that they and their world will change in unspecified ways? Asking gang members about the past creates a situation in which affective material that may have been dormant for significant periods of time can be revisited. Indicators of such a process may not be verbalized directly but may become obvious as a result of careful questioning. During the course of the interview, the client may become sad or less verbal as the subjects of past losses or disappointments emerge. Clinicians must be observant of such affective shifts and use them as the basis of interpretations to keep the interview moving.

The purpose of the mental status examination is to give a comprehensive clinical assessment of clients' functioning in the here and now. A variety of textbooks describe the content of and techniques for conducting a mental status examination. Interested readers are referred to the *Comprehensive Textbook of Psychiatry* (Kaplan & Sadock, 1989) for a detailed description. In this chapter, I cover the basic content areas of a comprehensive examination with a particular focus on gang affiliation and how the gang potentially contributes to the affective life of its members. Note that care must be exercised to distinguish between the objective reporting of data and clinicians' interpretation of information.

The exact style that clinicians choose to employ for conducting mental status examinations flows from their level of clinical expertise and comfort with the client. Without overgeneralizing or being stereotypic in our approach to gang youths, a few words of caution are in order about safety and volatility as ongoing concerns for clinicians. Some very simple rules of thumb that are not unique to working with gang members but are appropriate for any psychiatric patient are as follows:

1. Do not enter a closed room without a clear path for escape in the event the client becomes hostile and belligerent.
2. Whenever possible, position yourself between the client and the door to the room.
3. Confirm that the client understands the purpose of the examination and that some parts of it may seem intrusive. This should be done before beginning the examination procedure.
4. If the examiner anticipates recording any part of the interview, this should be discussed with the client before starting the actual examination.
5. Rules concerning confidentiality should be clearly established with the client before beginning the interview.

Rules

Appearance.   All dimensions of the client's presentation that are observable, quantifiable, and objectively verifiable should be covered. The most obvious dimension of this assessment point is the client's physical appearance, including manner of dress. Leon, Bowden, and Faber (1989) offer a word of caution to clinicians concerning assessments of client's appearance: "Current social trends must be respected when assessing appearance, however, inasmuch as multicolored dyed hair, pins through the earlobe, and bones through the nasal septum may all be acceptable in some subcultures" (p. 457). A direct statement about the client's physical stature and manner of presentation (i.e., dressed appropriately for the season, tidy, and so on) offers insights into his or her attention to details of hygiene and appearance.

A lot of attention has been given to the wearing of gang colors and clothing in the recent literature (Johnson, 1994; Monti, 1994). Johnson's (1993) guide to gangs includes an extensive discussion of the meanings that should be attached to variations in gang attire. It is useful as an introductory guide for understanding adolescents and their attempts to generate symbols indicative of their internal states. But it is of questionable value to focus heavily on the colors worn by young people or the associations made to them. Things change, including the ways in which adolescents attempt to distinguish themselves from others.

In addition to describing and assessing the client's physical appearance, the clinician should be attentive to the issues of manner of relating, overt emotional displays, and level of cooperation. Data for some of these areas can be obtained by direct methods. For example, a client who appears to be uninterested in the interview, evidenced by repeatedly looking down and avoiding eye contact with the examiner, could be conveying a variety of messages. Common interpretations of such behavior usually revolve around the absence of an appropriate affective connection to the interviewer. Often, cultural imperatives dictate that an adolescent should show deference toward elders. This pattern may be intensified when the adult is a physician. Still other interpretations of the lack of eye contact may be as evidence of shame or guilt associated with gang membership, an interpersonal style, depression, after-effects of drugs or alcohol, or a combination these factors. In reporting the behavior, offer details that qualify whether it persisted throughout the interview or only occurred at certain points.

Activity. The domain of activity is concerned with the client's manner of conducting himself or herself during the interview. Specific emphasis should be devoted to extremes of behavior. The clinician should exercise care when describing the behavior, making certain to locate it accurately in the context of the interview. Special behaviors that persist throughout the interview without fluctuation should be considered significant. The usual convention is to think of behaviors that occur frequently as hyperactivity. They may punctuate a point that has been made verbally or they can be emotional markers suggestive of internal tension related to the material being discussed. Hand gestures are a good example of physical activity that may become pronounced during an interview.

A variety of interpretations can be attached to frequent hand gestures. The client may be reflecting an ethnic cultural norm in which hand gestures are a common nonverbal expression or engaging in a particularly adolescent convention of hand gesturing, as one can frequently observe among rappers. In reporting, the clinician should describe the behavior, its frequency, and context in the interview. The clinician's report should include a summary or interpretative statement, with care taken to distinguish the descriptive from the interpretive sections of the report.

Behaviors frequently observed in mental status examinations with adolescents include foot tapping, hand wringing, face rubbing, and carphologic movements (picking at clothing). In reporting the presence of these behaviors, the clinician should note if the behaviors are purposeful. Extreme examples of nonpurposeful behaviors such as pacing and foot tapping are usually clinical indicators that the client is upset. The behavior is significant because the client is probably trying to tell the clinician something that he or she is unable to express directly in words.

Decreased activity, or psychomotor retardation, manifests by diminution of movement, speech, and thinking. It includes excessive speech latency before answering a question (Leon, Bowden, & Faber, 1989). Unusual physical activity or inactivity during the examination should be described in detail and localized within the life of the interview.

Speech and Language.   Language refers to a complex system of communication including both the capacity to send messages to others (expressive language) and the ability to understand and internalize messages from others (receptive language). Speech is a specific type of expressive language. Other examples of expressive language include body gestures and nonverbal facial expressions. Most adolescent gang members have a gang lexicon consisting of slang and other nonstandard word usages. Many adolescent gang members are fluent in at least two language systems, standard English as it exists in the client's reference community and the gang-specific dialect. Gang members from a recently immigrated family may also function in a third language. This bi- and even trilingual capacity has major implications for evaluating the client's functioning.

Clients who function in more than one language often switch language codes when they experience a high level of emotional charge. Language code switching has been observed in bilingual (Spanish and English) clients as well as among bilingual therapists performing technical assessments during a clinical session.

The client's style of linguistic presentation should be noted throughout the session, beginning with the initial greeting. The examination itself should be structured so there is a balance between questions, reflective statements, and ongoing dialogue. Too many questions from the interviewer can place the subject in a defensive posture. The same result occurs with statements beginning with "Why"? With the exception of a few well-seasoned veterans, most individuals who go to see a therapist are already feeling a bit fragile and defensive. The same probably can be said about gang members. Bombarding them with questions at the beginning of an interview is likely to earn a display of recalcitrance and avoidance. A better strategy would be to invite adolescent clients to tell the examiner about themselves and their world. Such an approach often successfully dissipates client resistance. It also provides an opportunity to discuss a comfortable subject and to eliminate the possibility that the novelty of the experience of seeing a therapist interferes with productivity. And as clients share information, they reveal significant details about internal states.

Assessment of speech and language should focus on two dimensions, content and form. Leon, Bowden, and Faber (1989) offer this summary of the assessment of speech and language areas: "The speech and language productions of patients frequently provide examiners with an indirect view of their thoughts, since thoughts as such cannot be directly observed. Formal speech or language abnormalities can reflect brain pathology or a psychiatric disorder, or both" (p. 457).

A host of speech and language variations are found to be predictive of underlying thought disorders and psychiatric disturbances. Box 4.1 provides a glossary of commonly observed speech and language variations.

Clinicians should observe the linguistic behavior of clients to determine if a significant change occurs when conversation focuses directly on gang membership and activity. Qualitative changes in a client's demeanor when the gang is mentioned may be a valuable clinical indicator, offering leads for more productive conversation and greater diagnostic understanding of the client.

Mood and Affect.   Some confusion exists about the terms mood and affect. The terms are often used interchangeably, albeit incorrectly. As used here, *mood* refers to "a sustained feeling tone or range of tones, pleasurable or unpleasurable, experienced by a person for periods of time lasting for hours to years" (Kaplan & Sadock, 1989, p. 572). *Affect* is a more immediate and transitory state, here-and-now expressions reflective of inner states. To clarify the relationship of these two domains, Kaplan and Sadock compare mood to a musical instrument and affect to the specific notes of a song played on the instrument.

It is not enough to simply observe and describe mood and affect in a global fashion. A degree of specificity is necessary. Range, intensity, stability, reactivity to external events, and congruence with thought contents are qualities of affect and mood that are generally covered in an assessment. Each quality provides some insight into the client's internal life, for although individual traits by themselves reveal little, a constellation of symptoms may aid the clinician in formulating hypotheses about the client. Box 4.2 pro-

BOX 4.1   Common Disorders of Speech and Language

Anarthria—an inability to produce sounds.

Aphasia—a pervasive disturbance of spoken language once the skills have been acquired.

Cluttering—rapid-fire production of speech with sounds and ideas blended in an unintelligible way.

Dysarthria—a speech impediment in which there is an imperfection of sounds for matching letters and words. The result is often nasal or blurred speech.

Dysphonia—a loss of voice volume.

Mutism—an inability to express oneself verbally. This inability may be selective, occurring only in limited settings.

Neologistic—a tendency to construct new words by combining unrelated ideas and concepts, without any awareness of the nonsensical result. This behavior is common in schizophrenics.

Overarticulating—placing stress on unaccented portions of words or adding inappropriate endings to words.

Palilalia—repetition of the last word or words of a sentence. This pattern is not to be confused with echolalia, a tendency to repeat an entire sentence before responding to it.

Stuttering—a pronounced tendency to repeat the initial syllable of a word, resulting in disfluency of speech. Anxiety intensifies the severity of stuttering.

vides clinical vignettes illustrating a range of affect and mood presentations I have observed among gang members.

Data obtained during a mental status examination are only a sampling of the client's behavioral repertoire, but they provide useful insights into the client's baseline of functioning. If very pronounced behavioral patterns, suggestive of underlying psychopathology, are observed during the mental status examination, these patterns are likely to recur outside the examination setting. Because clinical assessment of gang members often occurs outside the boundaries of the gang, clinicians are dependent on gang members' recreation of their gang experience in an assessment session. This arrangement gives a clinician valuable insights into the client's gang experience even when only second-person retrospective accounts are available. A preferred alternative to this once-removed accounting is to arrange a meeting with other gang members and the client's family of origin. This approach provides an opportunity to see the client relating to family members in another group setting. Family assessment as a method of understanding the mood

BOX 4.2   Affect and Mood Variations

Affect can be described in a variety of ways, ranging from appropriate to inappropriate. Between these extremes are types of affective expressions that give descriptive richness to understanding how the client is presenting during the clinical sessions. It is very important to note the range of affect expressed and its congruence to the subject matter being discussed. Therefore, it is imperative that the clinician localize the affect within the stages of the sessions. It is not enough to simply say that the client was "sad" or "happy" without noting how these affects matched what was being discussed at the moment they were expressed.

Appropriate Affect

Appropriate is usually reserved for use in describing a full range of affect considered to be in harmony with the expressed idea, thought, or speech.

Labile Affect

Labile denotes rapid and abrupt changes in emotional tone, unrelated to external stimuli. Examples:

Client   My girl is always trying to track me down . . . see what I'm doin' when I be hangin' out. . . . I don't like that shit . . . (Bangs fist on arm of chair) . . . (Long pause) . . . I guess she must love me (laughter) . . . at least that's what she says (smile).

Client   We was at a houseparty . . . just chillin' and . . . (smile) . . . some of the guys in the _____(gang)_____ were there but they left early. . . . Then I saw my partner from juvenile hall. He wanted to go get something to smoke (crack?) but I didn't want to do that. . . . I didn't want to go home either . . . (flat facial expression) . . . (fidgeting in the chair) . . . (hand gestures, but no words issue forth) . . . (smile) . . . (more hand gestures, termination of eye contact). I'm not sure why I stayed at the party. It was tired.

Ambivalent Affect

Mixed feelings of opposing valence with regard to a given idea are described as ambivalent affect. Example:

Therapist   So how do you feel about losing your job?
Client   I don't know. How am I suppose to feel? . . . They was wrong for doing that. . . . I didn't do nothin' wrong. (Chuckle) I guess this means I can stay home all day now.

and affective dimensions of a client's psychological life are discussed later in this chapter.

Thought Content.   Thought content concerns what the client discusses and how viewpoints are shared. Thematic material that is illogical and unrelated to the issues being discussed may be evidence of a thought disorder or a speech or language problem.

Gang members are often consumed by thoughts concerning affiliation and feelings of belonging. Many join gangs because the gang is "like family"(i.e., a source of unconditional acceptance). This affiliation theme may permeate conversations even when the focus moves on to other issues, a behavior that suggests that the themes of attachment and affiliation are obsessions.

Some judgments about the quality of the discussion are necessary. Clinicians may need to ask very pointed questions to gain an understanding of the client's mood and affect. Specific questions to which clinicians should seek answers include, Are the ideas expressed by the client congruent with his or her affective presentation? Or are they tangential and unrelated to the issues at hand? How does the gang member feel about the role he or she plays in the gang?

Clinicians may periodically challenge adolescent clients' thought content and processes by introducing conflicting ideas. The responses of gang members to the ideas of others, particularly ideas that run counter to their own, may reveal flexibility in thinking and capacity to tolerate contrary views.

Box 4.3 offers illustrations of thought contents and processes observed in gang members.

Insight and Judgment.   Insight is subjective awareness of one's inner life and the nature of the match between one's desires and needs. The absence of insight generally is considered to be a prognostic sign among psychiatric patients suggesting that a patient does not have the capacity to review his or her situation and to seek help when difficult situations are imminent. Conversely, the presence of insight is deemed to be a positive indicator among young people, including gang members, attempting to gain control over their lives to become more productive and socially appropriate. The capacity for insight suggests that an individual has the ability to be introspective and a level of language proficiency that permits internal states to be described, to oneself if not to others. Insight also suggests that an individual possesses the capacity for observing and critiquing his own behaviors and thoughts. "Insight correlates strongly but not absolutely with judgement, in that lack of insight predicts poor judgement, but the presence of insight does not assure sure judgement" (Leon, Bowden, & Faber, 1989, p. 459).

BOX 4.3   Thought Content and Processes

Preoccupations

Many gang adolescents are preoccupied with themes of affiliation or revenge for offenses that others have committed against them. Those themes, when present, seem to find expression in all of their conversations, relevant or not.

Ramon   I think I want to go to college, maybe become a psychologist or something like that.
Therapist   I see.
Ramon   That would probably mean that I'd have to get a scholarship. You know, my mom probably won't help me. She thinks I've been a traitor to the family.
Therapist   What do you mean?
Ramon   She thinks I should spend all of my time at home baby-sitting and taking care of the kids. And stuff like that . . .
Therapist   Let's go back for a moment to your plans for after college. . . . Do you think your behavior now is helping you get ready for college?
Ramon   Sort of . . . I get good grades, mostly As and a few Bs. That should be good enough. I knew a guy who went to community college and he almost didn't graduate from high school.
Therapist   Are there other things you think you might need to do to get ready for college?
Ramon   Not really. . . . Maybe get my mom off my back. She probably . . .

Language Impairments

Frequently, language impairments reflect disordered thinking, which may manifest in the form of clang associations, incomprehensible speech, or neologisms. The clinician should consider the possibility that the gang member may engage in such behavior to be resistant.

Therapist   Tell me a little bit more about the new homies.
Dwayne   What can I tell you? . . . Cool, man wit' a plan. _____(part of town)_____ we rule. Check this out. . . . They be guys who don't take no shit off nobody.
Therapist   So how is it that you all wound up in the same gang?
Dwayne   We all want respect . . . we cool, just out of school.
Therapist   And . . .
Dwayne   And nothin' . . . we don't do dope cause we "up with hope" (chuckle).

Productivity

Some adolescents meet the opportunity to tell their story in an unbiased setting with eagerness and an overinclusion of details. This may also represent a speech style they have employed for a number of years. This is not a pattern that is unique to gang adolescents.

Sheila   I don't want my little sister to have to go through all of that . . . like my sisters and me.
Therapist   I think it's a good idea to be concerned about your sister's safety.
Sheila   You're damn right . . . 'cause there is some sick motherfuckers in this neighborhood. You know, some men like to mess around with little girls . . . 'cause they won't tell nobody. They be scared. They be givin' 'em candy and stuff like that. If I find the son-of-a-bitch, I'm gonna kick his ass myself. That shit pisses me off. . . . When I was a little girl, there was a man who used to sit in the park and try to get me to play with his dick. Now, that's really sick. A grown-ass man trying to get a nine-year old girl to stroke him . . .

*   *   *

Therapist   What would you like to see happen?
Thomas   You mean now?
Therapist   Yes, you said you don't want to move with your family to _____.
Thomas   That's right. It's so boring there. Ain't nothing to do, and I don't have any friends there. Now, here, . . . that's different. Me and my homies, we be kickin' it. Sometimes, we go over to the park and play a little ball. If ain't nobody there that we can play we might go for a cruise on _____ see if there be some girls who want to get into somethin'. But sometime we have a little business we have to take care of. You know, make a few deliveries and stuff like that. I don't ever know when the crew is going to need me, 'cause somethin' might happen real fast. . . . Like las' Saturday . . .

For many gang members, self-examination is a new task and one at which they are not very skilled. This is particularly true of individuals in a state of foreclosed identity development (Marcia, 1966). Such individuals accept the identity others create for them without questioning the goodness of fit of the "preassembled" identity.

Traditional mental status examinations use questions about mailing letters, reacting to fire in theaters, and so forth, as indices of a person's capacity to exhibit sound judgment. These questions are problematic when dealing with gang youths because they assume a linearity of thought and language that may not be pronounced, or even detectable, in the performance of the gang member. Better questions address decisions and actions about gang activity and membership. Obvious and subtle patterns in thought processes and morality issues should be noted. In formulating an analysis of a gang member, examining the impact of his or her behavior on the lives of family, friends, and cohorts is important. Answers to the following questions may be helpful: Does the client show a capacity to assume the perspective of others that is developmentally appropriate? Does the client recognize being part of ongoing fluid relationships, in and out of the gang?

Perceptual Disturbances. Perceptual disturbances concern functioning in the sensory modalities. This area is difficult to assess because of limited opportunities to observe functioning in these domains without first asking the client to do something or to reflect in a special way on a set of experiences. For many suspicious and highly vigilant clients, such requests arouse suspicion and make them self-conscious and guarded. Distortions can, of course, occur in any of the sensory modalities. Table 4.1 provides a list of types of disturbances of perception. Any, or all, of these may occur with regularity among gang members. In completing a mental status examination, it is not enough to simply indicate the presence of a distortion; the nature of it (i.e., distortion of intensity, distortion of quality of stimuli) should also be noted.

The use of drugs is responsible for many perceptual disturbances. In evaluating a gang member, some form of objective verification of drug and alcohol use is necessary. Some professionals practicing in medical settings utilize laboratory tests to assist in this evaluation. Urine tests completed by independent laboratories are an option for independent and nonmedical practitioners.

Evaluations of perceptual disturbances are often confounded by the client's lack of speech and language skills. Client descriptions of significant events may be hampered by inadequate expressive language skills, inability to share a personal experience, and a general lack of cooperation during the evaluation.

Neuropsychological Evaluation. In addition to the clinical interview, a comprehensive assessment of a client's mental status ideally should include a neuropsychological evaluation. The testing itself should be completed by a qualified neuropsychologist. Currently, the Halstead-Reitan and Luria-Nebraska are the two batteries that are most commonly used. Both give an impairment index, a quantitative statement identifying the domains in which the client experiences problems (i.e., impaired memory, reading difficulties, understanding spoken language, and so on). Table 4.2 provides a description of the subtests included in both batteries as well as their clinical utility.

The neuropsychological battery for children is designed with an appreciation for the emerging status of neurological functions among youngsters. Different theoretical orientations toward the development and refinement of brain functions have given rise to different types of batteries. Rourke, Fisk, & Strang (1986) present a battery that is a modification of the Halstead-Reitan battery. It includes tests that assess the following brain functions: perceptual skills—tactile, auditory, visual, and language related; problem solving, concept formation, and reasoning skills; motor and psychomotor skills; and other general skills. Another approach, designed to assess basic competences, is pro-

TABLE 4.1 Common Disturbances of Perception[a]

Type	Definition	Examples
Illusion	Distortion or misinterpretation of real stimuli	1. Floating clouds come to represent angels in flight to deliver a message to the client. 2. Body shadows are seen as evidence of "evil beings" attempting to invade the body of the client.
Delusions	A persistent false psychotic belief regarding the self or persons or objects outside the self	1. An individual believes himself to be the "devil's child." 2. Messages instructing others on how to persecute the client are written in the sky.
Hallucinations	Sensory experiences that cannot be objectively verified	1. Flashes of light, noises, or sounds that are not integrated into a whole. 2. Hearing voices in the basement whenever a red car passes the house.
Pseudohallucinations	Hallucinations accompanied by the client's insight that they are not true	A gang member reporting having had a visit from a fellow gang member who was killed in a recent drive-by shooting. The gang member, however, is able to recognize that such could not have possibly have happened because his partner is dead.

[a] Disturbances of perception are of two types: Misrepresentations (misinterpretations) of stimuli and the creation of stimuli that cannot be objectively verified.

TABLE 4.2 Neuropsychological Test Batteries

Halstead-Reitan Battery	Halstead-Reitan Tests	Luria-Nebraska Battery	Luria-Nebraska Tests
The Halstead-Reitan produces seven scores, which collectively create an impairment index as the arithmetic average of the individual scores.	1. Category Test: requires the subject to discover through trial and error the correct principle utilized in successive presentations of visual stimuli 2. Tactile Performance Test: requires subjects to place the variously shaped block of the Sequin-Goddard Form Board without the aid of vision 3. Rhythm Test: an adaptation of the Seashore's Test of Musical Talent, requires the subject to judge whether two rhythmic patterns are the same or different (in pitch) 4. Speech Sounds Perception Test: requires the subject to identify spoken nonsense syllables from visual presentations 5. Finger Oscillation: requires the subject to tap a mechanical counter as rapidly as possible for 10 seconds 6. Trail Mailing Test: requires subjects to draw a line between scattered circles in alphabetic or alphanumeric sequence 7. Alpha Screening Test 8. Somatosensory Examination 9. Strength of Grip Test 10. Wechsler Memory Test	The Golden revision of the Luria approach to neuro-psychology	Scales of the Golden revision of the Luria Battery 1. Motor Functioning 2. Rhythm 3. Tactile 4. Visual 5. Receptive and Expressive Language 6. Writing 7. Reading 8. Arithmetic 9. Amnestic 10. Intellectual

posed by Fletcher (1988). Specifically, it evaluates performance in six broad areas: language, visual-spatial and constructional, somatosensory, motor-sequential, motor and learning, and attention. The Luria-Nebraska (Golden, Hammeke, & Purisch, 1978), a modification of the original Luria battery, includes scales that assess motor, rhythm, tactile (cutaneous and kinesthetic), visual, receptive and expressive speech, writing, reading, arithmetic, amnestic, and intellectual skills. In addition, there is a scale called the pathognomic scale.

All of the batteries operate on the principle of an impairment statement: how well the brain is functioning considering the subject's age and general level of overall development. The batteries also consider that children are still in the process of refining neurological skills.

Referring a client for a full neuropsychological battery is often a luxury for clinicians working with gang-affiliated youth. Limitations of time and resources and clients' unwillingness to cooperate are common barriers. Despite these obstacles, a neuropsychological evaluation should be considered when the potential negative effects of an inaccurate or incomplete diagnostic picture are high, especially in instances when a gang member is charged with a serious crime (i.e., drive-by shooting, serious assault) or is believed to be psychiatrically impaired.

Summarizing and Integrating Data. How clinicians summarize initial evaluations of gang-affiliated youths is a function of the clinician's work setting. Questions of mental competence and volition provide the typical backdrop of referrals from the criminal justice system. Other referring agencies may be more interested in the client's ability to make effective use of psychological counseling or ability (and motivation) to complete a job-training program. The nature of the referral creates the framework and perspective for approaching a gang member. This focusing has the unfortunate result of framing the perspective in which the client is presented to the clinician. Although this perspective may represent the area causing the most concern to the community, less-disruptive dimensions of the adolescent's life may go unnoticed, eventually leading to serious problems.

The Written Evaluation

The clinician's final report on the mental status examination will revisit the reason why the gang member was evaluated and provide a comprehensive clinical assessment addressing critical areas of functioning (e.g., affect, behavior, cognition).

The mental status examination is a first line of assessment of multiple domains in the life of the client. It provides information prognostic of future

BOX 4.4   Example of Mental Status Examination Report

a. Long Version

Jason is a 19-year-old African American male who looks his stated age. He presented as a neatly dressed young man who was overly polite and compliant during the examination. Questions presented to him were answered promptly with a flurry of details that made his answers appear to be exaggerations. Jason had a pronounced tendency to engage in echolalic behavior before responding to a question. Eye contact was established early in the interview process. There was a tendency on his part to look at the examiner when listening but to look away when responding to a question. Jason's level of activity during the examination was somewhat constricted, like his affect. He sat rigidly in the chair with his hands clasped and only spoke in response to questions from the examiner. Even when he became agitated near the end of the interview, he raised his voice in a controlled sort of way. The elevations in the volume of speech were regulated. Jason's constricted affect slowly dissipated into one of lability when his mother became the focus of the conversation. Speech and language were deemed to be age and culture appropriate. There was, however, a significant amount of profanity liberally sprinkled throughout his verbalizations. "Shit" was a particularly common phrase, used as a statement of exclamation as well as a noun. Women were often described as "bitches," void of any emotional punctuation. Jason demonstrated an intense proclivity for recursive thought. He seems to believe that many of his difficulties stem from others misunderstanding him and his needs. Jason accepts little or no responsibility for his problems. Judgment and insight were deemed to be poor. In response to standard proverbs and problem-solving tasks, Jason showed a pattern of being concerned primarily about his own needs being met, with little or no regard for others. When asked, "If you were in a theater and saw smoke what would you do," he replied, "Run out of the side door." He had a fair amount of difficulty responding to verbal abstractions (i.e., "One swallow doesn't a summer make"; "Don't buy a pig in a poke"; "If you lie down with dogs, you'll get up with fleas"). Jason idolizes the gang. He sees it as the answer to all of his psychological needs. Despite that, he also romanticizes leaving the gang and having a life of his own that he won't "have to share with nobody." I estimate that Jason is of at least average intelligence. His fund of general information is considered to be average for a 19-year-old. He was able to do serial 7s and 3s without error. Jason could name the last ten U.S. presidents, in reverse order. His knowledge of recent world and U.S. news was good. Jason does, however, have problems with logic and moral reasoning. There is a pronounced tendency to discount the perspective or needs of others. Despite his egocentric thought processes, there is no evidence to suggest that Jason has an underlying thought disorder that might compromise his ability to function in daily social situations. I am of the opinion that the information obtained in this interview is an accurate portrayal of his inner psychological life.

Diagnostic impression: Narcissistic personality disorder (?)
Ability to make use of therapy: Fair
Prognosis: Guarded

b. Short Version

Jason is a 19-year-old African American male who looks his stated age. He presented as a neatly dressed young man who was overly polite and compliant during the examination. Jason was oriented to person, place, time, and circumstance. He was reasonably informed about world and U.S. current events. I think he is of at least average intelligence. Mood and affect were somewhat constricted throughout most of the examination. Near the end of the hour, he became a bit more labile and occasionally laughed at things that would not strike most people as being humorous (i.e., his neighbor's car and truck were stolen within a 3-day period). Speech was slightly pressured, especially when talking about his mother and his girlfriend. Thought content evidenced some overvalued ideas (i.e., the importance of the gang to him). There were no other evidences of thought disorders or underlying psychosis. No perceptual disturbances were noted. Insight and judgment are poor and of a self-centered nature. A neuropsychological examination is not deemed necessary at this time. Jason appears to be able to cognitively understand and process information at a level such that he can make good use of psychotherapy.

---

functioning. Based on the results of this examination, neuropsychological testing may be recommended to establish a comprehensive profile of the client. Another aspect of preparing a report occurs when a referring party, such as a court, is not in agreement with the outcomes or the recommendations offered. This situation offers a wonderful opportunity for the clinician to educate the referring agency by carefully crafting the report to describe multiple facets of the client and offer new pieces of information that might help in formulating the case in new ways.

Frequently, in situations with open-ended referral questions, the mental health professional is expected to produce insights that will prevent the gang member, and his or her family, from behaving in maladaptive ways. When the referring professional is not sure what to ask of the clinician, the results of a well-crafted mental status examination will help to define the at-risk behaviors the referring agency may need to be sensitive to in later interactions with the client and other family members. For example, excessive and bizarre motor disturbances, delayed mentation, lapses of concentration, and bizarre thought content may be behavioral patterns the referring agency needs interpreted. If the client shows several of these behaviors, the possibility of serious affective disturbance (i.e., depression, bipolar disorder) should be considered.

The mental status examination is a useful tool to establish the possibility of such a syndrome, but often more evaluation will be used to rule out a problem or specify the severity of a recognized problem. Psychological testing completed by a licensed psychologist or a medication evaluation by a psychiatrist may also be useful diagnostic aids. They should be recommended to the referring agency in the written evaluation when appropriate.

Finally, the clinician may want to consider adding a brief report, minus technical terms and ideas, that can serve as a condensed report. Such a report is often useful to parents. Box 4.4 presents a mental status examination report in abridged and unabridged formats.

Family Intervention Project Examination

In the absence of a full mental status examination, critical dimensions of the presentation of the gang member (i.e., affect, behavior, cognition) should be evaluated by the clinician. To increase the utility of the clinical data obtained in such abbreviated evaluations, similar assessments should be completed on each adult member of the gang member's family. Wherever possible, the evaluation should be made relevant to the gang membership. The Family Intervention Project (FIP) provides an ideal setting for making these assessments. When a viable option for the clinician, the assessments should be completed concurrently during a protracted single session. The behavior exhibited in such a session is diagnostic of family member behavior in the outside world.

It is not sufficient to note the range of affects expressed by adolescents and their families without evaluating the richness, depth, and stability of the affects. Perhaps even more basic than these dimensions is a simple judgment of the appropriateness of the affect in the context. At least four descriptors of affective presentations should be considered in evaluating adolescents and their families:

1. Blunted—indifference that causes clients to look neutral, neither happy or sad
2. Flattened—restricted or constricted range of feelings expressed
3. Anhedonia—lack of pleasurable feelings from activities that ordinarily provide pleasure
4. Inappropriate affect—incongruency of affective expression and thought content

Finally, the clinician must evaluate the setting and how much it affects the results. Do the affective states gang members experience in the artificial and safe environs of a clinician's office transfer to the real world?

When an emotionally troubling roadblock occurs, a client demonstrates bewilderment. With this as a clinical marker, inviting families to participate in two structured exercises taken from the FIP is a useful beginning-level diagnostic procedure. A word of caution, however, is necessary about undertaking brief assessment procedures outside of the full context for which they were developed. The more compact and abbreviated the procedure, the less discriminating it tends to be. Taking a procedure out of a constellation of other procedures also reduces its explanatory power. Despite these two haunting realities, these first two structured activities of the FIP do provide valuable clues to the strengths and weaknesses of gang-affiliated families, information that can be useful in determining which clients have the capacity and motivation to make major changes in their behavior and thinking.

Unlike the medical model–oriented mental status examination, the FIP evaluates the whole family simultaneously under the theory that the problems experienced by the adolescent reflect a larger set of family dynamics. Although it may be difficult to convince some family members to attend a diagnostic session primarily concerned with a marginalized family member, it is critical to try to engage them. This type of global, communal, and extended-family approach to understanding the client has been written about extensively by Boyd-Franklin (1986). This approach is not therapeutic but diagnostic, intended to gather information and understanding about exactly who and what a clinician may encounter when working with an adolescent.

The two structured activities presented here are drawn from a larger collection of FIP exercises. They are not intended, of course, as definitive diagnostic tools, but rather as nonintrusive means to gain insight into the developmental phases and functioning of the family. The first exercise, titled "Why Are We Here?" is a structured interview. It allows the clinician to ascertain each member's perceptions of what it is that has brought the family together and what are reasonable goals to be set subsequent to the meeting. A useful outcome of this exercise is to create a forum for previously silent members to voice individual concerns and to correct misperceptions about what other family members believe can be achieved in the clinical setting.

"Why Are We Here?" Exercise

The exercise "Why Are We Here?" begins with the clinician offering a brief overview of why the identified client was referred. Near the end of this recitation period, the family is encouraged to share views about possible reasons for and desirable outcomes from this exercise. It may be difficult to sustain family members' interest during the introductory and background information phase, but it is critical to encourage discussion during this nonconfrontational section of the exercise. Some family members use this period as a point of departure to explain their perceptions of the reasons for the meeting. They may verbally attack the client or exhibit recalcitrance in their level of engagement with the group. Recalcitrant behavior may be attributed to anger toward the clinician for misrepresentations or toward the larger system that is responsible for "failing" the adolescent. This is good clinical information to collect about the affect and mood states of family members and their styles of verbal engagement with others. Allow each member of the group the opportunity to share views about the meeting's purpose before allowing interactions with and questions of each other.

Staying focused on the reasons for the presence of the family may be difficult for some members. The clinician should document who is subject to cognitive intrusions and whether the individual can recognize that his or her digressions are at variance with the stated agenda for the meeting. Other clinical indicators of the internal states of the family members are nonverbal responses members make to the verbalizations of others. Common responses include blank stares into space, fidgeting in the chair, and similar signals of lack of interest or symbolic denial of what was verbalized by someone else. The clinician can use these behaviors to explore the individual's range of affects and moods; these are significant revelations about internal emotional states and cognitive processing abilities. (The clinical issues related to cognitive processing ability are discussed in Chapter 6.)

The affective repertoire of family members can be recorded through sociograms and pictorial representations of the affective tone of statements made in the rebuttal or discussion phase of the exercise. Occasionally, exchanges between family members are so swift and intense it becomes difficult to capture all of the verbalizations. The primary emphasis of this exercise should be on the affective tone of interfamily communications. If intent on capturing this sort of emotional sociogram, a clinician may be unable to fully participate in the ongoing dialogue and may wish to include a second clinician in the family meeting. Families should be advised of the participation of this second clinician prior to the session. Finally, the family may lack sophistication regarding the techniques of a typical session. Prior explanation of the mechanics of a session, especially the clinician's note taking, can prevent suspicion or shutting down by individual members.

"Black Delinquent Gang Youth Values" Exercise

A second structured exercise that has been found to be useful in the beginning stages of family assessments is the "Black Delinquent Gang Youth Values" exercise. This pencil-and-paper test requires each family member to rate a series of values as he or she believes a group of Black delinquent gang members would rank-order the items. The exercise is designed to be used in a group of ten or more—a group large enough to be divided into subgroups. The exercise is useful also with families of at least six to eight members. Subgroups of the family can be made along gender or generational lines or by any category that provides the clinician rich information about differences of opinion in the family. The task of rank-ordering a group of values as one perceives a group of Black delinquent gang youths would do often causes much consternation among family members. Non-Black families often resist the task, indicating they do not know any Blacks. Other families, to exonerate themselves from expressing racial or ethnic stereotypes, insist that because the task is racist in nature they cannot comply with the request. All of this information can be used to help families examine how attributions are made to others, often without any factual information, on a daily basis. Each individual should be urged to complete the inventory. Once individual responses are complete, the small groups repeat the task and pool the individual data to arrive at a group consensus. Results from each subgroup are displayed for the large group, and similarities and differences in the rankings produced by each group are discussed.

This exercise is discussed in greater detail in Chapter 10. For the purposes of the current chapter, the deconstruction of the exercise should focus not on the factual responses, but on the affective reactions of the subgroups to the similarities or differences revealed by their answers. Frequently, persons whose subgroups produce dissimilar answers immediately review the chain of events that led to their agreed-on answers. Invariably, someone in the group expresses dissatisfaction about his or her contributions being dismissed or disregarded by the group. For a detailed accounting of this exercise, see Short and Strodbeck (1965); for more recent variations on the exercise, see Branch (1995).

Affective Life: Before the Gang

I conclude the chapter with a brief synthesis of some of the issues and ideas clinicians may use to make a preliminary determination about the stability and quality of a gang member's functioning in the areas of affect and mood in the context of a family setting. A detailed historical picture of the adolescent's pregang affect can be obtained from the adolescent and family members. The role of friends and presence or lack of stable friendships should be evaluated. Family members may exaggerate personal characteristics from the pregang period, often reporting a sudden unexplained conversion to the gang or out-of-control response patterns. Dramatic transformation is quite rare, however, and such reports likely evidence that family members were not particularly observant of or responsive to the adolescent. Such reports may also indicate that the family is in denial about changes that occurred in the adolescent's life day by day. Clinical research indicates most transformations occur gradually and without major warning signs.

Friendships

A client's history of interpersonal relationships holds vital pieces of information relative to affective states. If the client had friends, were the friends of similar age and gender as the client? Dissimilarities of major proportion, such as a ten-year-old having teenage friends or vice versa, are potential indicators of pathognomic social development for sustained periods of time. These kinds of incongruencies are valuable clues for discerning inappropriate responses to social situations. Reconstruction of an adolescent's affective life should also be reviewed against the developmental psychology literature relative to early bloomers and late maturers (Brooks-Gunn, 1987).

Present State of Mind

In addition to a detailed accounting of the affective and interpersonal experience of gang membership, information should be gathered on the adolescent's present status. Asking the gang member how it feels to be part of a gang enables the clinician to gauge the client's ability to articulate feelings, to note the range and richness of affects that are revealed in the answer, and to determine how others present react verbally and nonverbally to the response. Avoid directly asking the client why he or she joined the gang. Such a question is judgmental in ways that are counterproductive to diagnostic and psychotherapeutic relationship building with clients. It is more useful to ask, "What were you thinking when you joined the gang?" or "What were the events that led you to the decision?" or "What has this provided for you?"

Finally, provide an opportunity for other family members to discuss their feelings about the family member actively involved in a gang. Frequently, parents express responsibility for the adolescent's decision to join the gang by claiming to be overprotective or underresponsive to the adolescent's emotional needs. This is useful clinical data that will enhance a clinician's grasp of the dynamics and stages of conflict that exist in the family.

Disengaging

Disengaging refers to the tendency to emotionally withdraw from an experience that otherwise might provoke anxiety. Some individuals disengage early in a session as a way of saving face even before they have made any type of disclosure. They are often afraid of what might happen. Others withdraw as the session unfolds and they realize that they have made self-disclosures that are causing them to experience regret or some other form of emotional pain. Still others disengage in response to feelings stirred up by the verbalizations of others. They disengage as a way to diffuse the tension in the group.

Styles of disengaging and the tendency to use this approach to reduce anxiety are useful concepts for the clinician who is attempting to understand how a family functions in the face of anxiety. Disengaging can occur in a variety of ways, ranging from nonparticipation to inappropriate verbalizations masking the speaker's true feelings. Laughter and humor are often used as devices of disengagement.

The mental status examination is a very significant tool for the professional working with gang adolescents and their families. A carefully executed examination can provide great insight into how and why the family is in a state of dissonance. The flexibility of the parameters of the examination makes it especially suitable for working with clients from varied sociocultural backgrounds. It should be kept in mind, however, that the mental status examination measures internal and mental processes. The other part of the family's presentation, overt behaviors, must also be examined and understood. Behavioral assessments are discussed in the next chapter.

5

Behavior

The assessment of the behavior of an adolescent juxtaposed against that of his or her family is a complex task that requires special skills on the part of clinician; add gang affiliation into that relationship and the task becomes even more daunting. One pervasive problem has to do with the nature of behavior assessments, irrespective of gang status. Unlike the case with affect and mood assessments, the clinician has little firsthand data available for observation. Rather, when making behavioral assessments the clinician must respond to historic accounts of the behaviors that have been engaged in by the clients. Problems of selectivity of memory can be substantial. Another difficulty with behavior assessments in general is that they concern overt and observable events associated with assumed underlying thoughts and feelings. Third, behavior assessments are assumed to represent an adequate sampling of the subject's behavioral repertoire to provide an overview of the person. Finally, when the issue of gangs, and behavior in that context, is added to the assessment, the level of assumptions is increased dramatically.

Because the literature on gangs historically is demographic and descriptive in nature, there is virtually no clinically validated knowledge base for understanding the behavior of gang members. The result is that clinicians are left to interpret those behaviors without benefit of clinical reference points. A similar problem arises with the generally stereotypic images that families have of gang members. Families of gang members, like much of the general public, assume that gangs are exclusively committed to antisocial behaviors and a state of continuous antagonism with the larger society. Limited knowledge and fixed attitudes on the part of clinicians and families often make it difficult for the behaviors of gang members to be viewed objectively.

These issues add up to a formidable challenge to anyone trying to assess the behavior of gang members with the intent of creating some type of therapeutic intervention. But the problems are not insurmountable. In this chapter, I explore strategies for completing clinically based assessments of the behavior of gang-affiliated youths and their families. To accomplish that task, it is first necessary to discuss behavior as a developmental task that occurs in adolescents and family responses to it. Here, I highlight autonomy, intimacy, loneliness and attachment, interpersonal relationships, and self-esteem. Then, I present a scheme for describing and evaluating behavior in adolescents (and their families) before and after gang affiliation. I include the diagnostic criteria of the *Diagnostic and Statistical Manual of Mental Disorders* (*DSM-IV;* American Psychiatric Association, 1994) for conduct disorder as one clinical scheme for understanding the nature and presentation of antisocial behavior. I discuss the strengths and weaknesses of that medical model. Because behaviors are invariably assumed to be an indicator of values, I explore this association as it relates to adolescent gang members and their families.

Issues in Adolescent Development

The word *adolescence* literally means "to transition." In the human development scheme, that transition is from childhood to adulthood. The process can be stormy and protracted or it can be reasonably smooth and of a short duration. Despite disagreement about the upper limit of adolescence, theorists agree that it starts at puberty. The terminal point is less universally agreed on, with opinions ranging from the specific age twenty-one to functional definitions such as, "When a young person assumes adult responsibilities in the society and culture in which he or she lives." It is clear that adolescence is a period of dramatic changes and radical shifts in how young persons view themselves and are viewed by others. One of the critical areas of shifts is autonomy. Changes in this domain also inherently change the family system in which the adolescent functions.

Autonomy

Autonomy is defined variously but generally is thought of as individuals' ability to assess their needs, seek out information that allows them to satisfy their needs, and act consciously and deliberately in light of the newly acquired data. Put simply, it means to be self-sufficient. Being able to act independently is part of autonomy but not the entire story. As a developmental attribute, autonomy has two major components: emotional autonomy, or an ability to serve as one's own source of emotional strength rather than childishly depending on parents or others to provide comfort and emotional security, and behavioral autonomy, or an ability to make one's own decisions to govern one's affairs and take care of oneself (Steinberg, 1985).

As adolescents grow physically and cognitively they discover more nuances in themselves and how they impact others. "The increased independence that typifies adolescence is labeled as rebellious by some parents, but in many instances, the adolescent's push for autonomy has little to do with the adolescent's feelings toward the parent" (Santrock, 1993, p. 200). Unfortunately, as adolescents strive for autonomy, many families interpret their behavior as rejection and react by trying to exercise more control. In many situations, the growing autonomy of the adolescent is a painful reminder to parents of their own unresolved issues of adolescence and the imminent reality of their losing control over their child. The family is being replaced by others (i.e., peers, teachers) and significant events in the child's life. This idea has been eloquently expressed by Peter Blos (1962, 1979). He reports that in an attempt to psychologically separate themselves from parents, many adolescents experience a period of individuation and separation much like the childhood process described by Mahler, Pine, and Bergman (1975). "The second individuation process is Blos's term for adolescents' development of a distinctiveness from parents, which he believes is an attempt to transcend earlier parent-child ties and develop more self responsibility" (Santrock, 1993, p. 203).

The exact function of the quest for autonomy is less important than the fact that it occurs almost universally. Recent research suggests that seeking autonomy is not necessarily a sign that an adolescent's life will be filled with storm and stress. Instead, the process may proceed quite smoothly if the parents and family of the adolescent are reasonably healthy and accepting of the inevitable change.

Both the emotional and behavioral dimensions of autonomy can be observed in action as adolescents attempt to negotiate relationships with new individuals in their lives and to become self-sufficient. Choice of friends, regulation of emotions, and social problem solving are concrete ways in which adolescents express their growing sense of behavioral and emotional autonomy. In most situations their positions are apparent to others. In the area of emotional autonomy, especially, adolescents are expected to exhibit two seemingly discrepant qualities simultaneously—connectedness to family members and individuation from them. This conflict of thrusts is described in detail by Grotevant and Cooper (1985).

A third dimension of autonomy that is sometimes seen as being distinct from behavioral and emotional autonomy is *cognitive autonomy*. Sessa and Steinberg (1991) describe cognitive autonomy as a sense that one can make decisions without seeking the approval of others. Douvan and Adelson (1966) use the phrase *value autonomy* to connote a similar process that they operationalize as a sense that judgment and choices are based on one's own individually held principles, as opposed to those of parents and others.

The quest for autonomy causes adolescents to move away from their family into a social arena that is new, different, and sometimes frightening. In so doing, they are required to develop skills to perform new tasks. During middle adolescence, the peer group offers a sanctum for such autonomy-seeking behaviors to occur by replacing the family as the primary agent of socialization for the adolescent. Sometimes, in seeking relief for feelings of anxiety, adolescents turn to gangs for a quick, popular, and seemingly irreversible resolution to their developmental task of becoming autonomous.

Often, as adolescents seek more answers to the multiple variations of the question "Who am I?" the family becomes increasingly reactive to being shut out of the adolescent's life. Santrock (1993) notes

> Psychologically healthy families adjust to adolescents' push for independence by treating the adolescents in more adult ways and including them more in family decision making. Psychologically unhealthy families often remain locked into power-oriented parent control, and parents move even more heavily toward an authoritarian posture in their relationships with their adolescents. (p. 200)

Intimacy

Intimacy, a characteristic that is noticeably absent in childhood friendships and relationships, may be described as everything in a relationship that makes it seem close or intense. Concrete evidences of intimacy are willingness to engage in self-disclosing behavior and openness to sharing private thoughts with others. In the case of adolescents, private thoughts include fears and anxieties that they would not be inclined to acknowledge or share with others (i.e., fears regarding sexuality, concerns about physical attractiveness, and so on).

Friendships are perhaps the best forum for assessing the level of intimacy an adolescent is capable of accomplishing. Three findings in the psychological literature inform us about adolescents' capacity for intimacy. First, there is a gender difference. Girls are noted to be more likely than boys to share intimate thoughts with a friend. Duck (1975) notes that girls are more likely than boys to make references to empathy and sensitivity as a characteristic of a close friend. In so doing, they frequently indirectly make similar attributions to themselves. Boys, on the other hand, tend to shy away from openly discussing intimate matters even with someone they consider to be a friend. Maccoby (1991) interprets the reluctance of boys to self-disclose to be a by-product of their highly protective masculine veneer. Most children and adolescents choose friends whom they perceive to be like themselves on critical demographic characteristics such as age, sex, ethnicity, and personal interests. Such a congruence of features should facilitate an egalitarian relationship, making it easy to share with each other. Berndt and Perry (1990) find that significant age differentials in friendships are often prognostic of developmental disruptions. Large age differences between friends also raise questions about the functions of the friendship and what opportunities for intimacy rest in it.

Despite the increased rates of school desegregation and greater racial mixing of neighborhoods, cross-racial and cross-ethnic friendships among adolescents are rare. Those that do exist highlight youngsters' abilities to be intimate with and psychologically connect to someone unlike themselves. This same logic can be applied to friendships that extend across chasms of interests and family socioeconomic status. What functions are being served by the relationship? What level of intimacy, if any, is the adolescent able to establish and maintain in the relationship?

The need for intimacy becomes more pronounced as adolescents develop a wider range of interests, problems, and settings in which they function. Family becomes a less likely forum for them to share their "intimate stuff." Peers, and to a lesser degree teachers and coaches, become substitutes. In some situations, the need for someone with whom to share becomes so great that adolescents become blinded to the nonresponsiveness of their chosen partner. Such one-sided communication is quite prevalent among adolescents who fail to apply boundaries to how much they share or how indiscriminate they are in their sharing. In extreme cases, adolescents who lay bare their souls are exploited by older friends. The exploitation can take several forms, including psychological and sexual abuse. Recovery from naive unregulated attempts at intimacy with others can be difficult.

The adolescent who is propelled into gangs in search of satisfaction for intimacy needs is another extreme case. Many such young people hold idealized notions that the gang is like a family, with high levels of intimacy and connectedness. Once in the gang, the adolescent's experience is very much to the contrary.

Loneliness and Attachment

Loneliness is an issue often associated with old age. The logic for such an assumption is that older individuals are likely to have lost much of their family and many of their friends. From these losses comes a pervasive sense of isolation, helplessness, and lack of purpose in life. Loneliness is also very much an issue in the lives of children and adolescents, not because they have experienced loss of major relationships but because they may have never had them. Such is the case with children and adolescents with poor social skills who never developed friendships or who display levels of aggressiveness and antisocial acts that cause others to move away from them. These scenarios are more common than one might imagine. The psychological literature is very clear in its description of the profile of young people who are stuck in a web of loneliness and despair.

The connection between loneliness and attachment may not be obvious at first inquiry. But the history of attachment relationships with primary attachment objects (i.e., parents, caregivers) is prognostic of subsequent relationships. Most notable, the absence of strong and healthy attachments is frequently reported to be the common denominator among individuals who show patterns of unhealthy relationships in adolescence and adulthood. Attachment-disordered individuals often have anxious and avoidant-type attachment histories (Ainsworth, 1979). The categorization of attachment disordered also includes infants who are so *enmeshed* with their primary caregiver as to never individuate or separate. Such an individual grows up to have no will of his or her own except as given by others. Individuals with such an early attachment history are likely to evolve into a state of *foreclosed identity* (Marcia, 1966).

Weiss (1974) indicates that loneliness is virtually always a response to the absence of some particular type of relationship. He dichotomizes loneliness by proposing two types, emotional and social. The absence of an intimate attachment is what he terms *emotional isolation*. *Social isolation* is the result of a person lacking a sense of integrated involvement with others. Santrock (1993) suggests that "being deprived of participation in a group or community involving companionship, shared interests, organized activities, and meaningful roles causes a person to feel alienated, bored, and uneasy" (p. 359).

Developmentally, adolescence is a period of heightened social connectedness. The increased mobility of adolescents increases the number of microsystems in which they may be involved. Thus, adolescents who are unable to successfully negotiate attachments are at prime risk for loneliness and depression. To discern whether an adolescent is struggling with characterological loneliness, one should consider the possibility that the adolescent has grown accustomed to not being connected to others and therefore presents with little or no angst about the matter. Frequently, others are more concerned about such individuals and their lack of social engagement than they are. In contrast, many lonely and unattached youngsters are constantly in touch with the pain of being detached from others. They attempt to develop sustained friendships with peers but to no avail. Identity-foreclosed youngsters often fit in this category. Their need and desire to belong is so great and pervasive that they are willing to do almost anything to create a feeling of belonging—even join a gang. Because of their psychological vulnerability, such youngsters often become the targets of gang recruitment campaigns.

Interpersonal Relationships

Among the many other changes that occur during adolescence is an increase in active involvement in a variety of settings. One result is that young people become involved in a large number and multiple types of relationships. Family relationships continue as a constant, but the quality of these relationships changes dramatically, partly as a function of the adolescent's behavior but also as a function of the behavior of others. Friendships as a special case of relationships have already been discussed. The focus here is on relationships between the adolescent and his or her family members and relationships with others outside of the family, including peers.

As noted earlier, there are significant age differences in the quality and nature of friendships involving adolescents. Atwood (1996) characterizes the changes as follows: "The meaning and quality of friendships tend to change throughout adolescence, mostly because of the developmental and social changes occurring during the period. Friendship gradually evolves from rather superficial, activity-oriented relationships in early adolescence to more emotionally involved, intimate, and reciprocal relationships in late adolescence" (p. 214).

There is some evidence to suggest that adolescents who have close friendships tend to have high self-esteem, interpersonal competencies, and psychosocial adjustment, unlike their counterparts who show patterns of low self-esteem, anxiety, and depression (Buhrmester & Furman, 1990). It appears that adolescents who report having close friendships that are characterized by a reciprocal sense of intimacy are able to extract from those relationships intangibles that aid both partners in negotiating developmental tasks in their lives. One of the major difficulties in assessing the quality of the friendships is the reliability of the source of information. As suggested, adolescents are prone to overestimating the intensity and quality of a relationship. This tendency is due to their neediness, which compromises their ability to be objective. Shaffer (1994) suggests that the increasing intimacy and reciprocal nature of friendships beyond childhood may be responsible for the deep interpersonal sensitivity and commitment so often observed in stable adult love relationships. All of these factors seem to suggest that relating to others in a positive and age-appropriate manner produces a positive valence for prosocial development.

Evidence in support of close and deep friendships aiding in personal growth and development can also be found by looking at the lives of troubled adolescents who fail to experience close and deep friendships. Hartup and Overhauser (1991) observe that troubled adolescents tend to have fewer friends than well-adjusted peers and are more likely to associate with others who engage in deviant behavior, a finding corroborating similar results by Buhrmester and Furman (1990).

What is the developmental significance of friendships? Aside from the probability that friendships assist adolescents in creating a sense of social balance, they also serve the purpose of providing socially appropriate mechanisms for individuating, creating a sense of autonomy, and moving away from the family of origin to find one's way in the world. The process, however, is not a linear or simplistic one. Movement toward a peer group is not necessarily a smooth process or the antithesis of close alignment with family. Let me explain.

In middle adolescence—ages fourteen to seventeen—the peer group reigns supreme about matters of social relations (i.e., dating, manner of dress, choice of music, and so on), but parents and other adults are still relied on heavily for information concerning such matters as maintaining a bank account, applying to college, and occupational choice. It is also during middle adolescence that peer pressure is greatest. As the adolescent moves beyond this stage to late adolescence, peer pressure diminishes dramatically, partly because by this age most adolescents have self-selected a group of peers perceived to be like themselves and with similar interests. The dynamic relationship between family and adolescent peer groups emphasizes the importance of each aiding in the successful negotiation of the relationships with others. From parents and family members, adolescents learn valuable lessons about themselves and acquire some very basic social relations skills. In the context of peer groups, adolescents have multiple opportunities to display their social skills. Steinberg (1985) believes that the peer group also is vital for the development and expression of autonomy: "The process of developing more independent relationships with parents is accompanied by the establishment of more mature relationships with peers" (p. 179). Hill and Holmbeck (1986) characterize the peer group as a place where adolescents can try out decision-making skills with few adults present. (One assumes that they mean skills learned in the family.)

On another level, a conceptual connection can be made between the family and the peer group by rethinking what roles the adolescent has played in the family and how this pattern is replicated in peer group relationships. Specific issues include:

1. How does the adolescent relate to the power structure of the group? The issue of power relations directly draws on the psychoanalytic notion that early relationships become the blueprint for all subsequent relationships. The validity of that notion aside, it is reasonable to assume that the learning and experiential history an adolescent has had with authority figures is likely to find expression in all contexts in which the adolescent becomes, or is expected to become, subservient to the will of another.

2. How does the adolescent respond to directives and feedback from the group? In many families, feedback is unilaterally met with argument and debate about its accuracy and fairness. In some situations, these behaviors occur because they fit with the behaviors the parents are attempting to instill in their children—they want their children to question authority. In other families, there is no direct feedback, only circular, veiled messages. The indirectness of this feedback makes it hard, if not impossible, for recipients to know what others expect of them. A third variation in feedback occurs in the case of an adolescent spontaneously seeking feedback. The issue here is how, or if, the adolescent responds to feedback from others in the peer group compared to his or her response to feedback in the family.

3. How, if at all, does the adolescent make needs known to the peer group? Does the adolescent display an active style of telling others explicitly what is needed or wanted? Or does he or she engage in an indirect style of communication of intimating that something is wanted from others? Or does he or she simply wait for others to figure out what is needed?

The foregoing questions form the basis of a way of thinking about what happens in the family and its relevance in dictating an adolescent's behavioral style in the peer group. It is highly unlikely that the behavioral styles in the two contexts will be inversely correlated. It simply does not happen that overwhelmingly passive individuals become transfigured into aggressive and gregarious creatures in another setting and vice versa. Where significant variances in functioning are reported, consideration should be given to the possibility of a differential in the roles that the adolescent plays in different settings. Perhaps more important, the probability of widely fluctuating self-esteem should be considered.

Self-Esteem

Self-esteem refers to the evaluative and affective dimension of self-concept. It is also referred to as self-worth or self-image (Santrock, 1993). Historically, self-esteem has been confused with self-concept, the words often being used interchangeably. Until recently, it was thought that self-esteem differentiated from self-concept connoted a global statement about self. Research by several scholars in the area helps clarify the issue by showing that self-esteem covers multiple aspects of the lives of young people. This revelation inevitably led to psychologists concluding that it was difficult to measure self-worth or self-esteem (Harter, 1990; Wylie, 1989; Yardley, 1987) because it was hard to identify all of its constituent parts.

Knowing what adolescents think of themselves is an important component of the behavioral assessment. Because of its importance, I turn briefly to the issue of assessing self-esteem by some of the standardized tests that are available for that purpose.

One of the earliest instruments developed—and one that is still in use—is the Piers-Harris Self Concept Scale (Piers and Harris, 1964), a paper-and-pencil checklist in which subjects are asked to indicate how much a description (i.e., "I am very smart") applies to them. The sum of the scores on the items produces a self-esteem index, thought to be reflective of how a child feels self. Harter's (1989) two instruments are more precise than the Piers-Harris Self Concept Scale in self-esteem assessment. Her tests, for use with children and adolescents, contain scales to measure specific domains in which self-esteem might be manifest (i.e., scholastic competencies, athletic competencies, social competence, physical appearance, behavioral conduct) as well as global self-worth. Her most recent revision of the test (Harter, 1989), designed especially for use with adolescents, also contains three additional domains—job competence, romantic appeal, and close friendship.

Peterson and her colleagues (Peterson, Schulenberg, Abramovitz, Offer, & Jarcho, 1984) have also recently created a self-esteem inventory—the Self-Image Questionnaire for Young Adolescents (SIQYA)—which looks at different areas in which self-esteem may be readily discernible, such as emotional tone, impulse control, body image, peer relationships, family relationships, mastery and coping, vocational-educational goals, psychopathology, and superior adjustment. In the test, subjects are asked to indicate how closely they think ninety-eight different items describe them (i.e., "very well" to "not at all").

As is often the case in psychology, there is considerable debate among assessment experts as to what instruments clinicians should use to obtain the most useful data. For a review of the controversies surrounding approaches to assessing self-esteem and the tests themselves, the reader is referred to the Buros (1972) *Mental Measurement Yearbook*. Note that Santrock (1973) thinks self-esteem assessment necessarily should include evaluations by multiple individuals.

In addition to self-reports, rating of an adolescent's self-esteem by others and observations of the adolescent's behavior in various settings could provide a more complete and accurate picture of self-esteem. Peers, teachers, parents, and even those who do not know the adolescent can be asked to rate the adolescent's self-esteem (Santrock, 1993, p. 340).

Assessment Before and After Gang Involvement

The importance of assessment before and after gang involvement is rooted in understanding changes that occur in the adolescent as well as in the family and the dynamics between the two that result from the young person joining an adolescent gang. It is also important to note the behavioral changes that occur and the perceptions that each side has of the other, for such perceptions drive relationships. In the following pages, I outline the ways in which a clinician might go about assessing changes before and after gang involvement and how they give rise to changes in the behavioral dynamics between an adolescent and his or her family (see Table 5.1).

TABLE 5.1 Assessment Before and After Gang Involvement

Domain to Be Assessed	Ways of Assessing	Adolescent	Family	Notations
Intimacy	Clinical interview with adolescent and family	Who does the adolescent report to be his/her closest friends?	What has been the family's role in helping the adolescent get intimacy needs met?	
	Sociograms	Does the adolescent report sharing "secrets" with others?	Are these roles age-appropriate for the adolescent?	
Autonomy Behavioral	Objective statement of how much time the adolescent spends away from family	What is the nature of the activities (i.e., peers, other adults, sports, avoidant of family?)	How has the family encouraged or discouraged the adolescent's quests for behavioral autonomy?	
Emotional	Who provides relief when the adolescent has an emotional problem?	How does the adolescent understand his/her need of others?	How does the family view itself as an emotional support for the adolescent?	
Cognitive/ value	How does the adolescent arrive at major decisions in his/her life?	Are the opinions of others valued by the adolescent? In what areas?	Is the family consulted about major decisions the adolescent makes?	
Attachment and Loneliness	History of early attachments made by adolescent	Has the adolescent been a loner? If so, how has he/she felt about that?	How does the family view itself as an agent that has helped the adolescent get second individuation and separation needs met?	
Interpersonal Relationships	Listing of close friendships reported by the adolescent. Compare that list to a similar listing produced by the family	How much does the adolescent value friendships? Are the reported friendships age appropriate? What are the basis of the reported friendships?	How closely does the family's listing of friendships match that of the adolescent?	

(continues)

TABLE 5.1 (continued)

Domain to Be Assessed	Ways of Assessing	Adolescent	Family	Notations
Self-esteem	Piers-Harris Self Concept Scale Harter In addition to clinical interview	What are the areas in which the adolescent rates him/herself the lowest?	Are there incongruences in how the adolescent sees him/herself and how the family sees him/her? If so, how do these get acted out?	

One of the most critical elements of understanding how beliefs and expectations shift once an adolescent has joined or is suspected of joining a gang starts with a recognition of the gang membership. When an adolescent does join a gang, it is important to acknowledge the gang membership and the changes that occur in the family secondary to that fact. I suggest that the adolescent's recognition of changes in himself or herself and how that becomes a catalyst for changes in the family is important. It is a good idea to start the behavioral assessment with the adolescent, since it is his or her behavior that constitutes the catalyst for other behavioral changes. Likewise, it is important to note how family members recognize how they perceive and make attributions to the adolescent differently once the fact of gang membership is suspected or established.

How does the family alter its behavior based on the adolescent's decision to join a gang? According to the sociological literature, for some families having a young person join a gang is simply an extension of the family history with the gang organization (Vigil, 1983). In those situations, having a young person join a gang is hailed as a decision that fits with the family history and the script that others have created for the adolescent. But intergenerational gang legacies, with family members accepting gang membership as inevitable, are very much the exception rather than the rule. Even in families with multiple generations of men who have been a part of gangs, most notably in southern California, sentiments recently are turning against sons and grandsons joining gangs. And in other cases, concern about family image in the immediate community drives many families to disassociate psychologically from adolescent members who may choose to join a gang.

The purpose of the pre-post assessment is to discern concrete ways in which family statements of disapproval of the adolescent manifest in the dynamics of the family. Verbalizations that are direct and of an unambiguous nature, of course, need not be explored further, since they generally state the position of the individual uttering the statement. It is the nonverbal, or internal, changes that families make relative to their acceptance or nonacceptance of an adolescent family member who may choose to affiliate with a gang that need exploration.

In addition to thinking about how family dynamics shift with the change in gang membership status, it is also important to think about the developmental appropriateness of the behaviors that the gang member starts to display as a result of a change of gang status. I do not suggest that joining a gang is a developmentally appropriate or desirable behavior. But many young people join gangs in an attempt to get age-appropriate developmental needs met. Once in the gang, however, the adolescent discovers that the gang is unresponsive to these needs (Branch & Rennick, 1995). Then the adolescent faces a big decision: Realign with the family of origin or continue in the gang and potentially incur the wrath of the community, particularly the local police? This creates a major dilemma for many young people: continuing in the gang to show a sense of fidelity and commitment versus the autonomy of saying that joining the gang is a decision that is not in their best interest. Autonomous individuals can bounce back from the disappointment of the gang not meeting all of their needs.

Intimacy

The clinician evaluating a gang member and his or her family should pay particular attention to which persons the gang member identifies as belonging to an inner circle of confidantes. The question is whether the adolescent's list of close and special friends changes after joining the the gang. It seems logical that such would be the case, but it is not at all uncommon that individuals have two camps of friends, those who predate their involvement in the gang and those who come to be their special family once they have chosen to join the gang. When adolescents make the choice to join a gang, they often have difficulty terminating all of their pregang relationships or finding a way to reconcile two different types of relationships that seem to respond to two parts of their inner self. The family also should be assessed very closely with regard to ability and willingness to serve as an intimacy outlet for the gang member, both in the pre- and post-involvement stages. The clinical interview is the method of choice for obtaining this information from gang members and their families. It should be noted, however, that often families are unavailable to offer information about the adolescent's inner circle of confidantes, even in their pregang identity status. Such an occurrence should itself be considered information of major clinical significance.

Autonomy

Autonomy refers to behavioral, emotional, and cognitive self-sufficiency. Steinberg and Silverburg (1986) indicate that adolescents often abandon dependency on family only to create dependency on peer groups, in this case gangs. Such transferral of dependency is not to be construed as movement in the direction of being autonomous simply because the adolescent is no longer dependent on family. Adolescents may become dependent on peer groups in the same way that they were dependent on family.

In the area of behavioral autonomy, the evaluating clinician should explore how much time the adolescent spends away from the family in structured activities with peers and others. The nature of those activities (i.e., age appropriate) gives a strong indication of movement in the direction of behavioral autonomy. A big question in assessing the family is, Does it aid the adolescent in finding behavioral autonomy both before and after gang involvement? How much has the family encouraged the adolescent to be independent of the family?

A line of reasoning similar to that used to assess behavioral autonomy applies to evaluating an adolescent's sense of emotional autonomy as well. One way of assessing the level of emotional autonomy of an adolescent is to try to determine whom he or she turns to in times of emotional needs. The family is known to provide most emotional support for children up until they reach middle adolescence. It is critical to determine whether the same dynamics apply as individuals move in the direction of joining a gang. Do adolescents continue to look to the family for emotional bandages when they incur wounds in their relationships in the gang? A clinician making evaluations in this area would want to interview the family and the adolescent very closely about whom the adolescent perceives as his or her sources of emotional support. What is the basis of these relationships? Note that in any event changes would be expected to occur in that inner circle as an adolescent grows older and more discriminating about friends.

Cognitive autonomy is defined here as an adolescent's ability to arrive at major decisions, weighing information provided by others without undue reliance on family or friends. One way of evaluating shifts in an adolescent's tendency toward cognitive autonomy is to ask both the adolescent and other family members to talk about decisions made by the adolescent recently and how these were reached. There are likely to be significant differences of opinion as to what the decisions have been and even the ability of the adolescent to follow through on decisions made. Such discrepancies are vital sources of contradictory information, helping a clinician understand how each side seeks clarifications from the other when such mismatches occur. In some situations, there are no attempts to obtain clarification of information, but each person simply proceeds as if his or her version of the story is necessarily true and the only possible version. That sort of behavior helps the clinician to understand whether the adolescent or other family members are capable of seeking information from others or showing respect for the perspectives of others.

Attachment and Loneliness

Attachment and loneliness are perhaps the most difficult areas for a clinician to assess, partly because what is being assessed is internal states that give rise to behaviors. Frequently, these behaviors, in the form of isolation and absence of intense sustained relationships, are misinterpreted by family members and clinicians. A child who never experienced significant attachment in relationships may be described as always having been shy as opposed to always having had difficulty in affectively connecting to others. This is a diagnostic distinction that the clinician must make. The questions relative to loneliness also are difficult to answer because an adolescent's subjective experience is the best indicator of his or her perceptions of loneliness. Family members may always have considered the adolescent to be a loner. They conclude he or she must therefore be lonely. By contrast, the adolescent may report always having preferred to work and perform as an isolate as opposed to part of a large group.

The pre-post gang involvement dichotomy allows the clinician to gain an understanding as to whether there has been a major change in the adolescent's feelings of attachment and association with others. More important, it helps determine how the gang may have played a role in this regard. Many adolescents report that they join gangs in an attempt to get their affiliation needs met. The clinician needs to address this matter directly with the gang member without being judgmental about the decision to join the gang. Other family members should be asked to comment on how they see themselves as agents in the present (postgang state) as well as in the past (pregang state) with regard to the adolescent's affiliations.

Interpersonal Relationships

Many types of relationships exist in families. Some adolescents are able to create and sustain friendships with friends of siblings as well as friends of their parents. All of these possible combinations, in addition to relationships within the familial structure, should be considered as major indicators of an adolescent's capacity to function in sustained relationships. The before-and-after gang distinction should enable greater understanding as to whether the adolescent perceives a major change in his or her life relative to the number of meaningful sustained relationships that can be attributed to initiation into the gang culture. A useful way for stimulating discussion in this area is to ask the adolescent to prepare a list of close friends (first names only) before joining the gang. A second list, of close friends after joining the gang, should also be prepared. Family members could be asked to create similar lists. In addition to the obvious comparisons, this type of activity allows a clinician to estimate the adolescent's level of prosocial development and involvement before joining the gang. The exercise provides an opportunity for understanding how the family perceived the adolescent's social ability before joining the gang as well.

For many adolescents, transformation into a gang member follows several years of reasonably appropriate social development. The change to being a gang member does not occur spontaneously, nor is it an all-or-nothing progression in the lives of many young people. Giving up their previous lifestyle and social relations for the sake of blind allegiance and anticipated acceptance in the gang is often a major source of difficulty for adolescents. The result, when they are not able to resolve the task quickly and decisively, is often intermittent periods of depression.

Self-Esteem

The areas of self-esteem and self-concept have been the object of much discussion and mislabeling. Here, I refer to self-esteem as the affective component of self-concept. This is easily discerned from direct statements by the adolescent, reports from the family, and objective measures. I strongly suggest that if at all possible a pen-and-paper self-esteem measure be administered over the course of the extensive evaluation with the gang member and family. This process provides information about areas of weakness and uncovers objective information about areas of strength that can be used as a catalyst for moving an adolescent toward higher levels of self-affirmation. I encourage clinicians pondering the question of self-esteem among gang members to consider the possibility that self-esteem is multifaceted and that there may be multiple contributors to an adolescent's self-esteem, all operating at the same time. It is important to know what adolescents see as their strengths and weaknesses. Likewise, it is important to know what other family members identify as the areas of strength and weakness for the adolescent. The critical questions in this area of evaluation relate to family perceptions and can be summarized as follows: Are there incongruences in the adolescent's perception of self and other family members' views of the adolescent? If so, how are these discrepancies acted out? Again, I encourage clinicians to create a dichotomy of before-and-after involvement in the gang as the clinical interviews are conducted. Placing assessments in time may prove helpful to family members as they think about how their opinions of their adolescent family member may have changed over time and what is the basis of such change.

The foregoing information is intended as guidance for conducting clinical interviews with gang members and their families. The topics I selected for focus represent the issues that are integral to a developmental picture of adolescence and are most easily accessed through re-creation of histories by the gang member and other family members. There are other approaches and lines of diagnostic evaluation that a clinician may want to consider as a way of understanding the current level of functioning of the gang member and his or her family. It may be that the current functioning is a pattern of long-standing duration. If that is true, the before-and-after gang involvement dichotomy is problematic in that many individuals may not be able to accurately recall events or the status of things before the adolescent became a member of the gang or started to engage in disruptive behaviors. One approach, in addition to what has been offered so far, is the use of the medical

BOX 5.1   Evaluating Behavior in Different Settings

The clinician may want to consider asking the following questions as a way to assess the behavior of an adolescent across the multiple settings in which he or she functions.

1. How does the adolescent perceive himself or herself in the setting?
2. Does the adolescent want to be in the setting?
3. Are relationships in the setting mutually respectful?
4. What does the adolescent report as gains that result from participating in the setting?
5. Who are the other persons engaged in the setting? Are they like (unlike) the adolescent on critical dimensions?
6. How did the adolescent come to be involved in the relationships? Are they rewarding?
7. Does the adolescent desire to continue the relationships? If not, why?
8. What is the developmental and psychological nature of the relationships?

model diagnostic label. In the case of many gang members, the diagnostic category that seems to accurately reflect much of their activity is conduct disorder.

Diagnostic Label: Conduct Disorder

The conduct disorder diagnosis is a helpful way of describing the behavior of many adolescent gang members. Consistent with the atheoretical position of the *DSM-IV*, this diagnostic label includes no explanation as to why the behaviors have surfaced but merely gives a detailed description of the kinds of behaviors and their severity and longevity. The behavior is usually observed in the multiple settings (e.g., school, home, community) in which the child/adolescent functions. As noted in *DSM-IV*, "Because individuals with Conduct Disorder are likely to minimize their conduct problems the clinician often must rely on additional informants" (American Psychiatric Association, 1994, p. 86).

Clinicians using this medical model diagnostic category should be well versed in diagnostic procedures and the use of the *DSM-IV* (Branch, 1996; see also Box 5.1). Care should be taken in completing the history of the gang member to correctly determine if the conduct disorder is of childhood or adolescent onset, a distinction that is critically important. Childhood onset refers to individuals who began to display conduct disorder symptoms before age ten. Without major interventions, such individuals are likely to have persistent conduct disorder and to eventually develop into antisocial personality types. Adolescent onset is used to describe individuals who are

BOX 5.2 Diagnostic Criteria for 312.8 Conduct Disorder

A. A repetitive and persistent pattern of behavior in which the basic rights of others or major age-appropriate societal norms or rules are violated, as manifested by the presence of three (or more) of the following criteria in the past 12 months, with at least one criterion present in the past 6 months:

Aggression to People and Animals

(1) often bullies, threatens, or intimidates others
(2) often initiates physical fights
(3) has used a weapon that can cause serious physical harm to others (e.g., a bat, brick, broken bottle, knife, gun)
(4) has been physically cruel to people
(5) has been physically cruel to animals
(6) has stolen while confronting a victim (e.g., mugging, purse snatching, extortion, armed robbery)
(7) has forced someone into sexual activity

Destruction of Property

(8) has deliberately engaged in fire setting with the intention of causing serious damage
(9) has deliberately destroyed others' property (other than by fire setting)

Deceitfulness or Theft

(10) has broken into someone else's house, building, or car
(11) often lies to obtain goods or favors or to avoid obligations (i.e., "cons" others)
(12) has stolen items of nontrivial value without confronting a victim (e.g., shoplifting, but without breaking and entering; forgery)

Serious Violations of Rules

(13) often stays out at night despite parental prohibitions, beginning before age 13 years
(14) has run away from home overnight at least twice while living in parental or parental surrogate home (or once without returning for a lengthy period)
(15) is often truant from school, beginning before age 13 years

B. The disturbance in behavior causes clinically significant impairment in social, academic, or occupational functioning.
C. If the individual is age 18 years or older, criteria are not met for Antisocial Personality Disorder.
   Specify type based on age at onset:

Childhood-Onset Type: onset of at least one criterion characteristic of Conduct Disorder prior to age 10 years

Adolescent-Onset Type: absence of any criteria characteristic of Conduct Disorder prior to age 10 years

Specify severity:

Mild: few if any conduct problems in excess of those required to make diagnosis *and* conduct problems cause only minor harm to others

Moderate: number of conduct problems and effect on others intermediate between "mild" and "severe"

Severe: many conduct problems in excess of those required to make the diagnosis *or* conduct problems cause considerable harm to others

The shortcomings of a psychiatric diagnosis of this type are considerable. A few are listed here as a caution against seeing diagnosis as an answer in and of itself. Clinicians should consider the following:

(1) The conduct disorder diagnosis is atheoretical. It does not tell anything about the ideology of the subject's behavior. It is fairly well established that many adolescents and children who participate in violent behavior are simply responding to environmental cues that have suggested that such behavior is normal and acceptable. In addition, one should consider the possibility of conduct disorder being the result of long periods of lack of socialization and structure.

(2) The conduct disorder diagnosis is individualistic. Gang behavior, by contrast, is collectivistic. The question is whether the behavior in which the gang member is engaging is the result of gang membership and how the decision to engage in such behavior was reached. Or is it that the individual is out of control and indiscriminating in the expression of violent behavior toward others and property?

(3) The conduct disorder diagnosis does not identify how much of the behavior was engaged in by the subject as an isolate or as a member of a group of some sort.

(4) The conduct disorder diagnosis does not give any information on the subject's sense of remorse or lack thereof about the behavior.

(5) The conduct disorder diagnosis does not rule out contextual factors, including familial history, that may have normalized pathological behavior. Nor does the diagnosis rule out the possibility of contributions from substance abuse and other social toxicities facilitating the subject's engaging in behavior that is deemed to be disordered and inappropriate.

SOURCE: Reprinted with permission from the *Diagnostic and Statistical Manual of Mental Disorders,* 4th ed., copyright © 1994 American Psychiatric Association.

---

free of the disordered conduct until after age ten. The distinction is important here because adolescent onset suggests that a youngster has experienced a period of reasonably healthy and appropriate behaviors. It could be assumed that during that period the child had ample opportunity for acquiring

basic academic competencies and was available for age-appropriate friendships without the toxic influence of aggressive and maladapted behaviors.
Age of onset is also important because it indirectly helps identify the kinds of
issues with which a family may have been faced and can corroborate the accuracy of the developmental histories of the gang member offered by different family members.

Diagnosing clinicians should exercise special caution to make certain that
conduct disorder is used to describe the offender's behavior, not as an indirect labeling of the environment in which the child lives (see Box 5.2). As
noted in the *DSM-IV,*

> Concern has been raised that the conduct disorder diagnosis may at times be
> misapplied to individuals in settings where patterns of undesirable behavior are
> sometimes viewed as protective (e.g., threatening, impoverished, high crime).
> Consistent with the DSM-IV definition of mental disorder the conduct disorder
> diagnosis should be applied only when the behavior in question is symptomatic
> of an underlying dysfunction with the individual and not simply a reaction to
> the immediate social context. (American Psychiatric Association, 1994, p. 88)

6

Cognition

The final area to be assessed is cognitive functioning. As cognitive functioning is implicitly involved in the areas of affect and behavior, isolating its effects is virtually impossible. For the sake of demonstration, however, I discuss these effects individually. Unlike affect, cognitive activity can be inferred from nearly every behavioral expression a client or other family members engage in during their relationship with the clinician. Clinicians should be especially observant of verbalizations, affective presentations, and concrete behaviors that may give clues about the internal processes of the clients.

Cognition literally means "to become acquainted with" or "to come to know." The process includes both awareness and judgment and is accomplished through mental representations and manipulations made by the subject. The result usually manifests as words, affective presentations reflective of the subject's cognitive activity, or behavioral expressions that are driven by the mental scheme. The beginnings of cognitive development occur in infancy. Qualitative shifts in the capacity for abstract cognitive activity become more pronounced as the child enters school and has experience with a great variety of settings and persons. One should not assume, however, that development in all areas of social and intellectual functioning are parallel. Indeed, it is precisely unevenness of thinking that causes problems for many individuals. For example, a child may develop quite normally in the area of social cognition and interpersonal relationships, as evidenced by making lots of friends and adequately understanding the surrounding world. But the same child may have significant difficulties understanding abstract concepts such as mathematical calculations or the idea of geography, resulting in poor academic performance in school.

In this chapter, I discuss the importance of making a thorough evaluation of cognitive processes in gang members and their families as part of a clinical assessment. First, I briefly discuss normative cognitive development as it occurs across the life span. Next, I give descriptions and examples of common aberrations in thinking that may be observed in families in crisis. Then, I introduce strategies to use in evaluating cognitive processes. Finally, I apply the cognitive assessment process to issues of gang involvement. Throughout, I include clinical anecdotal vignettes demonstrating disordered thinking.

Cognitive Development Across the Life Span

Cognitive developmental theory originates from the work of Piaget. It is predicated on the assumption of normative changes in children's and adolescents' abilities to observe relationships in the world around them. Based on those observations, language and social relationships are adjusted. One major assumption of this theory is that there are universal stages of development that characterize the experiences of all individuals. That belief has been the subject of much debate, most notably as it relates to children who may have a different socialization experience than that captured by the theorists. It is not an issue that should be dismissed lightly. The clinician is urged to use extensive detailed interviews to determine the type of socialization experience gang members may have had in their pregang era.

Piaget (1952) proposes four major periods of cognitive development: the sensorimotor stage (extending from birth to two years of age), the preoperational stage (ages two to seven), the concrete operational stage (age seven to puberty at age eleven or twelve), and the formal operational stage (puberty and beyond). These periods constitute an invariant developmental sequence, occurring in the same order for all children in all cultures. Implicit in this idea is the assumption that cognitive skills as absolute entities are expressed at the same level across multiple domains of an individual's life. Piaget recognizes that in some situations a person may show uneven levels of performance, a pattern he calls *decaloge*. For example, a child who is quite advanced in logic when applied to mathematical problems may be at a rather primitive level in thinking about social relations problems. As I discuss later, similar patterns of incongruence are common among gang-affiliated youth.

The first two years of development constitute the sensorimotor stage of Piaget's (1965) theory: "According to him, infants evolve from reflexive creatures with very limited knowledge into playful problem solvers who have already learned a great deal about themselves, their close companions, and the objects and events in their everyday worlds" (Shaffer, 1994, p. 109). These changes in the sensorimotor period have profound implications for subsequent social and personality development.

In the following preoperational stage, children become more proficient at constructing and using mental symbols to think about the world that surrounds them. Much progress is made during this stage, but the child still is incapable of thinking abstractly or globally. Notable among the changes that occur during this period is the evolution of the ability to engage in symbolic and pretend play. Another area in which children make significant gains is that of preoperational thinking. Because most children are so egocentric, it is difficult for them to recognize that others may have views different from their own. This limitation makes it hard for preoperational children to engage in *perceptual perspective taking* (inferring what others can see and hear) and *conceptual perspective taking* (correctly inferring what another may be feeling, thinking, or intending) (Selman, 1980). Toward the end of the preoperational stage, egocentrism declines, making it possible for the child to classify objects on the basis of shared perceptual features, such as size, shape, and color. This classification ability is extended to people and situations.

Piaget's (1965) concrete operational stage (age seven to puberty) is characterized by the child being able to engage in relational logic. According to Shaffer (1994), "One of the hallmarks of concrete-operational thinking—an ability that permits us to sharpen our self-concepts by comparing our skill and attributes with those of other people—is a better understanding of relations and relational logic" (p. 116). At this stage, the ability appears to be limited to concrete objects and does not extend to situations or internal states of persons. Two additional characteristics necessary for the development of concrete operational thinking are that the objects must be physically present and the classification task must not violate the child's concept of reality.

Formal operations constitute the final stage of Piaget's (1965) theory. This stage is characterized by the abilities to engage in abstract thinking, to assume a mental set, to keep simultaneously in mind all aspects of a complex situation, to move from feature to feature as indicated by the situation, and to extract common properties. It is assumed that the capacity for abstract thinking is the result of an adolescent's development in the area of cognition. Implicit in the increased capacity for abstract reasoning is the idea that adolescents are more mobile than younger children and can make good use of the multiple situations in which they find themselves. Perspective taking increases dramatically during adolescence. That change too, it seems, adds to an individual's tendency to engage in formal operations.

Despite the controversy surrounding this theoretical orientation, the theory is useful in that it also proposes that there is a qualitative shift in the reasoning ability of children that is age related. Older adolescents think more abstractly and globally than younger children. It is assumed that this increasingly abstract reasoning gives rise to abstract thinking regarding morals and the social order in which an individual lives as well.

Cognitive developmental theory is useful in assessing the cognitive functioning of gang-affiliated youth and their families. The theory helps determine clients' stage of functioning and implicitly offers prescriptions for remediation. Preoperational individuals are notoriously poor prospects for gaining insight or adjusting their behavior in the absence of concrete evidence.

Establishing a client's stage of cognitive functioning also allows the evaluating clinician to better understand why there may be miscommunications between parents and children. Understanding their capacity for relational logic may also indicate how invested they are in changing their behaviors.

Common Errors in Thinking

Errors in thinking and formulating conclusions can occur for a variety of reasons. It is very common for adults to assume that children and adolescents make factual errors and corresponding behavioral errors as willful acts of disobedience. Sometimes, that is true, but very often errors in thinking and behavior are the logical sequelae to fundamental errors in receiving the information to be processed. Such distortions may be the result of multiple causations, including insufficient vocabulary to understand the incoming message, anxiety about the situation, emotional overlay of the relationship with the message sender, and a characterological style that causes the responder to make error-prone replies to communications. The last category is discussed here. Concrete thinking, loose associations, over- and underinclusion, and personalization are common causes for miscommunication.

Concrete Thinking

Concrete thinking refers to responding to things in an absolute either-or fashion not allowing for a subjective interpretation. Individuals who employ concrete thinking as a primary characteristic are inclined to disregard contextual cues (i.e., vocal inflections of the speaker, circumstances, and so on) and respond only to spoken or written words in a literal way. There are several reasons why an individual may behave in such a manner, including limited intellectual ability, emotional blockage that prevents them from becoming invested in the communication, limited language facility, and cultural factors.

Limited intellectual capability is an interpretation that is often applied to individuals who respond in a concrete and restricted manner. The logic of this interpretation is that the respondent simply lacks the ability to understand the statement other than in the straightforward, concrete way in which it was presented and hence the very concrete response. It is potentially dangerous to leap to this conclusion without testing a client's limits to verify why he or she responds in such a constricted manner. There is a large possibility of emotional factors creating a blockage and making it difficult, if not impossible, for the respondent to think or respond more expansively.

An often overlooked explanation for concrete thinking and responding in adolescents is that this style represents one way for the recalcitrant adolescent to make obvious "flaws" in the message, most often from parents, that was given to him or her. This response might be considered splitting hairs, but it can serve the purpose of the adolescent to resist adult controls and prove parents incapable. Consider the case of the adolescent who argues vehemently with parents about the limits placed on him having friends in the house when his parents are out of town:

Adolescent I think you're being unfair, punishing me when I didn't do nothin' wrong.

Mother But I told you not to have any girls in here when I was out of town. . . . You've ruined the basement.

Adolescent You told me not to have any girls in the living room while you was out of town, and I didn't.

Loose Associations

The blending of unrelated ideas as if they make a logical connection has been described as looseness of association. Individuals who engage in such behavior are inclined to do so based on similarity of sounds of words or other bases not apparent to the listener. Loose associations are generally considered to be evidence of an underlying thought disorder characterized by mixing and matching things for which there is no logical basis of association. Usually, the individuals are unaware of their performance. Pointing out the quality of their verbalizations can provoke a response of, "People tell me that all the time," suggesting that others too have noted the subject's behavior. The response also indicates that the subject is able to recall that others have on other occasions noted the illogical quality of his or her thinking.

Overinclusion

Overinclusive thinking is characterized by the combining of unimportant and often unrelated ideas as part of one's cognitive processing. Individuals who engage in such behavior add too many ingredients, so to speak, to create even the simplest of responses. Many clinicians feel that such behavior is related to more pervasive personality difficulties that find expression linguistically. The responses of others to overincluders cover a wide range. Because they cannot apply limits to their information gathering, invariably overincluders use an inordinate amount of others' time. Likewise, they cannot place good limits on how much they need to give in a reply. They never seem to know how much is enough. Their habitual query for more makes them vulnerable to losing the main point because they have so much data to manipulate. Although sensory overload is not likely to be a problem for such individuals, an inability to identify the main features of a question or reply is likely to be troublesome.

The exact psychological function served by overly inclusive behavior is likely to vary by the individual. One thing that is clear, however, is that such behavior makes it hard to get a direct answer from the subject. Avoidance of taking a position and reluctance to self-disclose are two functions that overly inclusive verbal and cognitive behavior have been noted to serve in clinical assessment and treatment settings.

In addition to the difficulty of discerning what overincluders are offering in a reply, it may be equally hard to disrupt their process and get them to re-focus their thinking. It is almost as if they have a global scheme that they must execute in total before they can respond to a question. The same ex-pansiveness of thought can be observed in their spontaneous messages to others, which leave listeners uncertain what pieces of the message they should respond to. At the other end of the spectrum fall individuals who produce a paucity of information in responses to others and spontaneous statements, the underincluders.

Underinclusion

Underinclusive thinking is characterized by a tendency to omit important, even basic, pieces of information and opt for a telegraphic style of response. Again, this cognitive processing style is inextricably linked to pervasive per-sonality traits. Like their expansive counterparts, underincluders evoke a wide range of responses in others. They tend to force others to fill in the blanks, literally and figuratively. One behavioral outcome associated with forcing others to do part of their work has been that underincluders tend to be nurtured by others. The logic supporting this behavior is often that under-includers are fragile and habitually in need of help. Of course, behav-ing toward them in such a way only reinforces their behavior. It is not clear if underincluders truly do not hear or value the full array of information pro-vided to them or if they simply eliminate much of the available data. It would be interesting to test whether underincluders are consistent in their behavior across contexts. Underinclusive behavior may be selectively, per-haps unconsciously, chosen based on the situation in which one is function-ing.

Personalization

Personalization as a cognitive error is best described as a style in which the respondent applies all information involved in a communication or cognitive manipulation to his or her own life. Objective and abstract conceptualizations are virtually impossible for personalizers. Information that cannot be fit into their personal life scheme is dismissed as being meaningless. Implicit in this thinking disorder is the idea that the subject cannot take the perspective of another person. It is often difficult to interact with personalizers because of their inability to move beyond self-reference. Consider the following example:

A clinician conducting an interview with an adolescent asked the client to think about why his mother may have come to the conclusion that the client could no longer reside in the mother's home.

Therapist   It sounds as if your mother is pretty upset with you.
Adolescent   Yeah.
Therapist   From what you're telling me, it sounds as if she thinks you'll have to go live with your father, or at least move out of her home.
Adolescent   Yeah . . . that's right.
Therapist   Why do you think she decided that?
Adolescent   That's wrong. . . . I'd never do that to anybody. . . . That is wrong.

Note that the adolescent is unable or unwilling to speculate about what might be the basis of his mother's decision. Instead, he shifts into a self-reflective mode and indicates that if he were in the mother's position he would not make such a decision. This, of course, misses the point of thinking about his mother's reasoning. Similar cases of personalizing are often observed among students writing examination essays.

Strategies for Evaluating Cognitive Processes

It is very important for clinicians to have an array of approaches available for assessing the cognitive processes of gang-affiliated youth and their families. One very frequently made assumption is that clients will cooperate with procedures as they are implemented by the clinician. Such is often not the case. Rather, some clients invest significant time and energy in being uncooperative. This tendency may take the form of overt resistance or more subtle attempts at catching the clinician off guard. Posing difficult dilemmas for the clinician to resolve is an example of trying to "get" the doctor. In the following pages, I suggest ways to overcome these problems and accomplish the much-needed assessment of cognitive processes.

One of the most obvious strategies for assessing the cognitive processes of a client is to simply note the processes as they are spontaneously presented during the course of the interview. This sounds simple but is a task that requires the clinician to preplan questions to be asked and observations to be made relative to the verbalizations and thought processes that the client may exhibit. It usually is useful to allow the client to lead the way in providing new information and clarifying old information. Sometimes, a carefully placed question, such as "What were you thinking when you did that?" or "What led you to that conclusion?" will provide the clinician with a wonderfully detailed description of the thought processes that underlie the client's verbalizations and behaviors. At other times, it is helpful to allow discussions that occur in a family to continue a bit longer than if an adolescent was being seen alone as an individual client. The benefit of this strategy is that it increases opportunities to note who talks to whom and the affective tones associated with those exchanges.

When working with families of gang members and others who may be in the office against their will, it is often useful to create a list of very focused questions to be sure to obtain all of the critical information during the interview hour. The very simple question, "Why are we here?" has tremendous power. That question can be read at multiple levels, including the obvious level of what conditions in the here and now prompted our being present at this place and the deeper level of what conditions preceded the clinical evaluation. Families that are not particularly invested in the clinical assessment process tend to respond to "Why are we here?" in a much more concrete fashion, the idea being that the less they say the sooner the ordeal will come to an end. Others who are more introspective and open to seriously reflecting on their behavior are inclined to answer in ways that suggest thinking in a more global way and beyond the urgent situation of the moment.

Testing the Limits

The term *testing the limits* is drawn from psychological testing. It refers to pressing a client to defend the rationale of an answer produced during a testing procedure. This approach dictates that the clinician quietly but directly challenge many of the statements made by the family, the gang member in particular. It has been useful to me in talking with gang members to test the limits relative to their frequent report of joining the gang because it is "like family." A typical response to testing such a statement would be for the client to explain how the gang is like a family.

Additionally, testing the limits allows the clinician to note whether or not the person who is being challenged becomes more cognitively disoriented, personalizes the questions, responds with anger, or makes some other illogical response. Even a "nonanswer" is a prognostic sign of how the person probably responds in the real world when his or her verbalizations are not accepted at face value.

Standardized Psychological Tests

In some situations, it becomes difficult, if not impossible, to complete a detailed and reliable cognitive assessment in a single family meeting. This occurs when family members are agitated and unstructured in their responses to questions. The clinician may observe that several family members talk at the same time, apparently with no one listening to anyone else. Needless to say, in such situations attempts to track the quality of the interactions and who says what to whom are futile. The clinician should determine whether this situation is part of a long-standing style of communication or due to anxiety about the referral and an impending court appearance. If the clinician determines that more objectively administered evaluation procedures are necessary, I strongly recommend that one of the standardized cognitive assessment tests be employed. A carefully crafted set of questions should determine which standardized test to use based on the reported strengths and weaknesses of the test as documented in the *Mental Measurement Yearbook* (Buros, 1972) and *Tests in Print* (Mitchell, 1983).

It is virtually impossible to evaluate thought processes without noting the content that arises as the conclusion of the process. Two levels must be carefully noted in any impressions that the clinician offers concerning the clients. Box 6.1 lists common disturbances in forms of thinking with examples that may be presented. The box provides a quick reference for clinicians but is not intended as an exhaustive list of all possible variations that may be presented during a clinical evaluation.

Applying Cognitive Assessment to the Gang Situation

Here, I discuss how to apply the clinical assessment ideas presented in this chapter. It is important for clinicians to understand how gang members and their families understand their current situation. Reasonable areas for exploration include their understanding of what gang involvement entails. It is striking how many families are able to engage in denial relative to possible outcomes of their behavior or the behavior of family members as a way of defending against anxiety-provoking realities. Ask family members to tell what they know, think, and feel about gangs as an issue separate and apart from their ongoing life situation. Most striking in such assessments is the inability of some families to distance themselves from the issue and their very strong tendency to personalize all of the information that they provide. At the other extreme are families whose members truly are ignorant or profess to be completely ignorant about the realities of gangs and violence in the communities in which they live. These individuals are likely to say it is incon-

BOX 6.1   Evaluating Thinking

Thinking: goal-directed flow of ideas, symbols, and associations initiated by a problem of tasks and leading toward a reality-oriented conclusion; when a logical sequence occurs, thinking is normal.

A. Disturbances in Form of Thinking

1. Neurosis—mental disorder in which reality testing is intact and symptoms are experienced as distressing and unacceptable
2. Psychosis—inability to distinguish reality from fantasy; impaired reality testing; includes creation of a new reality
3. Formal Thought Disorder—disturbance in the form of thought instead of the content of thought
4. Illogical Thinking—thinking containing erroneous conclusions or internal contradictions
5. Concrete Thinking—literal thinking; limited use of metaphor without understanding of nuances of meaning

B. Specific Disturbances in Form of Thought

1. Tangentiality—inability to have goal-directed associations of thought; wandering verbally
2. Incoherence—speech that generally is not understandable
3. Perseveration—persisting response to a prior stimulus after a new stimulus has been presented
4. Condensation—fusion of various concepts into one
5. Irrelevant Answer—answer not in harmony with question asked
6. Flight of Ideas—rapid, continuous verbalizations or plays on words producing constant shifting from one idea to another; ideas connected without any logical reason
7. Blocking—abrupt interruption in train of thinking before a thought or idea is finished; after a brief pause, person indicates no recall of what was being said or was going to be said

SOURCE: Adapted from Kaplan and Sadock (1989, chap. 9.2).

---

ceivable that a member of their family would be a member of a gang—despite the fact that they themselves profess not to know very much about gangs.

Another way in which information about cognitive processing and thinking can be utilized is in examining the logical or illogical quality of the decisions that families make about what they need to do in response to a member being at risk for participation in a gang. Often, family members talk about what they can do as a way to make their family situation better. Options include relocating the at-risk family member, physically defending themselves against attacks from community members, or simply settling into helplessness and accepting the decision that the young person appears to have made about his or her life. A good way of utilizing the cognitive assessment procedures relative to these matters would be to ask the family if those actions would make the situation better. If so, how? It becomes very clear that in many families there is no long-range planning or thinking about how their actions will have an impact other than in the immediate moment.

Cognitive processes also can be observed as family members talk about what they would like to see happen or where they would like to see things move beyond the immediate situation they face. Again, some families are able to show an astonishing ability to take perspectives of multiple individuals and use that as a basis for formulating a game plan. Others are impressive in their inability to move beyond the situation, their limited capacity for problem solving, or their tendency to be immobilized by a long history of fractured relationship with the identified gang member.

There are many other ways in which clinicians can use the assessment procedures outlined here to gain a better understanding of the strengths and weaknesses of a family. It is useful to occasionally talk with the family about matters other than the situation that brought them to the clinician and provide them an opportunity to talk about something that is not a source of anxiety for them. Such conversations might focus on work, school, and family activities in which members have participated with more enthusiasm. Families tend to react to this seeming diversion from the issue of gangs in one of two ways: Some families find it a waste of their time to talk about other times and places in the family's history. They think it would be more beneficial to focus on relief from their current crisis. Other families welcome the seeming digression as an opportunity to reveal something of who they are and how they see themselves beyond their present crisis. Remembering that how people share information with others is often as important as the information that is shared, clinicians should use judgment about how much time should be spent talking about other things.

7

Family Assessment

The purpose of family assessment is to evaluate the strengths and weaknesses of a family as perceived by its members and by the evaluating clinician. The assessment should be conducted in the spirit of understanding the family from its indigenous perspective as well as from the perspective of the larger society in which the family functions. Assessment data can be obtained from the family's present behavior faced with a member becoming an active gang member as well as from a historic context. Both yield information about how the family functions under different circumstances. This chapter is devoted to issues that may significantly impact the outcome of a family assessment. But before I present the basics of completing such an evaluation, I must describe some theories and concepts concerning families.

Relevant issues include matters as elementary as defining a family and understanding how clinicians' views about families might influence their ability to work with families of diverse backgrounds. Here, I use ecological theory to explore the idea that families, as units, function in different settings and from each setting receive an array of social and emotional contributions that influence their stability and functioning. Finally, I present two specific assessment procedures.

A Definitional Dilemma

One of the first major decisions confronting a clinician working with a gang-affiliated family is to decide who should be included in work that is deemed "family work." There are widely divergent attitudes about what constitutes a family and the significance of members' contributions to the life and energy of a family unit. The historic image of a family consisting of two parents, 2.5 children, and a family pet are more of a fantasy than a reality these days. In recent forecasting reports, the U.S. Department of Labor and other bodies predict that the pattern of fifty percent of all first-time marriages ending in divorce will continue for several years. This grim statistic, coupled with the uncertainty of economic trends, suggests that family boundaries will continue to change as the social environment in which families function continues to change.

The idea that a family unit provides for the well-being of its members is a basic assumption. Historically, this function has been performed by the nuclear family unit. The recent trend of *blended families,* a high divorce rate, and an even higher rate of separations is changing this historic pattern dramatically. With many parents also choosing alternative lifestyles that do not find widespread acceptance in many communities, the number of variations and permutations on the theme of family increases enormously.

Extended-family living arrangements play a vital role in many ethnic groups. It is quite common to find multiple generations of a family living in one residence, each making a major contribution to the safety and well-being of the younger family members. This practice as it exists in the African American and Latino communities is discussed extensively by behavioral and social scientists. The practice appears to be just as pronounced among families that recently immigrated to the United States. The reasons for such an arrangement include psychological connectedness (occasionally bordering on individuals being too connected to family, i.e., enmeshment), economic survival, and safety. Frequently, extended families include relatives with limited formal education and no understanding of U.S. folkways and mores. This cast of characters may create a compromising environment for adolescents attempting to resolve questions of self-identity.

Recently immigrated adolescents are often embarrassed about their family living arrangement and actively seek to distance themselves from the "old customs" (i.e., language) and a life of economic poverty. Street gangs are often seen as way out of the trap of poverty and marginal existence in a community. In moving toward the gang for redefinition of self, many adolescents come to regard the gang "family" as replacement for their biological family. Such a replacement is usually more fantasy than anything that can be objectively verified by level of altruism and concern.

Clinicians working with gang adolescents must have a clear idea about the composition of a family and the identities of the persons to be included in an intervention. Are distant relatives who contributed to the life of the family and the development of the adolescent to be excluded just because they fail to meet the legal definition for a nuclear family? On the other hand, are other gang members to be included simply because they are called "family"? What has been the contribution of the different people to the family system? The clinician may want to consider asking the family to invite other relatives to the session when appropriate. A requirement for such an arrangement should be that all members of the family must agree that the invited person is indeed a member of the family and should be invited. It is occasionally necessary for the clinician to contact individual family members, especially fathers who are absent from the home, before the first session. The purposes of such contacts are to obtain the absent member's perspective on the problem and to request their presence at the family meeting. It is helpful to briefly review expectations for the family meeting with the "absent" family member. A premeeting contact also provides the clinician with an opportunity to assess the absent member's willingness and ability to cooperate in the process. Contacting absent family members often sparks controversy and rage in other family members. Anger may be expressed toward the clinician for including the absent member. All of the family members, including the absent parent, who have had less than optimal experiences with mental health professionals may use this situation as an occasion to band together against the professional attempting to assess their family.

Once the question of defining the family is settled, it is imperative that all family members be allowed an opportunity to express any concerns about who should or should not be involved in the family work. Failure to do so only produces a lingering point of discontent that will continue to surface throughout the course of subsequent therapeutic work with the family. Once everyone is on board as a certified family member, the real work of looking at the family as a unit can begin. Critical questions the clinician must seek to answer even before the first group session are, What has been the history of the family as a unit? And what has been the contribution of each member to that history?

The Family's History

The history that a family has experienced as a unit is vital to understanding family members' range of experiences and how they feel about them. Clinicians should always keep in mind that asking families to talk about their histories can evoke a range of responses. Unresolved feelings that family members may have about events in the remote past are likely to surface very quickly. Indeed, the anguish that can result from such catharsis can be overwhelming. This seems to be especially true of families that have sustained significant losses and never had occasion to collectively share members' feelings about the losses.

A very important consideration in looking at a family is to see the collection of individuals as constituting a united whole. To do so requires that the clinician shift from individual responses to think about the collective—the family as an institution is more than the sum of its constituent parts. Thinking of the family as a unit has implications for how the clinician proceeds to integrate the experiences of individual family members. The focus should be on two dimensions: what the subjective experience means to the person having the experience and how the experience affects the family.

Getting to the level of familial response often is difficult. Frequently, family members are unaware of significant experiences of other family members. That reality is itself a clinical sign worth noting. Perhaps, it is suggestive of a lack of communication in the family. Another reason for difficulty in familial sharing of experiences is the anticipation that "Nobody will care." The frequency with which that excuse is offered by troubled adolescents is amazing. Such a statement is helpful to the clinician in a couple of ways. It demonstrates how the adolescent, or whoever else makes the statement, perceives his or her concerns in the larger scheme of familial dynamics. A belief that nobody cares about an individual's concerns and therefore the concerns should not be verbalized is often observed in depressives.

Ideally, the clinician wants to be able to view the strengths and weaknesses of the family as a unit. Is there any clear pattern of roles in the family? Do the parents lead the way in modeling appropriate behaviors? Or are the parents so consumed by their own developmental issues that they are not available to their children? Remember, the family assessment is meant to evaluate and gain an understanding of the family. It is not meant to be therapy, although it will undoubtedly have a therapeutic impact on the family.

Care should be taken to allow families to tell their stories, verbally and dynamically. Having heard a story, the clinician must act responsibly and sometimes quickly, as in the case of uncovering information with legal implications. These possibilities all reinforce the need for the clinician to be explicitly clear with families about what is or is not the purpose of a session.

An area of the family's collective identity and history that is likely to become an issue in the evaluation process is the racial and ethnic identity of the family. This issue is especially true if the family is of a different racial or ethnic group than the evaluating clinician.

Racial and Ethnic Identity

Race and ethnicity are two issues with checkered but intense histories in U.S. society. Recent emphases on multiculturalism and affirmative action have reacquainted the general public with the historic significance associated with these topics. Clinicians and families are likely to have to confront these issues in their work on multiple levels. Of course, it would be a grievous error on the part of the clinician to pretend that race and ethnicity are nonissues and therefore should not be addressed directly. This pattern of pretending that differences do not exist has been discussed in the psychotherapy and assessment literatures as the illusion of color blindness (Branch, 1995; Griffith, 1977; Vontress, 1969). Avoiding the issue ultimately only creates complications in the work relationship. It should be discussed very openly and directly, along with other clinical issues. The reader is referred to a recent text by Carter (1995), which provides a detailed exploration of how race affects therapeutic relationships. Carter does not specifically discuss the traditional evaluations at issue here, but many of his observations are generic and apply in any situation involving a mental health provider and clients.

Several dynamics concerning race and ethnicity are likely to occur when a clinician and clients are from different groups. Three creative statements of resistance around the issues of race and ethnicity are frequently voiced by families in treatment: "All people are the same, aren't they?" "You don't understand us because we are _____"; and "My sons are being harassed by the system because they are _____."

One of the most common errors of clinicians is to homogenize people in categories that permit a prescriptive approach to assessment and psychotherapy. Some of this behavior is a naive attempt to reduce the complexity of a client's life to a more manageable number of factors. Such behavior is also often an attempt on the part of the clinician to eliminate race and ethnicity as factors to consider in understanding the human developmental process. The behavior is usually emitted because of the clinician's discomfort with the topics. To behave in such a manner of course means that the clinician is guilty of redefining the client to reduce his or her own anxiety. This behavioral presentation is a fairly common one for White clinicians working with people of color, but it also occurs with other less visible minority groups (i.e., minority religious group members, minority language group members, first-generation White immigrants, and so on). The behavior can be interpreted as resistance on the part of the clinician, that is, a lack of openness to exploring all of the key elements of clients' identity that may provide clues for understanding their behavior. In the same way that care should be taken to determine whether race and ethnicity are factors that should be considered, all of clients' difficulties should not be attributed to race and ethnicity. Attribution of all of a family's problems to race and ethnicity is a dynamic that becomes reinforcing for resistive families.

"You don't understand us because we are _____"; "Nobody understands us": This is a position that many families of color have taken as a way to explain why they receive unfair or unequal treatment in the justice system or social systems designed to provide services for those in need. I caution clinicians against being deceived by such verbalizations. It is often true that a significant amount of misattribution and misunderstanding is caused because race and ethnicity cloud the picture. That does not sufficiently explain how and why a family may find itself in its current troubled state. Families use the defense of race and ethnicity as a way to resist looking at their dynamics and the events that led them to their current situation. To invoke these issues sometimes serves the purpose of diverting an evaluation away from a needed course in addition to invoking feelings of guilt and discomfort on the part of the mental health professional. The introduction of race and ethnicity in the dynamics of the assessment relationship often derails the clinician—which may be the result desired by the clients. Brief inquiries about how the clients conducted themselves in similar situations of incongruence of their racial identity and that of a person with whom they were required to work is sometimes a productive route to pursue. Also, noting when in the process of the treatment the issue of race is introduced and the affective tone that accompanies the verbalization helps the clinician understand the dynamics of the session. The point here is that the clinician should not allow such verbalizations to interfere with the appointed task. The reader is referred to Griffith (1977) for a detailed discussion of possible clinical interpretations of such behavior.

Another variation on the theme of race and ethnicity occurs in the form of "My sons are being harassed because they are _____." Many families see themselves as being victims of police and community harassment because they belong to an ethnic or racial minority group. This is a variation on the idea that their minority status is what prompts others to act in an unfair or unjust manner against them. Inherent in this clinical presentation is a large amount of denial. Parents are frequently unwilling to face the objectively verifiable facts of their child's misbehavior. Rather, they obsess about what others have done to their child. The capacity for self-examination and reflection in persons who use the defense of race or ethnicity is poor. Parents' behaving in this way is likely to be indicative of how they behave in the larger world about a variety of issues. Children and adolescents who observe this type of behavior acquire race and ethnicity as ready-made excuses to explain away all of their inappropriate behaviors that are called into question.

It is not enough to simply note the use of these explanations to explain otherwise dissonant experiences for families. The ways in which they are introduced is just as important as the fact that they are used. In assessing a family, a clinician should note when the race or ethnicity issue is verbalized and what views different family members have on the issue. A determination also has to be made as to what function these statements are intended to serve in the session. Asking the family member who introduces the issue how he or she has dealt with this reality in other situations is an idea worthy of serious consideration. In addition, the clinician should encourage all family members to think about the implications their racial and ethnic experiences have for the present work. Sometimes, the resulting family discussion about the salience of these factors in the life of the family is very illuminating. Some members will believe that race and ethnicity are realities that are facts of life inherent in living in the United States and have little or nothing to do with the issue at hand, such as the gang involvement or misbehavior of a family member. Others will think these factors have a lot to do with the general plight of the family. When such splits occur, the clinician should seize the moment to explore the bases for the different opinions and how they may reflect other philosophical divisions in the family.

The defenses of race and ethnicity are used not only in cross-ethnic or cross-racial dyads, but also, for slightly different reasons, when there is a racial and ethnic match between the clients and the service providers. For example, people of color who are not accustomed to making use of mental health professional services may attempt to determine if the clinician is really "like them" by testing "the doctor" (i.e., level of ethnic or racial identity attitudes). In some ways, these clients are really testing the clinician to see if there is a match between the clinician's attitudes and their own. This challenge requires that the clinician be firmly resolved in his or her own identity and not allow the client to turn the evaluation session into an extended interrogation of the mental health professional. This issue is also discussed at length in Griffith's (1977) classic.

Ecological Systems Theory Applied to the Family

An important dimension of the family is its developmental status. How did it come to be the way that it is? Who and what have been the identifiable contributors to the evolution of the family? How many of these contributions do all family members acknowledge? These are questions that are best answered through a fairly detailed description of the family's development and functioning as a unit prior to the onset of the gang problem. To gather this information, it is essential for each member to talk about the significant settings in which they function with others in addition to nuclear family members. This can often be accomplished by asking members to bring a list of their friends or groups to which they belong to an evaluation session. In addition to learning about their affiliation needs and how they get met, the clinician quickly gains insights into how family members evaluate each other's friends and associates. Ecological systems theory as articulated by Bronfenbrenner (1979) is ideally suited for exploring contributors to the life of the family and their sources. The theory is most frequently invoked as an approach for examining individual development, but it applies well to the family as a unit.

According to Bronfenbrenner's (1979) ecological systems theory, human development is a process occurring in, and arising from, a matrix of intersecting systems. These systems are organized in various levels, extending from the most proximal level, which he calls the self system, through the most distal level, the macrosystem. Santrock (1993) provides a pictorial representation of the systems and how they relate to each other, reproduced in Figure 7.1.

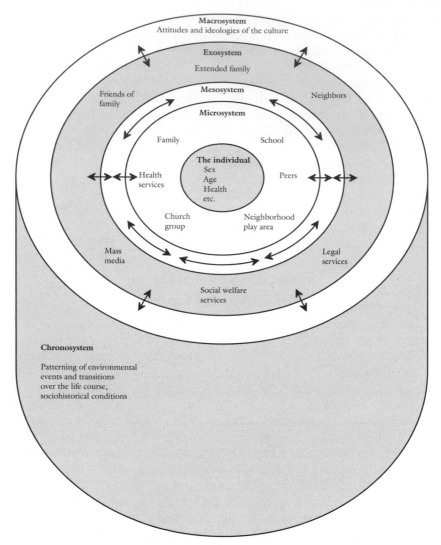

FIGURE 7.1   *Bronfenbrenner's (1979) Ecological Theory of Development (consisting of five environmental systems: microsystems, mesosystems, exosystems, macrosystems, and chronosystems).* SOURCE: *Kopp/Krakow,* Child Development in Social Context, *© 1982 by Addison Wesley Publishing Co., Inc. Reprinted by permission of Addison-Wesley Longman, Inc.*

Microsystems are the immediate setting in which an individual develops and in so doing experiences and creates reality. Microsystems include people and objects with whom the individual has face-to face relationships.

Mesosystems are relationships between microsystems that extend across settings. Examples of mesosystems include home-school, home-church, and school-neighborhood. *Exosystems* are settings in which an individual does not directly participate but is very much influenced. Frequently discussed exosystems for adolescents include parents' places of employment and parents' peer group. Exosystems for parents include the adolescent's circle of close friends and athletic teams on which an adolescent may participate. The largest systems in Bronfenbrenner's (1979) taxonomy are *macrosystems*. Simply put, they are the "Blueprints for defining and organizing the institutional life of the society" (Garbarino, 1985, p. 74). The dimension of time, the chronosystem, intersects with each of the other systems in an overarching way. Bronfenbrenner's model constitutes a comprehensive, powerful investigative and explanatory tool for understanding the multiple systems that simultaneously influence human development.

Bronfenbrenner's (1979) theory is most often used to explain individual development, but its premise that development is the result of direct interaction between persons and the environments in which they function can also be applied to the family. According to the theory, the individual is not passive, as other theorists have suggested, but an active agent in constructing the environments, which then contribute to the individual's further development.

The basic assumptions of Bronfenbrenner's (1979) theory can be used as a way of organizing the multiple contributors to the development of a family through graphically representing all of the significant sources of socialization that are identified by family members. This strategy is particularly useful to account for values and behaviors that seem to be incongruent with those espoused by members of the family. It sometimes helps to uncover information, such as names of friends or a confirmation that an object is indeed important to a family. The theory is used to structure thinking about how the family becomes, not to change the family. Sharing information gathered from family members about their systems also often produces major surprises in family meetings. A classic example is hearing adolescents value nonfamily adults as being more available than the parents. The procedure has the potential for generating templates for evaluating a family *risk index* for producing adolescents who are likely gang recruits. Bronfenbrenner defines the point in time at which the systems interact in a way to facilitate development of a certain type of behavior or thinking as an *ecological niche*.

The concept of ecological niche is discussed in relationship to gangs in communities, but it has not been called by that name. The researchers and planners who have looked at the issue of what conditions and which adolescents are ripe for gang membership have identified a host of social and economic factors but have paid little attention to psychological attributes or family dynamics.

Completing the Family Assessment

With all clinical evaluations, the question of how to proceed looms large. Family assessments are no different. There is no one absolutely correct way because circumstances in each situation are different, dictating that a different, perhaps idiosyncratic, procedure be followed. In the case of gang-affiliated families the issues of involvement with the justice system and a high level of potential resistance should not been taken lightly. Such realities pose special problems for a clinician who is trying to complete a comprehensive and objective appraisal of a family's level of development, its strengths and weaknesses, and its availability to help the troubled adolescent. The guiding principles should be to think about the family as a collection, not just an additive summation of individual members. To do so may mean putting aside views of individual members of the family as isolates and thinking about them in a redefined way as persons functioning as a part of an interactive system. All of the foregoing procedures used to assess members of the family also need to be temporarily abandoned in favor of new procedures that give data about the group. Ideally, family assessment process should be concurrent with the individual evaluations, but I encourage clinicians to think about what works for them in gathering information from groups. Does it make sense to try to assess both systems as suggested here or is it more manageable to complete individual assessments first? That is a critical decision. Consideration should be given to how individual assessments may adversely affect what the clinician might obtain in a later group assessment.

A second question of process concerns the type of instruments to be used. Reliance on pencil and paper procedures runs the risk of alienating family members who are not very comfortable with things that remind them of school. Proficiency in English should also be considered whenever written instruments are the procedure of choice. Translated versions of tests should be screened very carefully. Clinicians must make certain that there is a linguistic match between the concepts being explored and the language system into which they are being translated.

A final issue that must be resolved is multifaceted. It concerns the assumptions that are inherent in a clinician's decision to use standardized instruments with families. Box 7.1 presents a list of questions that clinicians should consider before and after assessing a family. The assessment process itself is likely to have a therapeutic impact on families that are ready to work. More resistive or unhealthy families, too, will derive benefits from the assessment process, but the benefits will be less obvious than in the less-troubled families.

Negative answers to preintervention questions may impact the expectations of clinician and family about the effectiveness of intervention and pose a serious threat to the credibility and validity of the family assessment. Of course, all of the fault may not rest with the clinician. It is often the case that

BOX 7.1   Family Assessment Questions

The clinician needs to gain a clear understanding of how the family perceives itself. Those perceptions often become the basis of family interactions with outside entities, such as schools, courts, and mental health professionals. Following is a list of questions the clinician may want to consider asking before and after working with a family. Answers to the questions can be obtained from direct verbal reports as well as from observations of the family.

Preintervention

1. What is the structural hierarchy in the family? (Who makes the major decisions in the family? When does the power shift? Are family members aware of the power structure?)
2. Does everyone accept his or her role in the family?
3. How much influence do exosystems (i.e., parents' places of employment, adolescents' peer groups, the gang) have on the family's cohesiveness?
4. How does the family see itself as a unit?
5. How does the family think it is regarded by neighbors? What is its response to neighbors?

Postintervention

One of the anticipated outcomes of a family intervention is that the unit will develop new ways of being with itself and others. It is to be hoped that at the conclusion of clinical work with a family some new insights and behavioral changes will occur. To determine if there is development in the family, the clinician may want to repeat the preintervention assessment questions *plus* ask the following:

1. What significant behavioral changes have occurred in the family during the course of the clinical work? How does the family explain those changes? Feel about those changes?
2. Is there a change in the level of introspection in family members or increased perspective taking?

families cannot cooperate because of anxiety or misgivings about the assessment process. In other cases, the process of being introspective becomes cathartic for family members. The more they reflect on their history and their feelings about it, the more information suddenly becomes available to them. But the information the family provided during the initial assessment may be incomplete. To control for these and related problems, two procedures for completing the family assessment are useful, a formal structured inventory (i.e., Family Adaptability and Cohesion Evaluation Scales III [FACES III]; Olson, Lavee, & Portner, 1985) and an open-ended clinical assessment.

BOX 7.2   Sample Items from FACES III: Family Version

Answer options are 1. Almost never, 2. Once in a while, 3. Sometimes, 4. Frequently, and 5. Almost Always.

_____ 1. Family members are supportive of each other during difficult times.
_____ 6. Children have a say in the discipline.
_____ 10. We shift household responsibilities from person to person.
_____ 16. In solving problems, the children's suggestions are followed.
_____ 20. Our family tries new ways of dealing with problems.
_____ 26. When problems arise, we compromise.
_____ 30. Family members share hobbies with each other.

SOURCE: Data from Olson, Lavee, and Portner (1985).

Using a Structured Inventory

FACES III is a psychological instrument designed to assess a family's level of organization and cohesion. A sampling of items from FACES III is presented in Box 7.2. This inventory has a reputation of being a good research instrument, but it is equally useful in clinical settings because of its strong psychometric properties, its extensive history of being used in a vast array of studies on family members' adjustment to different stressors, and the fact that it has been translated into several languages.

The measure consists of twenty items to assess the frequency of the occurrence of relevant events. A Likert-type scale is used to score the items. Response options are from 1 ("Almost never") to 5 ("Almost always"). Cohesion variables include emotional bonding, family boundaries, coalitions, time spent together, space, friends, decision making and interests, and recreation. The dimension of adaptability is also measured. Cohesion and Adaptability dimensions are divided into four levels each as follows: Cohesion—disengagement (low scores), separateness, connectedness, very connected (highest score); and Adaptability—rigidity (low score), structure, flexibility, and very flexible (highest score).

Psychometric properties of the test show it to be quite strong. Cronbach alpha coefficients for internal consistency are r (cohesion) = .87, r (adaptability) = .78, and r (total scale) = .90. Test-retest reliability is reported to be .84 (Mathis & Yingling, 1990).

When FACES III is used with families, it should be given directly to individual family members before they attend the first session. They should be asked to complete the inventory and bring it with them to the first session. The response to the task is often a beginning of the evaluation process of the level of investment the family member has in the assessment. Frequently, the forms are not completed. Family members offer a variety of excuses for this noncompliance: not having enough time; not understanding the relevance to the task facing the family; wanting to " protect" the business of the family from disclosure to outsiders. Whatever the reactions to the task, they can be used as assessment data and the beginning of insights into the dynamics of the family. On rare occasions, members come to the session and immediately start to talk about how their answers to the "test" were different from those provided by other family members. Such a revelation evidences at the very least that they have compared their responses.

Individuals who do not complete the FACES III inventory before the first session should be encouraged to finish the task, even if it means taking time from the first session. The clinician should remember that noncompletion of the task may be a creative attempt at sabotaging the work. Not finishing the assignment could also be an unsophisticated effort to anger others, clinician included. Listening very carefully to what excuse an individual offers for not completing the inventory can yield critical insights into that person's mode of operation in the family. Observing how others react to the noncompletion provides another valuable source of information.

Clinical Sources of Data

Clinical data refers to information acquired in the ongoing process of meeting with a family. It often provides vital pieces of information about who family members are, what struggles they have, and how open they are to changing. The recent affiliation of one member with a gang should not be taken as evidence of failure on the part of the family but rather as a developmental dilemma that faces the family. The task of the clinician is to understand how the family goes about the business of being a family unit. Asking a few questions about the family as a unit often helps. These clinical questions are in addition to the data obtained from individual members. Here, I discuss three avenues of exploration I have found to be immensely revealing about the life of the family. They are not intended as an exhaustive list but rather are a sample of the type of family assessment questions reflected in the longer list in Box 7.3.

Is there an executive structure in place? Who is the leader in setting examples and empowering other family members to overcome the individual challenges that they face on a daily basis? Insights into this question can be obtained by asking the family who the members think is in charge of the family. Expect different answers concerning different aspects of the family's life. Another way of uncovering this information is to note when and to whom family members defer about different matters. The deferring can be direct, as in asking the "in-charge" person for an opinion, or indirect, as waiting to speak in anticipation that the more powerful person will answer first. When

BOX 7.3   Family Functioning Questions

Clinicians need to know how the family sees itself (see Box 7.1) as well as how the family functions. Listed below are questions clinicians may want to consider asking to gain a better understanding of how the family goes about its business of being a family. These probes are intended to serve as catalysts for more information about the workings of the family.

1. How often does the family participate in leisure activities together? When was the last time?
2. How are the leisure activities decided?
3. Do all members participate in leisure activities? If no, please explain.
4. Are non–family members ever invited to be a part of family activities? Whose friends are they?
5. What are special holiday routines of the family?
6. Does the family collectively participate in a religious community? If no, explain.
7. Has the amount of time the family spends together changed dramatically in the past few months? How? What has caused the change?
8. What was one of the pleasant things the family did together in the past year? What made it so much fun?
9. What was one of the most unpleasant things the family did together in the past year? What made it so unpleasant?
10. How would the family like to see itself change? Be specific.

---

the family looks in the direction of the power broker, such behavior gives the clinician cues about whom questions should be directed to. It is not uncommon for a family member to perceive himself or herself as the spokesperson on a topic although other family members fail to share in that assessment. This situation is often demonstrated by parents offering answers on behalf of teenagers only to have the latter interrupt and assert themselves by offering a different answer. Significant differences of opinion often occur around the issue of who exerts the most power in the family, mother or father. This is especially true if one parent is absent from the home.

Procedurally, it may be helpful to ask a few open ended questions at the beginning of the session, making certain not to direct them to any specific individual. The clinician should note who answers first and whether this pattern continues throughout the early phases of the evaluation. A word of caution concerning cultural differences that may account for a high level of deference to adults and parents should be added here. Ethnic behaviors may account for some of the reluctance of young children and adolescents to speak before their parents have had a chance to respond to a question. This comment is not meant to be judgmental of such a system but merely to point out that in such situations there is an executive structure in place based on ethnic imperatives.

A special note should also be made about the use of a language interpreter. Whenever it is necessary to use an interpreter, this individual should not be a member of the family but rather someone who has a firm understanding of the assessment process and shares the clinician's concern about the well-being of the family. A child should never be used as an interpreter.

Establishing the presence of a functional executive structure in the family is an initial part of the assessment. A larger question is, How has that system reacted to the gang involvement of the adolescent in the family? It is not uncommon to find mothers very much in charge of daily functioning of the family but powerless when matters of economics or relating to outside agencies are involved. A similar pattern is of exclusion of the nurturing parent from situations that require intense and high levels of assertiveness. This behavior represents an interaction of an exaggeration of gender roles in the family with personal dynamics that exist between the parents.

How has the family responded to one of its members joining a gang? Is there a discernible sense of concern? Or is the gang involvement treated in a cavalier and matter-of-fact manner? Concern may find expression through efforts to help the adolescent get out of the gang, despite the fact that such a desire has not been voiced by the adolescent. A lack of interest may be expressed in the form of denial whereby family members refuse to discuss the issue or they minimize the level of risk that may be associated with membership in a gang. Again, verbal and nonverbal behaviors may be clues for the clinician trying to figure out where the family stands on the issue. Knowing glances between silent family members are often more telling than spoken words. Parents who are constantly in conflict with each other sometimes use the gang affiliation of a family member as one more battleground for their own fights. One parent, typically the mother, is blamed for not being able to control the children. A common retort is that the father's unavailability to the sons has prompted them to seek to get their affiliation needs met somewhere else. While this war of words rages, other family members frequently give clues as to where they fit in the scheme of the conflict by their own nonverbal expressions, such as glancing at the ceiling, appearing very disinterested, sighing heavily, or on very rare occasions asking if the group can talk about something else.

What is the level of cohesion within the family? How the family functions as a unit is one of the areas the clinician will want to explore in great detail. There are some very simple and direct methods that can be employed to gather this information. Inquiring about shared family activities usually is sufficient to get family members engaged in some level of appraisal of the life of the family. Avoid asking about family vacations or other prototypical activities that may require substantial levels of financial commitment. A less assumption-laden probe about time and activities shared is likely to be received more positively. Answers that are often given include things such as attending church, participating in activities with the extended family, and even participating in community activities. It is very important to note the history of the family, as reported by different members, concerning doing things together. Perhaps more telling is their reporting a change in the level of family participation in group activities. When did the change occur? How do they explain the change? Why do they think things changed?

Under normal circumstances one would expect that as adolescents grow older and develop intense friendships and romantic interests of their own they are less available for activities with the nuclear family. Does the family seem to have any awareness or tolerance for such a pattern of individuation and separation? Or do other members personalize the changes? Feuding parents often blame each other for their teenagers' movement away from the family. It is quite common that the gang is blamed for taking a family member away. The truth of the matter, however, is that the family member may have already started to move away from the family even before he or she made the decision to join the gang. With careful listening, the clinician can plot the adolescent's movement away from the family and into a network of peers.

8

Developmental Assessment

In the four preceding chapters, I have examined specific psychological dimensions as they exist in the lives of individuals. The idea of evaluating clients along those dimensions has been introduced but not explored in detail. This chapter is designed to provide detailed and specific coverage of the assessment procedure from a developmental perspective. Developmental theory is revisited and integrated with clinical assessment procedures as a way to obtain a maximally effective clinical evaluation. Practical suggestions, designed to help the clinician think about comprehensive evaluations, are also provided. A lengthy case history, illustrating many of the concepts and issues discussed, concludes the chapter.

Developmental Theory Revisited

Chapter 2 was concerned with developmental issues related to gang membership and the gang itself, acquainting clinicians with organizational issues and how they may manifest. Ecological systems theory was introduced in Chapter 7 as a theoretical orientation for a conceptual foundation for understanding the gang as a unit. In this current chapter, the interest in developmental theory concerns its utility for understanding individual gang members. The reader is reminded that there are many developmental theories; only three will be explored here. Ecological systems theory (Bronfenbrenner, 1979), mentioned briefly in Chapter 7, will be revisited in this chapter, along with cognitive developmental theory (Piaget, 1965), introduced in Chapter 6, and psychosocial developmental theory (Erikson, 1968).

Ecological Systems Theory

Ecological systems theory posits that individuals function in a variety of settings (i.e., systems) and as a result obtain different messages about themselves. The basic concepts of ecological systems theory are explained in Chapter 7. Each of these systems is likely to validate the adolescent as a person and to give messages about what is expected of him or her. The accuracy of an adolescent's perceptions of these messages is very important. Indeed, it is the misinterpretation, or perhaps selective interpretation, of these messages that create social functioning difficulties for many adolescents. Notable examples are adolescents' insisting, "No one listens (to me)" and "No one cares what happens (to me)."

The belief that no one listens often stems from the fact that others often do not behave in a manner consistent with what the adolescent desires of them. Not giving some adolescents what they want causes them to conclude that the other party has not "heard" them. The adolescent overlooks the possibility that their message was heard, evaluated, and then negated. A similar logic can be applied to the complaint, "No one cares about me." Not doing what an adolescent wants to have done is often perceived by the adolescent as an indication of rejection. Such thinking is prevalent during much of adolescence, especially early adolescence. As the individual gets older, for most adolescents this type of reasoning and behavior diminishes. The notable exception is the personality disordered individual who continues to use an egocentric approach to relationships.

To return to ecological systems theory, if adolescents conclude that the microsystems with which they are involved are not sensitive to them, they are likely to seek out other microsystems that "listen to" and "care about" them. Seeking unconditional acceptance seems to be the basis for much of the heightened importance of peers during middle adolescence. Microsystems can exist in multiple settings, providing adolescents with opportunities to engage in interpersonal face-to-face relationships in different contexts and with different types of people.

A network of two or more microsystems that extend across settings is called a mesosystem. A common example is school-home, involving relationships with parents, siblings, teachers, and classmates. It is important to note that just as adolescents have relationships with different individuals, those individuals may also have relationships, of a different quality, with some of the same persons intimately involved with the adolescent. This makes for a cross-pollination of relationships that sometimes becomes problematic for the adolescent. Some overly simplistic adolescents have difficulty with the idea that an individual whom they consider a friend may also be friends with another individual with whom the adolescent has a negative relationship. This dilemma appears to be a developmental phenomenon. Adolescents who function in a large variety of settings are able to observe that friendships are not always mutually exclusive. Frequently, the pattern of noting the likelihood of sharing relationships with others appears in childhood, when the child recognizes that parents have relationships outside of the family. Maturing children and adolescents recognize that they do not have a monopoly on their friends and family members. They recognize that friends and relatives may participate in systems from which they are excluded. These constitute *exosystems* for the adolescent.

Individuals, as noted earlier, do not participate in exosystems, but are significantly impacted by what happens in those systems. For adolescents, common examples include parents' places of employment and parents' network of friends. Both of these are likely to have an impact on how the parents respond to the adolescent. The social views and child-rearing attitudes of parents' friends are likely to influence how the parents approach problem-solving situations with their own adolescent.

The exosystem is superseded by the macrosystem, the societal blueprint. Parents, adolescents, and everyone living in a society are influenced by it. Macrosystemic influences include "ideology, social policy, shared assumptions about human nature, and the social contract" (Garbarino, 1985). All lesser systems are nested in this larger all-inclusive realm of the social order. Other systems derive their energy and sense of direction from the messages given by the macrosystem.

Crossing all of the systems discussed, the *chronosystem* and *ecological niche* further shape and refine the impacts of the systems on the lives of individuals. Chronosystem refers to a point in time in a historical era (e.g., the 1960s) or in the life of an individual. This concept is vital for understanding the ways in which adolescents present themselves. I urge clinicians to think about the developmental appropriateness of the adolescent and whether the presenting problem fits the point in the developmental sequence at which the adolescent is located. This element of time should also be considered with regard to the social order and issues that arise in society. Do the behaviors and attitudes of the adolescent reflect these macrosystem realities?

Ecological niche refers to a point in time at which the convergence of conditions are conducive to development. A good niche is one that facilitates the development of a certain situation. For example, studying hard, consistently and continuously, is probably a good ecological niche for performing well on an examination. This of course assumes that all other things are equal (i.e., grading is fair, the exam is criterion based, and so on). A bad ecological niche is one that does not support an outcome. High levels of family cohesion, good-quality communication between parents and children, plus an atmosphere of emotional and financial support collectively form a bad niche for high levels of aggressive and antisocial behaviors.

This discussion of the basic ideas of ecological systems theory is intended as an introduction to a theory that highlights the salience of environment in shaping the backdrop against which people develop. Garbarino (1985) also summarizes these ideas (see Table 8.1).

TABLE 8.1 Ecology of Sociocultural Risk and Opportunity

Ecological Level	Definition	Examples	Issues Affecting Adolescents
Microsystem	Situation in which the adolescent has face-to-face encounters with influential others	Family, school, peer, group, church	Is the Adolescent regarded positively? Is the adolescent accepted? Is the adolescent reinforced for competent behavior? Is the adolescent exposed to enough diversity in roles and relationships? Is the adolescent given an active role in reciprocal relationships?
Mesosystem	Relationships between microsystems; the connections between situations	Home-school, home-church, school-neighborhood, peer group–home	Do settings respect each other? Do settings present basic consistency in values?
Exosystem	Settings in which the adolescent does not participate but in which significant decisions are made affecting the adolescent or adults who interact directly with the adolescent	Parent's place of employment, school board, local government, parents' peer group	Are decisions made with the interests of adolescents in mind? How well do supports for families balance stresses for parents?
Macrosystem	"Blueprints" for defining and organizing the institutional life of the society	Ideology, social policy, shared assumptions about human nature, the social contract	Are some groups valued at the expense of others (e.g., sexism, racism)? Is there an individualistic or a collectivistic orientation? Is violence a norm?

SOURCE: *Adolescent Development* by Garbarino, James, © 1985. Reprinted by permission of Prentice-Hall, Inc., Upper Saddle River, NJ.

Applying Ecological Systems Theory to Individual Gang Members

Ecological systems theory is useful as an adjunct for understanding the origins and facilitation of gang membership. It provides a structured way for discerning how an adolescent comes to view a gang as a viable option. Because the theory makes explicit that behavioral outcomes are the function of several interacting factors, it clearly implies that interventions to counteract gang involvement should also be multisystemic. Figure 8.1 provides a summary of the ways in which the different systems may create a good ecological niche for gang participation. Box 8.1 offers suggestions for how to intervene in gang involvement at different levels.

Cognitive Developmental Theory

The foundation for cognitive developmental theory is laid by Piaget (1965). He postulates that over the life span an individual undergoes various changes in ability to comprehend the world and the relationships that they encounter in it. These cognitive changes find expression in a child's language capacity, thought processes, and concrete behaviors. As adolescents mature, their capacity for abstract thinking increases as does their ability to understand the perspective of others. These changes make adolescents quite similar to adults. Steinberg (1985) notes that Piagetian theory encompasses changes that occur across the lifespan:

> Piaget stressed the adaptive nature of cognitive development. Advanced types of thinking develop as maturational gains and environmental demands combine to make old strategies less effective and new ones available. . . . Transitions into higher stages of reasoning are most likely to occur at times when the child's biological readiness and the increasing complexity of environmental demands interact to bring about cognitive disequilibrium. (p. 68)

Investigations into the utility of Piagetian concepts for explaining intellectual and social behavioral changes that occur in childhood and adolescence have been plentiful, ranging from studies of the classic conservation task (i.e., transferring liquid from a short, fat container to a tall, slender container) (Piaget, 1965) to moral dilemma (Kohlberg, 1969).

The assumption underlying Piagetian theory is that as children mature and have more increasingly complex experiences in their environment, they subject these experiences to increasingly more advanced logical analyses. This has been demonstrated empirically with children's changing concepts of friendship, moving from simple and unidimensional (i.e., "You are my friend because you do things for me") to more complex (i.e., "You are my friend because we have similar views and attitudes").

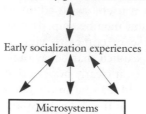

The individual organism

Individual characteristics as
determined by genetic endowment

Early socialization experiences

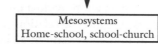

Microsystems

Negative Outcomes
•poor attachment rela-
tionship with mom

Face-to-face relationships
that provide the child with
messages about him/herself

Positive Outcomes
•good-quality early
attachment that
makes it possible to
have subsequent
good relationships

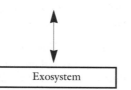

Mesosystems
Home-school, school-church

•poor adjustment to the
of social competence
•low level of mastery of basic
academics
•origin of a sense of
detachment

Network of two or more
microsystems across settings

•development of a sense
demands of school
•expansion of network
of places where she/he
is affirmed

Exosystem

•adolescent is not valued
•no support for the "issues"
confronting the adolescent
•helps to foster an antagonistic
relationship (i.e., concepts of
rebelliousness, defiant, etc.)
•limited opportunities for
remediation

Systems that exclude the
child/adolescent but influence
his/her life

•provides avenues for
the adolescent
•supportive environ-
ments, conducive
to risk taking and
remediation

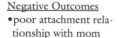

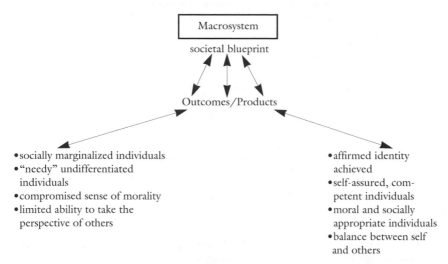

NOTE: "Good" and "bad" refer to the quality of the niche, *not* the outcome. A good ecological niche is one that facilitates a specific outcome. The outcome itself can be good (desirable) or bad (undesirable). A bad niche prevents the occurrence of certain outcomes.

FIGURE 8.1   *How Systems Create Good and Bad Niches for Gangs*

Much of the research concerning the utility of cognitive developmental theory is focused on functioning on intellectual tasks that are assumed to be indicative of capacity to function in the world. Adolescence is a critical stage at which individuals experience major shifts in their ability to interact with the world surrounding them and make good decisions about how to understand the world. Psychologists call this change in thinking *social cognition*— "thinking about people, thinking about social relationships, and thinking about social institutions" (Steinberg, 1985, p. 82).

This very important area of development provides insight into how adolescents form impressions of others and decide what roles they want to play in response to others. Hill and Palmquist (1978) assert that *impression formation,* the ability to synthesize information about persons and situations, becomes more differentiated and complex as adolescents grow older. Such changes are generally interpreted as being the result of cognitive growth.

A similar movement toward abstractness and complexity is noted by Selman (1980) in his description of adolescents' ability at perspective taking, the ability to observe events from the perspective of others. This is a critical ability for individuals to have if they are to negotiate complex situations involving others in the workplace or at school. The absence of an ability to take the perspective of another, characteristic of young children and developmentally arrested adolescents, leads to habitual conflicts with others. The problems with others are often associated with the one party being unable to

BOX 8.1   Interventions at Different Levels of Gang Involvement

Level I: Fantasy identification with gang
Interventions with adolescents at this "distal" level of gang involvement should focus on the cognitive component. Since the affiliation is make-believe, the clinician should engage in intense reality testing with the adolescents. Can they distinguish reality from fantasy? It is often helpful to have the adolescent identify other things that are not real but occupy a significant amount of his or her time. The most productive work with such adolescents seems to get accomplished when they can articulate what purpose the fantasy serves in their life. Does it help them avoid something or someone? Or does it propel them into arenas that they would not visit otherwise? An ideal outcome is to find socially condoned substitutes that allow the adolescent to meet psychological needs without being placed in a position of jeopardy.

Level II: At risk of gang involvement
The at-risk dimension associated with this level of involvement is strongly associated with neighborhood of residence. Interventions at this level require a restructuring of adolescents' time. It is essential that they have an investment in the "diversionary activities" planned for them. Simply sending them off to a "boring" time filler probably increases the likelihood that they will continue to move in the direction of the gang. Frequently, involving older adolescents who have a high degree of credibility with the client produces positive results.

Level III: Wanna-Be/Associate gang member
Cognitive and behavioral interventions again are the preferred practice for adolescents at this level. Renegotiating the relationship with the family of origin is vital for wanna-be gang members. The transition into the gang is not automatic or spontaneous. Because this is an evolutionary process, the family and community support systems can adjust their approaches as it becomes evident that old approaches are not working. Appealing to the adolescent's sense of belonging and long history with the family sometimes works. The greatest impact seems to come from pointing out the incongruences between public gang life and the inevitable outcomes. Well-defended adolescents often counteract those arguments with their myth of invincibility—"It won't happen to me." Getting any type of response increases the likelihood of continuing to engage the adolescent.

Level IV: Gang member
Interventions at this stage are far less likely to have an impact than at Levels I, II, or III. But this does not mean that family and others should give up on the adolescent. To do so would be confirming the belief that no one cares about him or her anyway. It appears that the purpose of intervention at this stage is to counteract movement to the ultimate level of being hard core. Wherever possible, the gang member as a person should be reinforced without reinforcing his or her gang membership. It is hard, but it can be done by focusing on the positive traits of the individual. Discussions with clients should be respectful of them and reassuring that often people change their minds about the directions of their lives. The tactic of choice here is to approach the individual, *not* the gang.

Level V: Hard-core gang member
The ultimate level of gang membership seriously negates the possibility of rehabilitation. In those rare instances where individuals are available to the possibility of an intervention, the strategy should be to dismantle their system of defensiveness. Frequently hard-core members spend a lot of time talking about how they "don't care because no one cares about them." This is a circular argument that can be dismantled very carefully and over a period of time. The secret to success here is to not take their defenses away without giving them a way to save face.

NOTE: The levels of gang membership referred to in this box are described in detail in Table 2.1.

---

participate in the socially required give-and-take of most interpersonal relationships. Cognitive developmental theory has also been applied to the area of moral reasoning. Kohlberg's (1969) work is usually cited as the prototype in this area. Kohlberg proposes six stages of moral reasoning, progressing from preconventional (Stage 1), in which obedience and punishment orientations prevail, through principled thinking (Stage 6), in which universal ethical principled orientations prevail. The Kohlbergian stages have been empirically tested by having subjects respond to a moral dilemma, such as the case of Heinz presented in Box 8.2. Table 8.2 presents the Kolhbergian stages, with examples drawn from responses to the dilemma given in Box 8.2. In scoring the response that the subject produces for this dilemma the emphasis is on the reasoning behind the answer, not the "yes" or "no" dimension of the answer. Consistent with the cognitive developmental theoretical orientation, the Kohlbergian stages assume that an individual proceeds from preconventional thinking (Stages 1 and 2) to universal ethical

---

BOX 8.2   A Moral Dilemma—The Case of Heinz

In Europe, a woman was near death from a very bad disease, a special kind of cancer. There was one drug that the doctors thought might save her. It was a form of radium that a druggist in the same town had recently discovered. The drug was expensive to make, but the druggist was charging ten times what the drug cost him to make. He paid $200 for the radium and charged $2,000 for a small dose of the drug. The sick woman's husband, Heinz, went to everyone he knew to borrow the money, but he could only get together about $1,000, which was half of what it cost. He told the druggist that his wife was dying and asked him to sell it cheaper or let him pay later. But the druggist said, "No, I discovered the drug and I'm going to make money from it." Heinz got desperate and broke into the man's store to steal the drug for his wife.

Should the husband have done that? Was it right or wrong?

SOURCE: Kohlberg (1969).

TABLE 8.2   Kohlberg's Stages of Moral Development

Level One: Preconventional	*Child's Response to Theft of Drug*	
Stage 1 *Obedience-and-punishment orientation:* The child obeys rules to avoid punishment. There is as yet no internalization of moral standards.	Pro:	Theft is justified because the drug did not cost much to produce.
	Con:	Theft is condemned because Heinz will be caught and go to jail.
Stage 2 *Naive hedonistic and instrumental orientation.* The child's behavior is motivated by a selfish desire to obtain rewards and benefits. Although reciprocity occurs, it is self-serving, manipulative, and based on a marketplace outlook: "You can play with my blocks if you let me play with your cars."	Pro:	Theft is justified because his wife needs the drug and Heinz needs his wife's companionship and help in life.
	Con:	Theft is condemned because his wife will probably die before Heinz gets out of jail, so it will not do him much good.
Level Two: Conventional	*Child's Response to Theft of Drug*	
Stage 3 *"Good boy–nice girl" morality.* The child is concerned with winning the approval of others and avoiding their disapproval. In judging the goodness or badness of behavior, consideration is given to a person's intentions. The child has a conception of a morally good person as one who possesses a set of virtues, hence the child places much emphasis upon being "nice."	Pro:	Theft is justified because Heinz is unselfish in looking after the needs of his wife.
	Con:	Theft is condemned because Heinz will feel bad thinking of how he brought dishonor on his family: his family will be ashamed of his act.
Stage 4: *"Law-and-order" orientation.* The individual blindly accepts social conventions and rules. Emphasis is on "doing one's duty," showing respect for authority, and maintaining a given social order for its own sake.	Pro:	Theft is justified because Heinz would otherwise have been responsible for his wife's death.
	Con:	Theft is condemned because Heinz is a lawbreaker.

(continues)

Stage 5 *Social-contract orientation.* The individual believes that the purpose of the law is to preserve human rights and that unjust laws should be changed. Morality is seen as based upon an agreement among individuals to conform to laws that are necessary for the community welfare. But since it is a social contract, it can be modified so long as basic rights like *life* and *liberty* are not impaired.

Pro: Theft is justified because the law was not fashioned for situations in which an individual would forfeit life by obeying the rules.

Con: Theft is condemned because others may also have great need.

Stage 6 *Universal ethical principle orientation.* Conduct is controlled by an internalized set of ideas, which, if violated, results in self-condemnation and guilt. The individual follows self-chosen ethical principles based upon abstract concepts (e.g., the equality of human rights, the Golden Rule, respect for the dignity of each human being) rather than concrete rules (e.g., the Ten Commandments). Unjust laws may be broken because they conflict with broad moral principles.

Pro: Theft is justified because Heinz would not have lived up to the standards of his conscience if he had allowed his wife to die.

Con: Theft is condemned because Heinz did not live up to the standards of his conscience when he engaged in stealing.

SOURCE: Steinberg (1985, p. 292). Reprinted with permission from McGraw-Hill Inc.

principled orientation (Stage 6) in a linear fashion. According to Kohlberg (1969) the higher-order thinking, represented by Stages 5 and 6, is more mature and more advanced than reasoning in the lower stages. It appears that "moral development is stimulated by having to struggle with moral conflicts and, in particular, from being exposed to levels of thinking that are more advanced" (Steinberg, 1985, p. 291).

Applying Cognitive Developmental Theory to Individual Gang Members

Several of the basic tenets of cognitive developmental theory have special relevance for working with gang adolescents. Cognitive development theory in its most elementary form suggests that older individuals develop more sophisticated and abstract styles of reasoning. This assumption is vital to understanding gang members' ability to reason. It is not enough to produce an intelligence index without an accompanying description of the quality of an adolescent's thinking. Are there *recursive thinking* errors (i.e., "I thought that you thought that I thought"; Hill & Palmquist, 1978) that make it difficult for the adolescent to objectively approach a problem situation? Are there any of the other errors in thinking described in Chapter 6 that might suggest an underlying thought disorder? An evaluation that fails to take such facts into consideration is incomplete.

In establishing a gang-involved adolescent's cognitive style and capacity, the clinician should consider asking the adolescent to explain his or her views about the gang. Special note should be made of the type of logic that is used to support conclusions. For example, some adolescents of color argue that their gang involvement is politically motivated or a response to the reality of racism in U.S. society. They do not consider how much of their disruptive violent behavior also occurs in and injures communities populated by other people of color. Pointing out such a contradiction may prove helpful in penetrating the veneer that many gang members erect as a defense against revealing their true selves. Pointing out the contradiction may also provoke the wrath of the gang member, sometimes resulting in the clinician being called a racist. The important thing to establish is how the gang member puts facts and opinions together. Is there a logical quality to the arguments that seems to fit in the developmental progression posited by Piaget (1965)?

The perspective-taking ability of an adolescent also holds valuable keys for understanding how he or she may justify acts of violence against others. Box 8.3 presents several examples of gang members trying to defend their acts of antisocial behavior. Note that in each situation there is little or no regard for other persons or their positions. These responses suggest an impaired ability to think beyond self. Also note the circular quality to the arguments.

BOX 8.3   Defending Gang Involvement

There are as many reasons for joining a gang as there are gang members. Asking adolescents about their decision to join a gang will provide a wonderful view of their thinking and their life space. The following excerpts are glimpses of what two young people view as their justification for the directions that their lives have taken since joining the gang.

Jason—a 19-year-old African American male who has been involved with gangs since he was 14 or 15 years of age. Despite his involvement with a local gang, he graduated from high school and briefly considered attending a trade school.

Jason   Well, see, it's like this . . . the gang is my family. They take care of you and look out for you and stuff like that.

Therapist   Tell me a little bit more about this family.

Jason   Watcha' wanna know? . . . I mean, we are just like any other family. We have good times and we have bad times. It's just a family.

Therapist   Bad times? . . . (long pause)

Jason   You wanna know who's in my family?

Therapist   Sure, if you wanna tell me.

Jason   (Chuckle) . . . I knew you was going to say somethin' like that. Man! Sometimes you can be a trip. Well, it's me and my partner _____ and all of our homies who live on _____. We been hangin' together since we were kids. A couple of the homies are in the county (jail) . . . but they still cool . . . when they start callin' me on the phone and whinin' like a little bitch . . .

Therapist   So, what is it like for you in the gang family?

Jason   Oh, it's alright . . . (pause) (looks away)

Therapist   Are you sure?

Jason   I'm sure, alright . . . (chuckle)

Therapist   Last week, you told me that you are tired of always fighting and taking care of other people.

Jason   You got a good memory.

Therapist   So, if you're tired, what is it that keeps you in the gang family?

Jason   You can't just walk away . . . you know. If I did that, I'd be just like those people who walked away from me when I needed somebody.

Therapist   Are you referring to your mom and dad?

Jason   You got it. . . . Damn, doc, you do have a good memory.

Therapist   Tell me more about what keeps you in the gang.

Jason   It's all I got. . . . Nobody else gives a fuck about me.

Therapist   You've got Trina.

Jason   Man! I can't count on her.

Therapist   Let me make sure I'm hearing exactly what you're saying. . . . You stay in the gang because they're the only people who care about you?

Jason   Right.

Therapist   What about when the baby comes?

Jason   I don't know. I don't want my child to go through the hell I lived in.

Therapist   It sounds like you might quit the gang after the baby is born.
Jason   Nah, nah . . . I didn't say that. I can't turn my back on my homies.

* * *

Ramon—a 16-year-old Latino who moved to the United States recently. He participates in gang activities by night but attends school by day. Per his reports, confirmed
in part by local newspaper stories, he excels at track and field.

Ramon   You know, sometimes I wonder why I keep gang bangin'.
Therapist   What do you mean?
Ramon   Last week, we were at a party and a fight broke out. I almost got shot.
   That's crazy.
Therapist   What's crazy?
Ramon   There I was crawling across the lawn . . . bullets were flying everywhere. I
   coulda got shot. But then I thought maybe my number's not up tonight.
   (laughter) Do you believe in predestination? We were talking about that in
   school. Some things are just gonna happen to us anyway, no matter what we
   do.
Therapist   Despite the danger, you continue to gang bang. Help me understand
   what it is that keeps you in the gang.
Ramon   That's easy! If I belong to a gang, people will respect me and stuff like
   that. . . . People will think you do heinous stuff, girls like you better if they
   think you are a gangsta. (chuckle)
Therapist   What about the danger?
Ramon   Oh that, nothin's gonna happen to me . . .

The issue of perspective taking is inextricably linked to the adolescent's social cognition, or how he or she views others. In many situations, victims of
attacks are seen as inferior, deserving maltreatment. These types of attributions are often made to entire groups of people as a way of defending the
gang's program of activity targeting that group.

Moral reasoning in gang members has been the subject of much debate.
Some researchers suggest that gang members exercise a type of morality that
runs counter to the larger culture's. Others see no discernible morality in
gang members. The evaluating clinician must decide which, if either, position seems tenable for a given client. Moral reasoning research offers a developmental scheme for critiquing the quality of an individual's moral decision
making. I offer several words of caution, however, about the Kohlbergian
stage theory, the most popular theory of moral development. First, the theory concerns moral reasoning, not behavior. There is no evidence that discussing moral dilemmas has any explanatory or predictive power in real-life
situations. Clinicians who decide to utilize the Kohlbergian progression as a
basis for thinking about a gang member's evolution should not take the the-

BOX 8.4   Using Cognitive Developmental Approaches with Gang Adolescents

The clinician should explore the thoughts and feelings a youngster may have about joining a gang by asking simple but direct questions.

General Cognitive Ability
1. What does being in the gang mean to you?
2. How do you know that you are really a member?
3. If you moved away for 5 years and then returned to this city, would you still be a gang member? Explain.
4. What do you say to people who think gangs should be put out of business?
5. Would you want your little brother to join your gang? Your little sister?

Perspective Taking
1. How do you feel about robbing others?
2. How do you think people feel after being robbed?
3. If you had to attend the funeral of a partner, what might you say to his mother?

Moral Reasoning
1. Is it okay to steal large quantities of supplies from the local city hospital?
2. What would you do if a kid much smaller than you tried to start a fight with you?
3. Do you think it is okay to sell drugs to middle school kids?
4. What would you do if someone tried to sell your little sister some crack?

---

ory too literally. Steinberg (1985) notes, "Studies have confirmed Kohlberg's suggestion that moral reasoning becomes more principled over the course of childhood and adolescence. . . . Kohlberg's suggestion that moral development proceeds in stages, however, has not been confirmed" (p. 293).

Box 8.4 offers some suggestions for using the cognitive developmental theoretical constructs when working with gang adolescents.

Psychosocial (Eriksonian) Theory

The psychosocial framework is embodied in the work of Erikson (1959), a neo-Freudian who proposes that development across the life span occurs as the result of life crises: "He views the developing person as moving through a series of eight psychosocial crises over the course of the life span. Each crisis, although present in one form or another at all ages, takes on significance at a given period of the life cycle because biological and social forces interact to bring the crises into prominence" (Steinberg, 1985, pp. 248–249).

According to Erikson's (1959) model, each developmental crisis is associated with an age period. To move on to the crisis of a higher period, the individual must resolve the developmental tasks of the lower age period. This is Erikson's *epignetic principle*—"Anything that grows has a ground plan. . . . Out of this ground plan the parts arise, each having its time of ascendancy, until all parts have arisen to form a functioning whole"(p. 92).

The implicit notion of the theory is that an active engagement between the developing person and his or her environment results in growth—it is the relationship of an individual's ego to the demands placed on it by society that result in higher levels of functioning. The ego must adapt to these new demands if healthy or optimal development is to occur. An inability to rise to the new demands of one's environment results in conflict between the individual and his or her community.

Erikson (1959) describes adolescence as characterized by the big issue (i.e., crisis) of identity (e.g., "Who am I?"). Individuals who do not adequately answer the question are left in a state of uncertainty (i.e., diffusion). For most individuals, the identity crisis is the hallmark of adolescence. Previous crises of trust versus mistrust, autonomy versus shame and doubt, initiative versus guilt, and industry versus inferiority contribute significantly to one's ability to develop a sense of identity. Just as the earlier crises have implications for identity development, likewise later life is influenced by how the identity crisis is resolved.

Identity formation during adolescence maintains a pivotal place in the psychosocial theory and has become the object of a rich research tradition. The process of identity development is not simple, linear, or unidimensional (Archer & Waterman, 1983, 1990; Marcia, 1966; Phinney, 1989). The early work of Marcia is central to the understanding of identity development. He proposes four ego-identity statuses:

Diffusion—not actively seeking an identity
Foreclosure—enacting an identity created by others
Moratorium—actively seeking an identity but has made no commitment
Achievement—has considered multiple options for identity and settled on a specific identity

The value of personal identity has received a significant amount of attention in the developmental literature. In so doing, researchers have posed a variety of explanations for how the process of identity acquisition occurs. "Identity can be viewed as a developmental outcome of early-childhood experiences, as a summary of adaptive accomplishments, and as a structural

BOX 8.5   Personality Characteristics of the Identity Statuses

Mallory (1989) has completed an investigation of perceived personality characteristics for each of the four identity statuses. Among other characteristics, the following four personality or social behaviors are viewed as pertinent to a general prototypical portrait for each status.

Identity Diffusion
Reluctant to act
Brittle ego-defense
Avoids close relations
Lacks personal meaning

Identity Moratorium
Introspective
Values own independence
Rebellious, conforming
Basically anxious

Identity Foreclosure
Overcontrol of impulses
Moralistic
Sex-appropriate behavior
Conventional

Identity Achievement
Clear, consistent personality
Warm and compassionate
Productive
Values own independence

SOURCE: From *Adolescent Life Experiences* by G. R. Adams, T. P. Gullotta, and C. Markstrom Adams (based on Mallory, 1989). Copyright © 1994, 1989, 1983 Brooks/Cole Publishing Company, a division of International Thomson Publishing Inc. By permission of the publisher.

configuration of personality. Above all else, identity is thought to be a dynamic process of testing, selecting, and integrating self-images and personal ideologies" (Adams, Gullotta, & Markstrom-Adams, 1994, p. 269).

The ego-identity status research has produced a detailed understanding of the process of ethnic identity development. It shows that there are clearly identifiable social and behavioral characteristics associated with different statuses (see Box 8.5). Mallory (1989) indicates that there are differences that show identity-diffused adolescents to be more restrictive in their relationships than adolescents of other ego-identity status types. Mallory's work, and that of others concerned with relating ego-identity status to behavioral and social characteristics, is particularly relevant for making developmental assessments of gang adolescents.

Applying Psychosocial Theory to Individual Gang Members

Understanding the social and behavioral repertoire of gang adolescents requires that clinicians have some understanding of their developmental history. An awareness of how early psychosocial crises are resolved is helpful. This information should be requested of the gang member and other family members. Clinicians should keep in mind, however, that parents are notori-

BOX 8.6   Psychosocial Stress Questions

In assessing the developmental stage of a client it is often necessary to also evaluate the developmental status of the other individuals with whom they form microsystems. The quality of parental relationships has direct implications for introducing stress into the lives of adolescents. One way to accomplish the goal of evaluating the family's stress quotient is to review the psychosocial stressors that have existed in the adolescent's life and his or her parents' for the past year. The following questions are offered as guides, not a prescription, to follow.

Conjugal
Has there been a significant change in the parents' conjugal relationship?
If there has been discord how has it been expressed?

Developmental
Have new developmental plateaus been reached?

Financial
What has been the family's financial situation over the past 12 months?
Is this a significant change?
How has the family adjusted to the change?

Legal
Are there legal problems? Ongoing? Resolved?
Have legal problems negatively impacted the family's financial status?

Living Circumstances
What changes have occurred in the living arrangement? What prompted them?

Occupational
What changes have occurred relative to school and work?
How have others been affected by these changes?

Parenting
Has there been a change in parenting status?
Has there been friction between parents and adolescent? Describe.

Other
Are other sources of psychosocial stressors identified by family members?
Describe whether these exist in the microsystem, mesosystem, exosystem, or macrosystem.
How has the family responded to the stress?

---

ously poor historians about the developmental paths of problem children. A review of school and medical records, if available, can help recreate the adolescent's development history.

Additional questions that clinicians may want to use to establish the developmental history of an adolescent's family from a psychosocial perspective are provided in Box 8.6.

A Critique of Developmental Theory

All of the developmental theories discussed here use a life-span perspective, except Marcia's (1966) ego-identity status theory. The theories are built on the belief that resolution of early developmental issues is essential if an individual is to negotiate the more complex and difficult tasks of adulthood. Inherent in each theory is also a belief that development is a linear progression. The environment in which the development occurs is not discussed directly in any of the theories except Bronfenbrenner's (1979) ecological systems theory. In each of the other theories, there is an implicit idea that the environment is maximally conducive for the conditions necessary for growth and development to occur. Table 8.3 shows the relationships among development theories. Despite the expansiveness of the period known as adolescence, little specificity is given to the exact tasks of adolescence except in the work of Marcia. Even the oft-cited psychosocial theory of Erikson, in which the identity crisis is the hallmark of adolescence, fails to offer a detailed breakdown of adolescence. Such a division appears to be important because of the dramatic changes that occur at different points in adolescence.

Steinberg (1985) shows that adolescence can be easily divided into three distinct periods: early, middle, and late. Early adolescence appears to be best described as a period in which the young person is defined primarily by dramatic changes in body image caused by sudden hormonal changes. Middle adolescence is punctuated by the heightened influence of the peer group and peer group pressure. By contrast, late adolescence is usually defined by a stabilization of peer pressure and a preoccupation with assumption of adult roles (i.e., getting married, job or career, and so on) as defined by the cultural context in which the individual resides.

An even more detailed articulation of adolescence is made by Blos (1979) in his four stages of adolescence: preadolescence, early adolescence, adolescence proper, and late adolescence. Blos stresses adolescence as a time of a second individuation and separation from parents. The delineations of both

TABLE 8.3   Relationships Among Development Theories

	Piaget: Cognition	Erikson: Ego	Marcia: Identity	Kohlberg: Morality
Infancy	Sensorimotor	Trust Autonomy		Punishment
Childhood	Preoperations	Initiative		Instrumental
Adolescence	Concrete operations	Industry	Foreclosure Diffusion	Interpersonal Law and order
Adulthood	Formal operations	Identity Intimacy	Moratorium Achievement	Social contract Universal ethical

Steinberg and Blos have implications for how individuals relate to the world around them. Level of autonomy and perceptions of others are two areas that have been shown to change across the span of adolescence. Treating adolescence as a unitary developmental period appears to be a gross oversimplification.

A second problem area with developmental theory has been its assumption that development occurs in a "normal" environment. None of the theories discussed here take into consideration the developmental impact of being socialized in other than "normal" and "healthy" environments on children—two adjectives synonymous with environments that approximate a middle-class White lifestyle. Issues of cultural variation (i.e., recent immigrants to the United States, belonging to an ethnic minority), ecological niche (i.e., economically deprived neighborhoods), or parental alternative lifestyles (i.e., gay or lesbian parents) are not addressed at any level by these theories. Such an oversight could be attributed to the historic era in which the theories were advanced, the reluctance of theorists to revise the canons, or a combination of the two. Whatever the reasons, traditional developmental theories have been limited in whose life course they describe. Of the theories cited in this chapter, the fault of exclusion is most heavily levied against Kohlberg's moral development stages, which are criticized for excluding females and people of color.

The assumption of "normality" is challenged in Garbarino's (1995) work on social toxicity. Gabarino contends that the assumption of normality of early socialization environments is biased against children and adolescents who live in what he calls *toxic environs*. Implicit in Garbarino's argument is also the idea that pervasive violence and other toxins make it difficult for children to make healthy choices. Indeed, options may not be a part of the repertoire of responses that children in toxic environs perceive to be available to them. Garbarino specifically notes that war and the destructive legacies associated with it are prime suspects for compromising the life choices available for young children. From wars, children learn the art of conflict and are explicitly reinforced for aggressive behaviors in certain contexts. It is, however, not clear when children are able to draw boundaries for which behaviors are acceptable on a macrosystemic level but not in microsystems. It is clear that children who grow up experiencing violence directly are likely to employ violence and control tactics in their relationships with others. A return to the young man introduced in Chapters 1 and 4 is in order.

The Case of Jason

The case of Jason, a nineteen-year-old African American male who was referred to me for psychotherapy, illustrates many of the issues and concepts discussed in this chapter. Immediately prior to the referral, Jason had had a domestic violence complaint filed against him by his live-in girlfriend. Jason is a high school graduate who reports that he has been "gang banging" since he was fourteen or fifteen years of age. Recently, several of his fellow gang members have gone to jail on a variety of charges. At least three friends have been killed in drive-by shootings within the previous eighteen months.

At the initial evaluation session, Jason presented himself as a neat, well-groomed, and friendly young man. He was on time for his appointment and was cooperative with me as the examiner, despite his verbalizations that he really did not want to go through with the evaluation. He seemed startled when I started the session by saying, "Tell me a little about yourself." His reply was, "Like, what do you want to know?" "Anything that you want to tell me," I told him. After a few minutes of chuckling and hand wringing, he started to describe his relationship with his girlfriend of two years.

Reflecting back over his high school years, Jason indicated that he had been a good student, earning As and Bs with a minimum of effort. Somewhere about the eighth grade, he recalled, he started to lose interest in school. At about that time, he also started to drink and to experiment with drugs. The first session ended with a discussion about the conditions of working together. Jason reiterated his position that he was not happy about the idea of coming to "a shrink" but was willing to do it if it helped keep him "out of the county [jail]."

Developmental History

Most of the information concerning his early developmental years was provided by Jason himself. School and medical records were not available, but some key points concerning his legal involvements were corroborated by his attorney.

Jason grew up in a family in which he was an only child. His parents "split up" when he was less than two years old. He reported having very faint memory traces of his father. According to Jason, his mother developed a serious drug problem during his toddlerhood. Because of that, he went to live with his maternal grandmother. When asked to reconstruct his earliest memory, he talked about an incident in which he was locked in a bathroom and crying for his mother. "It seemed like an eternity . . . and she never came for me."

During the years that he lived with his grandmother, he saw his mother intermittently but his father only infrequently. Jason was in the third grade the last time he remembers seeing his father. A few years later, his grandmother told Jason that his father had died. The elementary school years were "difficult." When he was in the fourth or fifth grade, Jason went to live with his mother again. He recalled those years as being "filled with bitterness and a shitload of conflicts with mom." He ran away from home a lot and got into trouble in school. Shortly after returning to his mother's home, he recalled, he fought a lot at school and then he would be afraid to go home, fearful that his mother would punish him severely. His maternal grandmother would often intervene and attempt to protect him from the wrath of his mother and her boyfriends. The relationship with his mother continued in a volatile state until she attempted to stab him when he was fourteen or fifteen. From his perspective, that was the turning point in their relationship. He started to look elsewhere for validation. The gang answered affirmatively.

Jason rarely offered any details of his middle adolescence years. He would gloss over the subject of friendships and school activities by saying, "It was just your ordinary high school bullshit" or some similar nondescriptive phase. The notable exception was his relationship with his girlfriend, Trina, whom he met in school. He noted with a great deal of pride that she was the person with whom he had his first "real sexual experience." Despite having been with a large number of girls since he met Trina, he insists that she is the one true love of his life.

Trina got pregnant a couple of months before Jason started psychotherapy. He was very excited about the prospect of becoming a father. Frequently, he talked about wanting to give his son a better life than he had. In order to do so, Jason thought prenatal care had to be scrupulously carried out. To make sure that things were orderly and under control, Jason would attend all of Trina's medical appointments. He also made it a point to speak with the doctor directly "to make sure I had the whole story."

The Call of the Wild: Jason's Life as a Gang Banger

Jason dates his active participation in gang life to when he was fourteen or fifteen years old. He was not very specific in identifying the events that directly led to his gang affiliation. Likewise, he avoided questions about his gang initiation. In one of the early sessions, he observed that he was very hard on himself. Efforts to get his family of origin to respond to him affirmatively were fruitless. "My family is a bunch of hypocrites . . . they are users." "My family was the street. I was a _____ [gang member]." Of all the things about the members of his family of origin, what bothered Jason the most was that they always wanted him to do things for them. He resented this greatly.

When he came to therapy, Jason indicated that he was trying to turn his life around. Several of his gang friends were in jail or recently had been released. Jason thought of them as being very needy. He no longer wanted to serve the role of meeting the needs of others: "I can't fight them all on my own. I'm always doing the fighting. I'm fuckin' tired of always helping others [being used], not receiving anything from others . . . [becomes teary-eyed] . . . I'm emotional now."

Efforts to engage Jason about his specific gang activities were not successful. No matter how indirectly I would phrase the inquiry, he was so guarded and well defended that he would avoid the questions. In a good spirited and relaxed manner, he would often reply "Shi-it, I'm not going to tell you that" or "Do you work for the police" or "Now, why do you really want to know that? . . . All of that gang bangin' shit is behind me" or some variation on these responses.

On two occasions, he momentarily dropped his guard and shared with me what it was like to participate in a drive-by shooting. After one of those disclosures, he became agitated, accused me of tricking him, and stormed out of the office, ending the session. Ironically, he showed up the next week at his regular appointment time.

Issues in Jason's Life

Jason presented several challenging and complex issues for resolution.

Relationship with Mother. Jason's developmental history was a point of great concern to him. He never really knew his father. He blamed his mother for that. During the period that he lived with his grandmother, he had limited contact with siblings who were born to his mother and her boyfriend. Jason indicated that he feels cheated out of the joy of having a brother because of his mother's explosive personality and deemed inability to parent him. When Jason finally returned to his mother's home, the friction between the two of them continued to escalate, culminating in her stabbing him when he was fourteen or fifteen years old. Conflicts between him and his mother figure prominently in his perception of himself and the world around him.

Jason expressed a lot of anger that his mother would not accept his help when she was being abused by any of her several boyfriends. This was interpreted by Jason as an indicator that she would rather be abused than to accept his help. He was outraged that his offers of assistance were declined. According to him, his mother does not like Trina but is inclined to align with Trina whenever she and Jason have conflicts. In almost every session, Jason devoted at least a few minutes to talking about his relationship with his mother. Despite the fact that he always raised her as an issue in his life, he would frequently deny any desire to repair the relationship with her. "I don't really care about the relationship with her . . . kick that bitch out of my life."

Other family members also figured in Jason's rage at his mother. He reported that his aunts seem to collude with his mother. At least, they were reluctant to confront her about her self-destructive behaviors (i.e., involvement with abusive men). Even worse, Jason thinks his aunts are unwilling to help him avoid the wrath of his mother. "It's almost like she has some magical power over them or something. . . . They know she's wrong for treating me like this. . . . She knows she's wrong. . . . Everybody knows that she's full of shit, but no one will do nothing about it. . . . Nobody seems to see my side."

Relationship with Girlfriend.   Jason has been in a live-in relationship for approximately twelve months. His girlfriend, Trina, is six months pregnant. From Jason's perspective, having a child will provide him with another opportunity to correct many of the things in his life that have not gone well. He is excited that he will have a chance to model for his "son" the kind of caring and nurturance he never received.

Jason seems to be conflicted about the relationship that Trina has with her own mother. On several occasions, he expressed jealousy and anger that the two of them spend so much time on the telephone with each other. In addition, he is resentful that Trina seeks her mother's advice about matters related to the pregnancy.

Because Jason is mistrustful of Trina, he does not allow any of his friends to call or come by to visit when he may not be at home. He could not provide any objective data to substantiate why he does not trust her, but he persisted in the belief. Despite his chauvinistic attitudes toward Trina, Jason reports continuing to have occasional brief, casual sexual liaisons with a variety of young women around town, including acquaintances of Trina's. He sees nothing wrong with this behavior.

Trina has filed domestic violence charges against Jason on two occasions. When asked about the incidents, he indicated that he never hit her, just yelled and screamed at her a bit, "Cause she was being stupid."

Relationship with the Gang.   Jason spoke about his gang experiences with mixed feelings. On one hand, he was quite proud of his leadership abilities and how they had earned him a position of respect in the gang. My efforts to gain a better understanding of the scope of his gang participation were only minimally successful. Jason was very protective and secretive about his gang life. Part of this nondisclosure had to do with him not trusting me. He repeatedly asked me if I worked for the police.

It appears that Jason was involved in several automobile thefts and at least two or three drive-by shootings. Questioning him about these incidents revealed that he was the "mastermind" behind them. He gave the orders that others followed. He showed no remorse or sense of guilt about his behavior. On one occasion, following a newspaper account of a drive-by shooting, he talked about how the family of the victim must have felt. All of that was tempered with a general feeling, however, that maybe the victim had gotten what he had deserved. "He probably wasn't taking care of business . . . that's what happen when you don't cover your back [chuckle]."

The relationships that Jason created in the gang continued even though he considered his days of "gang banging" to be over. Several gang members continued to call him from jail. Jason was annoyed—even outraged. The fact that they were appealing to him for a sense of validation and affirmation angered him tremendously. He did not want to be placed in the position of continuing to give to others, "especially since they couldn't do anything to help me. They are like a bunch of pussies, always whining."

Relationship with the Clinician. From the very beginning, Jason indicated that he did not want to see a "shrink." He thought the experience was demeaning. But when he considered the possibility that he could be sentenced to the county jail for domestic violence, he reassessed his position and agreed to make an effort to be minimally compliant. He seemed to enjoy the process and the attention being focused on him once the work actually began. It was difficult to convince him that there is such a thing as confidentiality. He was convinced that the therapist was an extension of the law enforcement agencies.

Despite his reservations about the process, Jason was happy to comply with requests to change appointments, to bring in dream material, to complete the Minnesota Multiphasic Personality Inventory (MMPI) and other standardized tests, and to answer many questions about what others might consider to be private matters. Jason never missed an appointment, suggesting either that he was invested in the process or that he did not want to run the risk having a negative evaluation sent to the court.

Jason was rather demanding. He would become upset if I was three minutes late starting the session. On one occasion, he pouted for approximately the first twenty minutes of a session because some other people were leaving the building just as he arrived for his appointment.

Jason Who are all of these damn people in here?
Therapist Oh, that was just a group of people who had a meeting here.
Jason [sarcastically] Right. . . . They all staring at me and shit . . . like they checkin' me out or something. . . . Man, I don't like that shit. [pause] You told me my appointment was at six [o'clock].
Therapist Yes, that's right.
Jason Well, it's now five minutes after six.

Jason exhibited a high level of concern about how he would be represented in progress reports to the court. It was standard practice that all clients be provided with a copy of the court report before it was submitted.

Jason not only insisted on receiving his report but underlined all of the technical terminology contained in it. He insisted on having a satisfactory explanation of the terms before the report was submitted.

His relationship with me could be described as being a symbolic representation of that with the father he had barely known. Despite his testy behavior, he would often ask the clinician what he personally thought about the issues being discussed. These queries were often punctuated with, "But you can understand where I'm coming from, can't you?" or some other phrase suggestive of seeking validation for his position.

Summary

Jason is a very needy young man. His history of poor relationships in the family and community is a major source of dissonance for him. He has been engaged in a volatile relationship with his mother for a number of years. It became apparent during the course of his work with me that his mother probably does not have the capacity to provide him what he wants and needs. He seems to have come to that conclusion but is unwilling to accept it. Rather, he continues to perseverate on the idea that she is an unfit mother. He also invests a significant amount of energy in trying to get others to adopt his viewpoint. When those efforts fail, he becomes angry with the other parties (i.e., aunts and grandmother). Jason seems to have an idealized notion of mothers. When he recognizes that his mother does not measure up to that standard, he is filled with rage. He blames his mother for all of his early developmental problems, even the fact that his father left the family. Jason's high level of demanding behavior also finds expression in his relationship with Trina.

In pursuing a romantic relationship with Trina, Jason expected her to be devoted to him exclusively. When it turned out that she maintained a close relationship with her own mother, he was filled with jealousy and rage. He acted to terminate her frequent telephone calls to her mother. Jason is suspicious that Trina might be unfaithful to him, despite there being no evidence to confirm this, other than his pervasive sense of mistrust. It is ironic that even as Jason mistrusts Trina, he himself continues to have brief sexual liaisons with several young women in the community, including acquaintances of Trina's.

The gang provided Jason with a forum where he could accomplish a measure of achievement. He did that by becoming a leader in a local chapter of a national gang. It is not clear, however, what was the exact nature of his gang activities. The only objectively verifiable data that could be obtained was that he had a few arrests for automobile theft.

Jason idolized the gang. He felt affirmed by the high level of need that the other gang members had for his approval. This fascination with the gang became a source of annoyance for him when the gang members started to call him from jail. He perceives their obvious neediness as evidence of weakness. The very behaviors that he himself engaged in with family members—becoming enraged when they did not respond affirmatively—are now the behaviors that others express toward him. He wants to walk away from these others. They served a purpose in his life at another time but not any longer.

Finally, his relationship with me as clinician embodies all of the foregoing dynamics. Jason appeared to have an on-and-off relationship with me. Avoiding time in the county jail was a reason to cooperate with me, but I also symbolically represented the father that Jason never knew. That was a good reason to cooperate with and please me, but he could not give me too much information because I might be "working for the police." Worse still, I might go away and abandon him, just as his father had done several years earlier.

The plethora of issues presented by Jason illustrate the complexity of working with gang adolescents who have had a life filled with family and personal problems. The focus of Jason's work with me was not on the gang per se but on issues that found expression in the gang culture and the wider world simultaneously (i.e., mistrust, modulating relationships with others, anger management, taking the perspective of others). Jason was chronologically in late adolescence and about to become a father. Developmentally, he was still involved in low-level behaviors characteristic of toddlerhood. He could be described as having a narcissistic personality disorder, but that would do little to explain the conditions that may have given rise to it.

Part 3
Interventions

9

Planning an Intervention

The relationship between a therapist and gang members and their families begins at the time of referral. At that point, all preconceived notions and history of contact or noncontact that the therapist has had with gang-affiliated families and vice versa become activated. This happens in a rather dramatic fashion, despite the fact that the two parties have not yet had face-to-face contact. The images that each has of the other are significantly impacted by media portrayals. Therapists, like the general public, are influenced by the sensationalism that the media use to report stories of gang activity. Jankowski (1991) describes in detail how such sensationalism gives rise to one-sided portrayals of gang youths. Because of such news-reporting practices, the public is often left with inaccurate and overwhelmingly negative images of all dimensions of the life of gang youths. Completely accepting the media portrayals of gangs increases the likelihood of perceiving gang members to be habitually out-of-control, indiscriminately violent individuals.

In most media coverage of gang members, there is no place for considering them as adolescents trying to find their place in a vast and troubling world. In my research, I find partial support for the idea that most adults have very fixed and limited images of gang-affiliated youths (Branch, 1995). Adults surveyed in two different regions of the country overwhelmingly perceive gang members as being out of control and antisocial, with no interest in education or good familial relationships. These adult images are incongruent with the images reported by gang and nongang adolescents. It appears that the adults have rather parochial views of gang members, owing in part to media portrayals of gangs. Therapists are likely also to have fixed ideas about gangs, many of which are the result of limited experiential exposure and biased news reporting. Gang members and their families are also at risk for having stereotypic a priori views of therapists and other mental health professionals.

The images that many gang-affiliated youths and their families have of mental health professionals are likely to be created from a mixture of media stereotypes, histories of direct exposure, and secondhand reports provided by other family members and friends. Movie and television depictions of therapists are the source of many initial impressions of the mental health profession. Television portrayals of therapists as witty or stiff and inflexible characters probably add to generic images that gang youths hold of them.

In addition to creating images of therapists, media portrayals also help develop images of therapy and what kind of people participate in it as consumers. Overwhelmingly, the images are of mildly neurotic middle-class individuals who can afford the luxury of "reflecting on things but taking no action." Personal experiences with clinicians greatly influence a family's receptivity to the idea of services in the future. Many gang members have a history of exposure to mental health professionals, perhaps a school psychologist or a social worker, because of behavioral or academic problems. The quality and outcome of those relationships are likely to color the expectations that gang-affiliated youths have when they learn that they are about to be referred for clinical services. In a similar fashion, parents of gang youths are likely to have memories of their child's last encounter with a mental health professional. For many parents of color, these memories include the belief that their children are often misdiagnosed and misunderstood, especially in school. These attitudes often lead to early termination of treatment and other remediation services that are offered to families of color.

Another source of attitudes about mental health service providers for gang-affiliated families may be extended-family members and friends. That information may be the most influential, even more powerful than media images. Relatives often share their impressions of social situations and service providers to help save family members from a fate like their own. It is rare that receivers of information stop to make qualifiers and appropriate differentiations. If a negative assessment is made of a professional or the experience of being in treatment, it is received as being absolute, expecially if the appraisal is made by a relative who has a high degree of credibility in the family.

An examination of both sides of the would-be therapeutic relationship, as outlined above, suggests that therapists and consumers (i.e., gang-affiliated youths and their families) are inclined to have formulated opinions about the other even before they meet. These precontact mind-sets are often built on information that is inconclusive, second- or thirdhand, or factually incorrect. Despite the shortcomings of the information, it gets incorporated into the receivers' memory banks and becomes the blueprint for dictating their behavior toward the "other," especially after a referral to treatment is made.

The Referral

All of the prereferral conditions mentioned in the opening of this chapter come to life the moment a referral is effected. The ensuing dynamics between the persons making the referral, the would-be client, and the service provider are potentially very interesting. Collectively, they account for much of the variance in whether or not the intervention is effective. Referrals themselves have the impact of motivating individuals to become introspective. The result can be that clients start to work on themselves and their situation. Or they shut down, becoming resentful of the referral, evidenced by an increase in recalcitrant and oppositional behavior. The subject of referrals for treatment could fill a treatise by itself, but here I address only issues surrounding referral of gang-affiliated adolescents. Practical issues of how to plan clinical interventions for them and their families will also be examined. This chapter concludes with some practical suggestions for developing clinical interventions for gang-affiliated adolescents and their families.

In thinking about referrals involving gang youths, several very basic clinical questions should be considered early in the process. The absence of a clinically well-grounded answer to any one of these questions can become a tremendous obstacle to treatment. Because services intended to help gang youths often cut across several organizational systems, it is often difficult, if not impossible, to arrive at an intervention philosophy that is supported by all parties involved. Consistent with that reality, it becomes even more of an imperative that clinicians intending to work in this area ask several pertinent questions and receive answers with which they can live. Perhaps the most basic question that needs to be asked is, Who is making the referral? At the level of a superficial reading, this question asks what agency is making the referral. A deeper reading might reveal an inquiry about what element in a community system finds gang members' behaviors and attitudes to be unacceptable. For the moment, I confine my exploration to the former.

Mental health referrals for gang-affiliated youths usually originate in some section of the criminal justice system. This suggests that young people who are referred because of gang involvement or suspected involvement are usually in trouble with the law before one is willing to state on the record that help is needed. This circumstance also raises the possibility that despite the fact that an adolescent may have been in emotional and academic trouble for a number of years, help is likely to be forthcoming only when the adolescent starts to engage in socially disruptive behavior such as violence or selling drugs. Thus, an important part of understanding the referral is to know what conditions led to the referral. Is therapeutic intervention being sought because everything else has failed? Or is the gang member being sent to therapy as a first step to try to gain greater insights into the range and depth of issues with which he or she is struggling? These two questions represent polar points on a continuum.

The first question suggests that other services have been attempted but the results have not been encouraging. In such a case, a referral for therapy is a setup for failure. Having experienced failure at several other types of intervention undoubtedly produces feelings of failure, and possibly anger, on the part of the gang member. If family members participated in any of the failed interventions, they too are likely to feel resentment about getting yet another referral when all of the preceding ones have not made a difference. On the other hand, if the family has not been involved in any of the earlier attempts at intervention, members are likely to be confused about why their involvement is now being requested, especially since things have continued on a downward spiral.

Where a mental health referral is made as a first step to understanding the nature and extent of disruption or impairment a youngster may be experiencing, the questions asked are likely to be diagnostic in nature. Referrals that are made after a long history of problem behaviors are usually treatment oriented. Clinical intervention as a beginning phase of interventions with gang-affiliated youths and their families has the advantage of conveying the message that the behavior that is being emitted is the result of very complex internal processes. In addition, clinical services that are family based suggest that long term sustained changes need to involve family members as well as the gang member. Perhaps most important, starting with mental health intervention can give the message that the root cause of gang affiliation may be traceable to multiple systems. The focus on assessment and diagnosis that is inherent in clinical interventions is a good place to begin identifying and evaluating the contributing factors. All of these things suggest that in addition to noting the source of a referral, attention should also be placed on where, developmentally speaking, in the child's difficulties the mental health referral occurs—early or late. The timing of the request for mental health services coupled with who is making the request conceptually creates a philosophical framework for the referral.

Referrals that originate in the criminal justice system usually occur after the youngster has been adjudicated to be in trouble. Courts and probation officers are also inclined to make cooperation with an evaluation or treatment a condition for probation. Under these conditions, referrals are likely to be viewed as means for staying out of further trouble with the court. A much better situation would be for young people awaiting adjudication to see a mental health professional for the purpose of creating a profile to be used by the judge in rendering his or her decision concerning conditions of probation. This could be accomplished in some cases where the issue of guilt or innocence is dealt with swiftly and the court is seen as a place that gives advice about prevention as well as after-the-fact consequences.

Mental health professionals should think of court evaluations as an opportunity to educate colleagues about the etiology of much adolescent misbehavior. If youngsters are referred from courts for mental health evaluations, there might be a high level of appreciation for mental health, or the lack thereof, being a causative agent in deviant behavior. Court referrals tend to be for the purpose of understanding what led to initial misbehavior. Little attention is given to extrapolating those findings for family and community intervention purposes. This is not to suggest that court officers are not interested in preventive intervention, but rather that the demands of very busy schedules preclude such activity. In less extreme situations, information obtained as the result of a mental health referral can be used for dual purposes: to stabilize a youngster's relationship with the community and family and to evaluate generic progress while on probation. I will return to special issues associated with referrals for mental health services that originate in court systems in discussing specific referral sources in detail. Whatever the origin of the referral, however, several issues should be examined carefully to maximize the likelihood of success in intervening with gang members and their families.

In addition to wanting to know who specifically is referring the family, a clinician should carefully review the following matters *before* agreeing to accept a case:

What has been the relationship of the individual making the referral to the referred family? An important condition that seems to directly impact the outcome of referrals for mental health services is the client's belief in his or her need of the service being offered. This gets expressed in a variety of ways, including acceptance or nonacceptance, metaphorically speaking, of the referral. Another way this has been expressed by some clients is in whether they trust the judgment and conclusions of the person making the referral. Put another way, "Does the person referring us really know what we need?" In the case of people of color and recently immigrated families, this is a critical issue. In community-based intervention programs, gang-affiliated youths often find themselves having multiple-layered relationships with counselors—one adult provides a troubled youngster with educational counsel as well as vocational and legal guidance. These multiple relationships are complicated and create ethical conflicts in many professions. Such arrangements are, however, a way of life in many communities, and clients sometimes find it desirable that a worker knows about all of the complexities of their lives. To be intimately involved with all facets of their lives is interpreted, by some clients, as evidence that the helper is genuinely concerned about them.

Individuals who have had significant relationships with clients that extend over long periods of time often have an easier time selling the idea of mental health services to the would-be mental health client. If clients trust the service provider and his or her sense of competence, they will accept the referral as what needs to be done.

What conditions or events led to the referral?   It is important to determine whether the referral is the result of a crisis or someone determining that the gang member is out of control and in need of help after a long history of disruptive behavior. Understanding whether there is a sense of urgency associated with the referral helps the clinician figure out how strongly others want something to happen. The greater the stakes in the minds of others, the more pressure there is to provide a "miracle cure," even when one does not exist. Referrals for preventive interventions are extremely rare. Part of the reason for their rarity is the high level of denial among many parents and communities. Many families are not willing to accept the reality of their family member's participation in gangs. Left unchecked, this denial moves to another level and finds expression in social contracts (Jankowski, 1991) between gangs and communities. Such alliances lead to complicity in accepting the gang and its illegal activity until it exceeds its boundaries.

Practical Issues in Developing an Intervention

One of the first issues that must be resolved in attempting to provide clinical services to gang-affiliated youths and their families is whether there is a clear and acknowledged need for clinical work. At face value, this sounds like a very simplistic idea, but it can make the difference between the intervention being successful or not. The major issue to be resolved is whether the clients accept the referral. A referral for clinical work suggests that there is an identifiable problem or array of problems that all parties acknowledge. One of the most critical issues in making this determination for gang-affiliated youths and their families is, From whose perspective has the need for work been determined? With many multiproblem families, gang membership among young people, particularly when it does not result in direct entanglements with the law, is not seen as being particularly problematic. Rather, some parents simply see their children as coming of age and making choices about friendships and social relations in the context of a troubled community. In other situations, the joining of adolescent gangs by young males is seen as part of the ritual of passage into manhood and as such is not problematic.

A related question is, How was the decision to recommend clinical services reached? In the mental health community, it is widely known that clients who enter services as involuntary clients are less likely to remain in treatment until its completion. Even among voluntary clients, the rate of premature termination from treatment is quite high. In communities of color, the figure of premature termination from treatment is no greater than in the larger community, but the pattern that exists has in some cases been greatly exaggerated because of the severity of the disruptions, from the perspective of the larger community, that led to the individuals being in therapy.

That simply means that for many people of color, referrals for mental health services by professionals are likely to occur when things have disintegrated to a state of crisis or individuals are heavily involved with the court system. This is not, of course, the best approach to providing preventive intervention, but it speaks to generic social attitudes about mental health professionals, mental health services, and the dynamics that exist between therapists and many people of color.

For gang-affiliated families, involuntary referrals for mental health services are often part of a package of conditions associated with probation or delay of sentencing by the court. This at face value provides families with yet another opportunity to redeem themselves and find a better quality of life. But closer examination of these kinds of situations suggests that entering treatment involuntarily as part of a probationary sentence increases the pressure on the family to work and find resolution for what may have been long-standing problems. Among involuntary referrals for families, the probability is high that many individuals in the family may have had less than optimal experiences with mental health services themselves. This history is reactivated once the identified patient is referred to treatment and other family members are expected to participate also. Sometimes, individuals offering referrals to families are not aware of the family's history and mistakenly interpret resistance or less than high levels of cooperation on the part of the individual family members as a statement that they are uncooperative or not interested in the well-being of their family member.

One of the last issues related to documenting the need for clinical work with gang-affiliated youths and their families has to do with understanding the source of the referral as having a major impact on what is likely to be identified as the issue of concern. Generally speaking, school officials who make referrals of gang-affiliated youths are more concerned with the learning difficulties and disruptions that gang members cause in the school community. There is a fair amount of literature on the impact of the presence of gang members in school settings (Kyle, 1984; Vigil, 1983), mostly concerning weapons, a sense of safety, and the psychological risks that are introduced by the presence of gang members in the school setting. Little attention has been given to the ambivalence gang members may feel about participating in gang activities outside of the school. The current literature gives the impression that *gangstas* who attend school want to be part of the school community and are interested in making preparations for a life in the future.

Referrals from law enforcement agencies are rooted in concerns that young people have violated social and legal codes. The intent of such referrals is to help young people not only change their behaviors to be consistent with prevailing standards but also to decrease the rate of recidivism. Thus, law enforcement personnel often are interested in preventive intervention as well as corrective actions. They use the opportunity of referring young people for mental health services as a way to suggest new ways of thinking and behaving to young people. Unfortunately, the court system is often so overcrowded with cases of delinquent behavior that preventive interventions become less emphasized in the programs of those courts. Indeed, in some court systems, the concern is exclusively with the handing out of justice based on past behaviors. Little attention is given to the role the court can play in maximizing the likelihood that young people will not return to the court system.

Many community-based intervention programs direct their resources toward preventing young people from affiliating with destructive elements that may exist in the community. Referrals from such programs tend to be multi-problem oriented, and it is less clearly discernible what those making the referral would like to have happen with the future client and his or her family.

Once the person making the referral has convinced the client and his or her family of the need for mental health services, the very difficult question of creating a context for the work arises. Multiple issues are inherent in this problem. Some of these issues are extensions of good clinical practice, but others are unique to working with individuals who are involved with the court system. One of the very first issues that must be resolved is that of a setting for the work.

There is much talk in psychology about community settings being preferable to individuals leaving their community to receive mental health services. Indeed, it is precisely this idea that was at the root of the Community Mental Health Centers Act of 1963 that led to the creation of community mental health centers. Individuals who are involved in delinquent gang activities react in a variety of ways concerning the setting in which the work occurs. Some individuals express a clear preference for receiving service in their own community, "on their own turf." This arrangement often signifies that the practitioner is indeed a member of the community and perhaps someone who can be trusted to work in the best interest of the client. On the other hand, some individuals note with a great deal of pride that their mental health practitioner is someone who is situated in a medical facility or in a more exclusive neighborhood of the larger community. These issues of residence sometimes have importance to clients.

Perhaps more important than the physical location of the service provider are the images and significance of this arrangement to the client. In rare instances, mental health practitioners have been known to provide services in a community-based facility even though that is not the usual place of their practice. This dilemma of where to provide the services is used by some community-oriented workers as an occasion to periodically provide services in the home of the client. Home-based services provide an opportunity to understand the ambiance of the family residence as well as to see what resources are available to all of the members of the family. I do not advocate one arrangement over others but simply highlight the fact that any particular arrangement can have positives as well as negatives associated with it.

The circumstances surrounding the provision of services are likely to also influence the success or failure of the clinical intervention. Issues that clinicians may want to consider as impacting the outcome of the work include frequency of visits, amount and method of payment for services, and personal characteristics of the service provider (i.e., age, race, gender, and so on). Some of these factors are not matters over which the individual provider may have control, but they certainly should be considered in planning an intervention.

The behavioral science literature is filled with discussion and debate about the match between therapist and client and how that affects the outcome of psychotherapy. Much of this literature is focused on racial congruence between therapist and client. Concerning the issue of race, it should be noted that the literature indicates that where possible a match between therapist and client is likely to be facilitative of a better work relationship. An oversight in this literature, however, is the fact that adolescents are still in the process of developing racial attitudes and thus are likely to change their position relative to who is, from their perspective, a person of high credibility. On the other hand, it could be argued that striving to make a racial match between clinician and families is often used as a creative form of resistance. The real issues should be the ability of the clinician to understand the issues of the family as best one person can understand another and to convey a genuine concern to the family, not the racial identity of the clinician. Of course, eliminating race as a variable in the work relationship is much easier said than done. It is a goal that may not come to fruition until after the passage of at least a couple of sessions, if ever.

Less pronounced in the literature is the issue of gender similarity and how it may impact the dynamics of the work between therapist and client. This issue may be particularly important in the area of working with gang-affiliated youths and their families, however. Given that the majority of adolescents who are actively involved in disruptive elements of gang membership are male and that many of these individuals have at best pejorative attitudes toward women, the gender of the clinician becomes a very critical issue for discussion. In the attempt to provide gang-affiliated adolescents and their families with a supportive and nurturing atmosphere in which to work on their issues, it could be argued that a female—an individual who is likely to be perceived as nonthreatening—may be more facilitative of therapeutic work. This could of course be reinterpreted as an example of the dynamics of the work relationship between the gang member and his or her family simply reinforcing stereotypes that individuals bring with them to therapy work. It could also make a difference in the tone of the work relationship. Clinicians must try to understand where the identified client and his or her family members stand on issues of race, ethnicity, and gender before beginning a therapeutic relationship with them.

One of the other issues that must be resolved very early in planning an intervention is how the identified work will be discussed with the gang member and other family members. It should be noted that the nature of what is requested in a referral is usually associated with the source of the referral. For the intervention to have a chance of succeeding, all parties involved in the work must at least acknowledge the presence of the set of problems and have a minimal level of commitment to exploring the possibility of working on the problems. This is often best accomplished by the clinician making a clear statement of parameters of the work, which should be explained to the identified client and his or her family even before a formal contract of work is made. This saves all parties from misunderstandings about the role of the clinician and the ultimate outcome of the work not being fulfilled. It also provides an opportunity for individuals who have other agendas to introduce them during the early stages of the work. An agreement to a contract in the early stages of the work should not be construed as a statement that the contract will continue unchanged throughout the work relationship. People change their minds, especially as new material emerges in the sessions.

In identifying the parameters of the work relationship with a gang member, it is vital that the clinician make a clear statement of behavioral expectations concerning keeping of appointments, payment of fees, and limits of confidentiality.

An important clinical issue that has been the source of some debate is the efficacy of group work versus individual therapeutic interventions with gang members. Social relationships are very important to many adolescents, and they spend a lot of time engaging with others—not just any others, but other adolescents. These interactions help adolescents develop and refine interpersonal skills that they will use as adults. Even adolescents who are troubled use social engagement with peers as a way to discover things about themselves and others. These are some of the arguments for group work being an ideal modality for use with adolescents. In addition, the medical model approach of doctor and patient is seen as too limiting and perhaps even artificial for many adolescents.

I believe the value of a group cannot be overestimated. Because so much learning occurs by observation, groups provide a wonderful setting for adolescents to see how peers relate to each other and to an adult who is perceived to be in charge. Groups also provide a sense of community, even collegiality, for adolescents who might otherwise be seen as outcasts. Individual therapeutic interventions provide none of these advantages.

Because the psychotherapeutic relationship between a gang adolescent and a clinician may be a new experience for either or both parties, it is vital that the nature of that relationship be discussed very openly in the beginning of the work. As noted earlier, some gang members, because of their long history of conduct disorder and special learning needs, may have a history of receiving special services in a variety of settings. Sometimes, these relationships are the basis for assumptions for future work relationships. Again, because some of these relationships may have been in settings other than mental health settings, it is incumbent on the therapist to dispel any expectations that the gang member may have that the present relationship will be like all its (failed) predecessors. In particular, the issues of confidentiality and working in the best interest of the client should be discussed at length. Some family members may also have a history with mental health professionals that may prove to be disruptive to subsequent relationships with mental health professionals. It is very important that thoughts and unspoken fantasies that family members may have about what the present relationship will be like are identified and corrected where necessary.

The very important issue that sometimes contaminates work with gang adolescents is the potential problem of how much information gets shared and with whom. Mental health professionals may have idiosyncratic rules about how specifically they work, but there seems to be consistency across disciplines that the confidentiality of clients must be assured except in situations of child abuse or other imminent danger to others. At the risk of being terribly repetitive and maybe even antagonizing clients by sounding paternalistic or implying they are slow to understand, I urge therapists to repeat this guiding principle with identified clients and family members several times in the early stages of the work.

There has been concern on the part of some mental health professionals that the intensity of work with gang members often causes them to move out of their usual mode of functioning with clients. Clinicians are occasionally called on to write multiple reports, answer numerous telephone calls, and even visit schools and other facilities during the course of work with a multiproblem family. This should be anticipated and is an issue that needs to be discussed with the family members. Clarification in this case should include a statement of what services are provided as part of the basic fee and what things will require that an additional fee be assessed. Clinicians should state ground rules concerning their availability outside of regular sessions as a part of the basic contract.

One last area that must be addressed is the overall intent of the work. There are occasions where a mental health clinician is involved as an auxiliary to an ongoing and more global systemic intervention with troubled adolescents and their families. In such cases, the mental health work is a supportive set of assessments that can be translated into concrete behavioral objectives and associated across domains of work. On other occasions, the mental health work itself is primary in helping to move troubled young people and their families to a new level of functioning. In the latter case, mental health work, as the primary focal point, is critical in introducing new ways of thinking and new ways of behaving that will find expression in all areas of the gang members' and family members' lives. It is most important that mental health clinicians clearly distinguish the goals of the referring agency from their own. Such clarification implicitly creates a statement as to what things are expected of the clinician and the way in which reports are generated, as well as a statement about relating with other professionals who may operate from a professional or theoretical framework that is not mental health focused.

Clinical Issues to Consider

The experience that a clinician has with a gang-affiliated family is idiosyncratic, representing the unique blend of the clinician's characteristics and the presentation of the referred family. It is difficult, if not impossible, to predict the ways in which gang adolescents and their families will respond to the experience of being sent for mental health services. Attempting to delineate the dynamics of gang members is also a daunting task. There are as many reasons for joining gangs as there are members. There does seem to be a core set of issues and behavioral responses with reasonable certainty of surfacing in most work relationships with gang youths and their families, however. I present them here in an abbreviated manner, not as a fixed prescription but rather with the hope of inspiring readers to anticipatory conceptualizing and planning.

Getting All Family Members Involved

The frequency with which family members are excluded, even as sources of information, from therapeutic work with troubled adolescents is amazing. Sometimes, this occurs as a result of the clinician's theoretical orientation, which dictates that all of the work should be focused on the identified client. At extreme levels, this even means not talking to others to receive additional information. Another reason that family members have been excluded from therapeutic work is the unspoken belief that family members are unavailable or not interested in participating. Frequently, this is not the case. Many family members, including extended family members, want to be of assistance to troubled adolescents but are not sure how to express their concern in a tangible way. Involving such individuals in providing corroborating information about the client's situation or being available as an emotional resource is often a powerful intervention. Boyd-Franklin (1986) articulates a model of multiple-family therapy in which extended-family members and *fictive kin* (i.e., imaginary relatives) are included in the therapeutic work.

In dealing with gang youths in trouble with the law, the struggle of getting the familial network actively involved may be problematic for several reasons. Many of the gang adolescents who come to the attention of the court immediately before a referral to mental health services have fractured so many relationships in the family that they have few allies left. Many gang adolescents also live in families that are headed by a single parent, usually the mother, for whom ensuring nurturance and support for a wayward child while trying to maintain the rest of the family can be overwhelming. Many single mothers in such situations lapse into helplessness and decide that continued intervention on behalf of an out-of-control youngster is not something they want to do. The absent father is rarely invited to be a part of the gang member's quest for a better life through therapy, but it is vital to make an effort to include absent parents in the therapeutic work at some level, as sources of information if not active, ongoing participants. In a clinical sense, reconstituting the family around the struggles of one member may be therapeutic. It may reopen old wounds and feuds in the process, but it also has the potential of setting the stage for a confrontation relative to a conflict that may have occurred years before. Whatever the outcome, the effort to involve the whole family can become a positive contributor to understanding the environs and relationships with which the identified client has had to struggle.

The early stages of work may prove to be very interesting if it is discovered that an absent father actually wants to take an active role in the life of his son or daughter. The initial struggles with getting full participation from both parents were partially solved, in the pilot phase of the FIP, by a judge ordering families to participate as a condition of their child's probation. In sending the directive to attend the FIP, he addressed the letter to "The Parents of _____." Invariably, the letters were received and read by the mothers. With few exceptions, they interpreted the letter to mean that the father, despite his absence from the home, was also required to attend. Frequently, the mother took it on herself to call the absent father to tell him about "the letter from the judge." The results were stunning. Several seemingly uninterested and unavailable fathers responded affirmatively. The by-product of all of this was that unfinished or dormant business between the parents was reawakened. This became material to be worked on at the FIP, obviously in the interests of the troubled child. For those conducting the FIP, the conflicts and how they got expressed in the very first minutes of the work session (i.e., greetings, seating arrangements, who accompanied whom to the FIP) provided rich clinical data.

The example of the judge's letter is an extreme and perhaps atypical situation, but it highlights the range of creative ways one might consider using to involve absent parents.

Educating the Family About the Clinician's
Approach to Therapeutic Work

It is very important that families coming for psychotherapeutic interventions regarding their teenagers being involved in adolescent gangs be given a very careful education about the psychotherapeutic process. Clinicians should not assume that their role has been explained to the family in any detailed way or that the family fully understands how mental health professionals function differently from law enforcement officers or school personnel. It is vital that therapists who will be working with gang members and associated family members offer some very basic understanding of this approach to the work. This can take many forms, but I recommend that a detailed written statement be given to families even before they come to the first appointment. The benefit of providing them with written information before the first appointment is that it allows them to review the therapist's ground rules and theoretical positions even before attending their first session and as often as is necessary. Relative to the issue of keeping the first appointment, it might be a good idea to call both parents, particularly if they do not live in the same household, to remind them of the appointment once it has been scheduled.

The matter of scheduling the first appointment is of clinical significance. Some clinicians prefer that individuals coming for services call to schedule their first appointment, according to the rule that "clients should never have done for them things that they can do for themselves." In working with gang-affiliated youths, there may be a need to be more flexible. With court-referred individuals and families, in the interest of saving time it may be necessary to provide the court with a series of time slots that are available to clients. The families are then given the responsibility of scheduling the first appointment hour. Whatever approach is used, it is vital that families gain an understanding very early in the process of how the clinician who will be working with them operates.

The Setting for the Work

The clinical issue of the setting for the work is slightly different from the practical issues of how much it costs to get to the office or how far it is from the client's home. Here, my emphasis is on the mental representations and psychological changes that arise as a result of the setting. For example, asking a client to travel forty-five minutes by bus to get to an appointment has both practical and clinical significance. It is a time commitment for clients (practical issue), but it is also an issue of how they feel about others making such demands of them (clinical issue). It is issues at the latter level of analysis that the following section raises. What does it mean to a client that the therapist has an office in an exclusive part of town? Or is there some implicit valuing of the mental health work because it is in an exclusive neighborhood?

The setting in which the work occurs should be one that is conducive to families becoming invested in the process of the psychotherapy. There are arguments on both sides of the issue concerning the proximity of the treatment site to family's place of residence. One argument is that providing services in a "community setting" is likely to increase families' feelings of being valued by the therapist and hence valuing what the therapist has to offer. This line of logic also suggests that being involved in the community in which a family lives gives the clinicians a better sense of the strengths, weaknesses, resources, and issues with which the family has to contend on a daily basis. Another argument for local community settings as intervention places of choice is that this reduces the time and financial resources that the family has to spend to participate in the process of therapy.

Arguments on the other side of the issue suggest that families should be seen in whatever setting the clinician normally operates. In some situations, clinicians are not situated in the communities in which families reside. To work with such a clinician means that family members have to travel outside of their home community to perhaps a new part of town. Before a definitive decision is reached concerning the accessibility or interpretations that families make of the setting in which the work occurs, the issue should be discussed directly with them. Some families are reluctant to travel significant distances to maintain the relationship with their clinician. They often complain of the travel time and the logistics of making arrangements to get to the office as yet one more burden that intrudes on their limited emotional and financial resources. Adolescents occasionally boast that their "shrink" has an office in the upscale portion of town. Again, before concluding what images the family has of the setting or how it will impact the treatment, it is necessary for this to become an issue of discussion early in the work relationship. A middle-ground solution in providing services to poor families or families who live a great distance from the clinician's office is to alternate sites for work. Some weeks, the clinician visits the family in its home, thereby gaining the valuable insights that come with home visit, but other weeks the family comes to the clinician's office, making whatever arrangements are necessary to keep such appointments.

Understanding the Family's Level of Functioning

It is very difficult for a therapist to obtain a good sense of what and how much families understand about mental health services without actually interacting with them. Thus, it is essential to assess family members' knowledge in this area before establishing a definitive program of intervention for working with a gang-affiliated family. A good clinical understanding of the dynamics of the family will help determine whether the members show up for an evaluation. This is to be distinguished from the dynamics of the family as an ongoing, evolving family unit that result from an intensive psychotherapeutic work relationship. I suggest that clinicians have some direct interaction with all adult members of the gang-affiliated youngster's family who may avail themselves of the opportunity to come for a family-oriented intervention. Obviously, the two parents and any stepparents should be contacted directly and encouraged to participate. Often, an absent parent will find it a source of validation, if not vindication, when a "doctor" calls to invite him or her to attend the family sessions. Direct contact with adult members of the family also minimizes the likelihood of a miscommunication relative to the purposes of the intervention or procedural matters. Sometimes, in contacting extended-family members who may be willing to participate as supportive family members, a clinician is able to gather valuable insights and pieces of information that may not be volunteered by the identified client or the parents. It is vital that in making contacts with auxiliary members of the family, the clinician gain some sense of these individuals' availability to participate in the ongoing work. With some individuals, such invitations may potentially raise ethical issues concerning who should be privy to the information relative to an adjudicated adolescent being referred for professional services. One way out of this potentially thorny issue is to ask the parents and identified client who they would like to invite to the first large family meeting and to ask their permission for clearance to contact these individuals directly. Of course, this permission arrangement should not be used to exclude absent parents who are still legally responsible for an adolescent. Such absent parents should automatically be contacted because of their continuing legal status with the child.

Beyond Cultural Sensitivity

The issue of cultural sensitivity among clinicians has been the subject of much discussion. Frequently, these discussions are focused on cultural sensitivity as an issue that is exclusively an ethnic minority concern. Nothing could be further the truth. In recent years, many White Americans have spent a great deal of time and energy searching for their ethnic roots. Some of these efforts lead to a reconceptualization of their histories and a deeper understanding of how families are affected by historical events. Cultural sensitivity, as a dimension of clinical interventions, is often overly simplified and invoked as reasons why clinicians and other persons working with families are not confronted for inappropriate behavior.

One of the issues that must be addressed in thinking of cultural sensitivity as a component of clinical work is the exact definition of the phrase.

Antisocial individuals frequently explain wildly inappropriate behaviors as being cultural expressions indigenous to their ethnic community. This kind of normalizing of pathological behavior is a syndrome that is likely to occur quite often with gang adolescents of color.

Cultural sensitivity also becomes a critical factor used by clients to gauge a clinician's level of "genuineness" in the treatment process. Clinicians who are judged to be unacceptable in this regard by clients are likely to be dismissed as exploitative and not interested in the well-being of the clients. Instead of sharing their feelings about this matter directly, many clients simply drop out of the therapeutic work or behave in passive-aggressive ways toward the therapist. These kinds of behaviors ultimately lead to the referred individuals and their families remaining in a state of dysfunctional and maladaptive behavior. One of the things that clinicians who anticipate working with gang members of color and their families must anticipate is the likelihood that they will be challenged on cultural awareness and sensitivity. This applies to clinicians of color also. In preparation for working with families from ethnic groups different from their own, clinicians need to carefully think about how they will respond to questions about credibility without appearing overly defensive or evasive.

Attention Span

Attention span is an issue that I introduce here simply because it is likely to appear as a problem in working with gang members who have documented histories of learning disabilities. It is an issue that a clinician must consider in devising the duration of appointments with an identified client and his or her family members. There is some evidence that in work with families of color, approaches other than the traditional fifty-minute treatment hour in a one-to-one modality should be considered. A clinical axiom that should be kept in mind in thinking about the attention span of troubled youngsters and their families is the idea that the closer people move to the source of their angst and dissonance, the more disturbed they are likely to become and the more they will lose their ability to remain focused.

Incentive for Attending

Motivation for attending therapy sessions is an issue that is not uniquely associated with gang adolescents and their families. It represents the more global concern that many helping professionals have to address in providing services to troubled individuals and their families. Why does the individual want to participate in the proposed intervention? Even more basic, does the individual want to participate in the proposed intervention? In many situations concerning gang adolescents, the incentive for participation is primarily to avoid prosecution in a court of law. Even in such situations, there is hope that the therapeutic alliance will enable clients to obtain new insights into their behavior and their impact on the lives of others. In some cases, the incentives for attending interventions and therapeutic work are not so obvious but become more apparent as the work unfolds. I suggest here that a clinician anticipating work with gang adolescents seriously consider ways of assessing how and why an individual is committed to engaging in psychotherapeutic work. Once answers are obtained for these questions, it is incumbent upon the clinician to use them as part of the therapeutic work. The goal should be to move the individual to new and higher developmental stages where appropriate.

Outcome and Follow-Up

One of the most difficult dimensions of working with gang adolescents and their families is to determine the efficacy of interventions. Clinicians anticipating working in this area are encouraged to think about what will be their indicators that the interventions have been more than minimally effective. Even for successful interventions, the amount of growth and development that is likely to occur in the lives of troubled youth and their families may be significant. The big question in this area is, Whose indicators will be applied as evidence of progress and by what standards? I urge clinicians to look beyond the oft reported rate of recidivism as an indicator of the effectiveness of treatment. Recidivism rates simply represent the frequency with which people are apprehended for being suspected of committing socially unacceptable acts. It could be argued that recidivists are people who are not very skilled at committing their acts. They get caught repeatedly. With the passage of time, many individuals who continue to engage in illegal and problematic behaviors become more skilled and proficient at eluding law enforcement officers. As a result, those individuals do not reappear in the literature and are often mistakenly assumed to have terminated their socially inappropriate behaviors.

10

The Family
Intervention Project

History of the FIP

In the early 1980s, the city of Denver, Colorado, experienced a significant increase in the level of adolescent gang activity. Gangs had operated in the city for a number of years but never in such an intense and disruptive way. Relatively easy access to firearms and widespread abuse of drugs made gangs a volatile and deadly problem. No one was quite sure what to do. Increased law enforcement efforts only served to increase the number of youngsters incarcerated and did nothing to suppress the recruitment of young people into gangs. Mental health practitioners were called on for clinical insight into the cycle of escalating gang involvement. They too were baffled as to what needed to be done. After a series of conferences, think tanks, and workshops, it became apparent that one approach to intervention with gang-affiliated youths was to make use of their families of origin. At the time it seemed like a novel revelation; now seen in retrospect, it was a statement of how program planners and policymakers had been blinded by their own good intentions.

Few people involved in the dialogue about what to do about the gang problem had considered the issue of utilizing the families of gang-affiliated or at-risk families as the basis of interventions. This was surprising, given that several people had implicated families as a causative factor in explaining why young people join gangs. The presiding judge finally decided that families had to be involved if the social systems of the community were to be effective in helping youth who had already joined gangs and those who were at risk for recruitment. An intervention model, designed by a group of mental health professionals to provide clinical assessment data and psychotherapy (intervention) process material, was developed. Aside from its usefulness to clinicians, the model was conceptualized as a way to help families and their gang adolescents reexamine their commonalities and differences. Particular emphasis was placed on values as opposed to behaviors.

The project was sponsored by the Denver municipal courts and probation department. Adjudicated youth and their parents were ordered to appear in court for two morning workshops. Most of the participants were adolescents of color (African American and Latino) from single-parent homes. Part I of the program consisted of an educational component designed to increase awareness of gang-related activities in Denver. The second part of the program closely approximated multiple-family therapy and was created for the purpose of helping families work through real problems. Throughout both parts of the program, clinicians assessed all of the family members, especially the gang adolescents, in the areas of affect, behavior, and cognition. Results from those assessments formed the basis for postworkshop feedback and prescriptive planning. After several revisions, this program came to be known as the Family Intervention Project (FIP). The resulting model was built on families struggling with gang-affiliated youth, but it can be applied effectively to any variety of at-risk youths and their families. In this chapter, I present the FIP model in its final form. The exercises of the FIP are presented along with commentary about how to analyze the results and integrate the analysis into clinical decisions about the participants.

The FIP Model

Rationale

The family of origin is the first setting of socialization for children and adolescents. Lessons learned in that context become the foundation on which all other lessons are superimposed. Basic skills as well as the capacity for new learning are acquired in the family of origin. It is often forgotten that adolescents who are affiliated with gangs frequently have had an early period of fairly normal socialization. Something happens along the developmental path and the adolescent goes awry, ultimately turning to the gang in an attempt to get psychological needs met. Popular images and portrayals of gang youths have created the lore that gangs are populated with social misfits who are, at best, marginalized by peers and the larger society. This has been shown not to be the case (Jankowski, 1991; Monti, 1994).

Many family members of gang adolescents exhibit atypical behavior and thinking relative to their gang-affiliated family member. A common response is denial, insisting that the family member is not associated with a gang when there is overwhelming evidence to the contrary. For a variety of reasons, many parents find it easier to distance themselves from their gang-affiliated children than to accept the reality of their children's participation in gang activities. When confronted with the contradiction between their attributions to their gang adolescent and the reality of his or her behavior, parents often resort to values incongruence as an explanation.

The values of gang adolescents are assumed to deviate from those of parents and the society at large. The reality, however, is that some research studies have shown that gang-affiliated youths, despite their behavioral proclivities, verbalize values that are prosocial (Branch, 1995; Jankowski, 1991). A distinction must be made between values and behaviors. The manner in which an individual behaves in a limited setting is not necessarily reflective of what he or she thinks or believes. Therapy operates on a principle that is not necessarily true. Hence, sociopaths, liars, and good actors deceive unsuspecting therapists into believing they have altered their behavior, based on what happens in the therapy session. In reality, they have not changed. They are good actors. Socially unacceptable behavior on the part of adolescents is inevitably the result of the interaction of many factors, including peer group affiliation patterns, substance abuse, alienation from the educational system, dysfunctional patterns of communication in the family, low self-esteem, financial stress, and so on.

The FIP is predicated on the idea that gang adolescents and their families share many commonalities that are often dormant. By having the family reunite in a safe, supportive environment, it is felt that they can engage in an introspective process, with assistance from clinicians. More important, it is believed that families need to rediscover their shared values and develop actions to accomplish meeting their needs as individuals and as families. Early experience with the FIP suggested that families are more responsive to other families with shared dilemmas than to professional clinicians, resulting in the design of multiple-family groupings. It appears that families are more apt to consider their adolescents' needs when they view other families, whom they perceive to be like themselves, struggling with adolescents around a similar dilemma. A major goal of the FIP is to create situations in which families can interact with other families and engage in community problem-solving around the misbehavior of adolescents.

Assumptions

Many clinical assumptions are readily observable in the FIP model. Perhaps the most pervasive of these is the belief that gang adolescents and their families have the capacity to make significant changes that are in their best interests. There is no empirical support to substantiate this critical assumption except a history of working with troubled families and clinical observations of their ability to do things for themselves. Similarly, there is a belief that taking this position with families has a therapeutic effect. It sends the message that the family has buried somewhere within its boundaries the ability to make things better. It is important to send this message to families that otherwise are in a state of less than optimal functioning. Urging families to look inward has the potential of empowering them. This approach is in direct contrast to the more common approach with gang adolescents and their families. Historically, the interventions of choice have been to isolate the out-of-control adolescent from the family, often eliminating any opportunity for family healing. The "isolating to rehabilitate" approach also sends pejorative messages to the adolescents and the family about the family's ability to help the troubled adolescent.

Another assumption of the FIP model is that families want things to be better. In the development of the model, all of the participating families were court ordered to attend. Once they actually arrived at the program, it became apparent that none of them wanted to continue in their fractured state. It is often problematic for families to consistently show behaviorally that they want their situation to improve. One of the goals of the program is to help family members recognize their shared goals and values, including the desire that things should be better in the family.

All participants in the program are assumed to have something of value to contribute. Everyone is invited to share in the exercises and to share his or her feelings about the exercises. Conventional family roles of hierarchy are suspended within the context of the FIP. This is a new experience for many families and has the potential of causing some dissonance that may become an interference in the groups.

A final assumption of the FIP is that the at-risk behavior being exhibited by the identified client, the adolescent, is symptomatic of deeper and more pervasive family dynamics. Because of that, it is necessary for the entire family to be involved to rectify the situation. It is important that the focus is on the family system as a totality rather than on the behaviors of the adolescent. All members of the family, including a parent who may be living in another household, should be invited to attend.

Getting Started

All of the behaviors emitted by families relative to participation in the FIP are significant clinical indicators. If examined carefully and consistently, those behaviors hold valuable clues for understanding the dynamics of the families and their troubled youngsters.

In its original staging, the FIP was conducted in the juvenile court of Denver. Anyone entering the courtroom must pass through a metal detector. This rule, of course, was applied to families participating in the FIP also. Needless to say, it created a point of conflict for some participants. They refused to be screened. Not only did they refuse to comply, but they stood outside the courtroom and taunted others who did submit to the screening. Ultimately, all persons who refused to comply, actually very few in number, left the building and the program began. Some of the reasons articulated for noncompliance with the screening included "invasion of privacy," "illegal," and so on. These verbalizations were interpreted by the clinicians as resistance. The defiant behavior created conflict between the facilitators and the families. The result of this conflict was to create an ongoing cycle of anger that made it difficult, if not impossible, for the defiant participants to make themselves open to the program. The resistive behaviors emitted before entering the courtroom also caused dissonance and disruption for other participants. Perhaps, these are the sort of dynamics that the offending parties generate with regularity in the context of their families. Above all else, the behavior had the effect of drawing special attention to otherwise disregarded individuals.

I suggest that clinicians planning an FIP-type program should be especially observant of behaviors emitted by participants *before* they actually arrive at the scene of the program. Hostile responses to letters of invitation to participate, re-creation of arguments between clinicians and clients, and accusations of racism and classism levied against "the system" are common ways in which anxious and avoidant clients are likely to act out their feelings. Upon observing such behaviors, clinicians are cautioned against making interpretations to the client. Such a response would only serve to further agitate the client. Rather, notations of such behavior should be made. Opportunities for sharing these observations occur in the first two hours of the FIP process. Clinicians should also note whether the client is willing to share feelings and behaviors relative to being invited to participate in the FIP.

Once everyone arrives at the designated work area, the dynamics continue, even without the formal exercises. Seating patterns and spontaneous dialogue among participants provide the facilitators with critical information about patterns of alliance. Table 10.1 lists the schedule of program activities presently used in the Denver program.

The FIP Exercises

Registration and Orientation

The opening activities provide the group facilitators with an opportunity to introduce themselves to the participants. The families are given an opportunity to share as much—or as little—as they would like about themselves and their perceptions of why they have been referred to the FIP. Everyone in attendance should be given an opportunity to share.

A common occurrence in the greetings period is that many family members express anger and resentment about having been directed, or even invited, to attend the program. Sometimes, these disclosures can be quite visceral and passionate, with a high potential for adversely affecting the other participants. It is helpful for the facilitators to acknowledge such feelings

TABLE 10.1   Activities of the Family Intervention Project

8:30–9:00	Registration and informal interactions with facilitators
9:00–10:00	Welcome and orientation
	"Why Are We Here?" exercise
10:00–10:15	Coffee/smoke break
10:15–10:45	"Black Delinquent Gang Youth Values" exercise (Individual performance)
10:45–11:30	"Black Delinquent Gang Youth Values" exercise (Group performance)
11:30–12:00	Debrief "Black Delinquent Gang Youth Values" exercise
12:00–1:15	Lunch
1:15–1:30	Review of the morning's activities
1:30–2:00	Discuss threats to good communication
2:00–2:30	Teach rules of good communication
	Discussion
2:30–2:45	Break
2:45–3:15	Practice sessions: good communication
3:15–4:00	Family work sessions
4:00–4:30	Debrief afternoon activities
	Planning the next steps

from participants and to gently encourage them to try to give the program the benefit of the doubt.

"Why Are We Here?" Exercise

The "Why Are We Here?" exercise is designed to help establish the goals and objectives to be accomplished over the course of the day. It should be conducted in one large gathering place. At face value, the question may seem rhetorical, if not insulting, but it has proved to be a direct and useful way for facilitators to get a complete understanding of participants' perceptions of what is likely to happen during the course of the day. Most people answer this question in a way that is positively correlated with their fantasy or hopes for the day. The reasons that family members offer for being present provide valuable insights into their cognitive processing of the letter of invitation or verbal interactions with the facilitators. Cognitive slippage (e.g., "Forgot why we're here"), loose associations, cognitive intrusions, and other forms of cognitive impairments become very pronounced at this point.

Often, before everyone has been given a chance to share on this issue, conflict ensues between individual family members, within and across families. This frequently takes the form of people arguing or being negatively responsive to statements of "why we are here" that are verbalized by other members of the program. Different groups require different amounts of time to come to even semi-closure on this issue. In developing and piloting the model, one hour proved to be the minimum time necessary to arrive at a general consensus as to why the group had been assembled. It is not uncommon for members of the group, because of their own angst concerning their presence and the lack of closure on the question, to angrily confront the group leader. Confrontation may take the form of challenging statements, complex questions, and even negative interpretations about the possible utility of the FIP. Such verbal exchanges usually come to closure with fairly good results when the leader can summarize the variety of reasons offered by individual group members and reframe them. The rewording, of course, should match the stated objectives of the FIP.

After "Why Are We Here?" the participants should be separated by age. Parents form one large group, adolescents another. If there are young children below the age of eight, they should be separated into a third group. This group of younger children is taken to another room where they reflect further on their perceptions of why their family has come to this place and what will happen during the day. Kinetic family drawings and story telling are effective techniques with the younger children.

"Black Delinquent Gang Youth Values" Exercise

In the parent and adolescent groups, all members are given a copy of the exercise "Black Delinquent Gang Youth Values." Individuals are encouraged to listen very carefully to the following instructions:

> The following list of 13 images were given to a large sample of individual Black delinquent gang youth. They were asked to rank these images in the order in which they valued them, with most valued at number 1 and least valued at number 13. Your task is to rank these images as you predict the Black delinquent gang youth did. Place number 1 by the highest valued image, number 2 by the next, and so on to number 13.

The items included on the rankings are sticks by his friends in a fight; has a steady job washing and greasing cars; saves his money; is a good fighter with a tough reputation; knows where to sell what he steals; gets his kicks by using drugs; stays cool and keeps to himself; works for good grades at school; has good connections to avoid trouble with the law; likes to read good books; likes to spend his spare time hanging on the corner with his friends; makes money by pimping and other illegal hustles; shares his money with his friends. Box 10.1 shows the decision form given to each participant.

Each adult and adolescent attending the FIP is encouraged to complete these rankings based on their perceptions of how Black delinquent gang members would rank the items. Once all participants indicate that they understand the directions, they should be allowed to work individually on the rankings. Participants should be given as long as they need to complete the

BOX 10.1   Black Delinquent Gang Youth Values

Name _____

Group _____

DECISION FORM

Instruction: The following list of 13 images was given to a large sample of individual Black delinquent gang youth. They were asked to rank these images in the order in which they valued them, with most valued at number 1 and least valued at number 13. Your task is to rank these images as you predict the Black delinquent gang youth did. Place number 1 by the highest valued image, number 2 by the next, and so on down to number 13.

_____ Sticks by his friends in a fight.

_____ Has a steady job washing and greasing cars.

_____ Saves his money.

_____ Is a good fighter with a tough reputation.

_____ Knows where to sell what he steals.

_____ Gets his kicks by using drugs.

_____ Stays cool and keeps to himself.

_____ Works for good grades at school.

_____ Has good connections to avoid trouble with the law.

_____ Likes to read good books.

_____ Likes to spend his spare time hanging on the corner with his friends.

_____ Makes money by pimping and other illegal hustles.

_____ Shares his money with his friends.

SOURCE: Short & Strodbeck, 1965. Original exercise and forms created by Jerry Spiegal.

task. When everyone has completed the ranking task, the participants are instructed to rejoin their age group. Referring to the same list of Black delinquent youth values, each group pools its members' understandings to arrive at a group consensus. The instructions for the group exercise are presented in Box 10.2. The group summary sheet is presented in Table 10.2.

The "Black Delinquent Gang Youth Values" exercise provides insight into perceptions that adolescents and adults have of gang members and what is important to them. Following is a brief description of how to make further use of these two approaches to the exercise.

The adult group should list its rankings for the value images followed by the adolescent group. Sometimes, there is a need to have two groups of adolescents. In that case, each group should indicate its listings of the rankings. Following these sets of rankings, the group leader should list the rankings given by the normative sample of Black gang youths on which this exercise was based. Adult and adolescent responses virtually never match. The rank-

BOX 10.2 Black Delinquent Gang Youth Values, Decision by Consensus

Instructions: This is an exercise in group decision making. Your group is to employ the method of *Group Consensus* in reaching its decision. This means that the prediction for each of the 13 images value ranked by the individual Black delinquent gang youth must be agreed upon by each group member before it becomes a part of the group decision. Consensus is difficult to reach. Therefore, not every ranking will meet with everyone's complete *approval*. Try, as a group, to make each ranking one on which all group members can at least partially agree. Here are some guides to use in reaching consensus.

1. Avoid arguing your own individual judgments. Approach the task on the basis of logic.
2. Avoid changing your mind only in order to reach agreement and avoid conflict. Support only solutions with which you are able to agree somewhat, at least.
3. Avoid conflict-reducing techniques such as majority vote, averaging, or trading in reaching decisions.
4. View differences of opinion as helpful rather than as a hindrance in decision making.

On the Group Summary Sheet, place the individual rankings made earlier by each group member. You will be given the time limit in which your consensus decision must be made.

---

ings provided by the normative sample are rarely replicated by adolescent groups, but adolescents tend to produce results closer to the list produced by the normative sample than the lists produced by their parents.

After each group has been given an opportunity to inspect the other groups' responses and the normative sample's responses, the participants discuss the exercise. There are a number of approaches that facilitators can take to the discussion. The first step is to ask the adults to talk about how they came to the decisions that they arrived at in the group. Invariably, participants talk about not believing the rankings provided by the normative sample, simply because "Likes to read good books" is listed as the number 1 value. The focus in this part of the exercise is intended to remain on the adult group. It is occasionally necessary to ask the adults to reflect on and deconstruct their approach to the task before they can clearly understand their behavior and its results (e.g., the rankings). While discussing the results of their group's deliberations, many adults come to understand that they interpreted the exercise in a manner slightly different from the instructions. People often interpret the exercise as a statement about the behaviors of adolescents, as opposed to images that they value. This is evidenced by many adults saying that most gang youths that they know do not even attend

TABLE 10.2   Group Summary Sheet, Individual Predictions

	1	2	3	4	5	6	7	*Group Prediction*
Sticks by his friends in a fight.								
Has a steady job washing and greasing cars.								
Saves his money.								
Knows where to sell what he steals.								
Is a good fighter with a tough reputation.								
Gets his kicks by using drugs.								
Stays cool and keeps to himself.								
Works for good grades at school.								
Has good connections to avoid trouble with the law.								
Likes to read good books.								
Likes to spend his spare time hanging on the corner with his friends.								
Makes money by pimping and other illegal hustles.								
Shares his money with his friends.								

school and therefore must not value it. Sometimes, adults defend their responses by saying they do not know any gang members as their familiarity with gang culture is very limited. These creative forms of resistance should not gain them a reprieve from the exercise. A similar procedure is employed in analyzing the responses produced by the adolescents, trying to understand what was the cognitive basis of the answers they produced and what procedures they utilized in the group to produce the rankings offered as the group's final consensus.

A second layer of analysis to this exercise has to do with group members reconstructing and verbalizing the psychological dimensions of their participation in the group consensus exercise. This is perhaps the most vital part of the FIP. Careful observation of who participates in the group actively and how others respond to their participation can provide invaluable information for the synthesis of clinical data. In both adult and adolescent groups, occasionally an individual's response is overruled by the group and that person becomes angry and withdraws from the rest of the activity. Conversely, there may be individuals who are reluctant to offer any responses to the group. The reasons for their nonparticipation may be unclear. Uncovering these reasons should be a goal for the facilitators.

After the "Black Delinquent Gang Youth Values" exercise is discussed, the young children are brought back into the room. All are thanked for their active participation in the morning program. Lunch follows. It is important to have a communal lunch activity with a mixing of FIP staff and family members.

The "Black Delinquent Gang Youth Values" exercise has been used in a variety of settings, almost invariably with the same results: Adult and adolescent group responses are inversely correlated. Would the adults rate the gang members differently if the task were presented in a different format? What is the role of social factors (e.g., age, gender) in affecting how others are perceived? Do the same variables affect adult and adolescent response patterns in the same way? In the review of the morning's activities scheduled immediately after lunch, it usually becomes overwhelmingly clear that the quality of communication directly influences the outcome. Communication skills, or the lack thereof, are highlighted as part of the reason for the incongruence of the adult and adolescent responses in the activities of the morning. A learning point for this review exercise is that because of poorly focused communication, individuals often misread the values and behaviors of others, as evidenced by the responses to the "Black Delinquent Gang Youth Values" exercise.

Communication Skills

The afternoon portion of the workshop is intended as a session for participants to practice good communication skills. This, of course, requires that they are able to observe and evaluate their current behaviors in this area. The history of a relationship is also a factor in shaping the quality of interactions in the present. Conflict-ridden relationships are often the cause of incomplete or inadequate communication. When the communication is incomplete or not fully reflective of the sender's intentions, receivers often make poor decisions. The purpose of good communication skills is to eliminate the frequency of miscommunication and poor decisions. A structured exercise focusing on rules of good communicating is offered at this point to help families better understand the concept of good communication skills. The five rules of good communication given to the participants are:

Rule 1. Offer ownership for our own statements. Use "I" statements to show personal responsibility for what is said.

Rule 2. Never make statements for a person who is not available to state his or her position.

Rule 3. Keep focused on the issue at hand.
Rule 4. Only one person speaks at a time.
Rule 5. Make certain if you are the sender of the message that the receiver
understands exactly what you meant.

These rules are read aloud to the participants. Each participant is given a 4×6 index card and a pencil. The rules of good communication are then dictated for the participants in the workshop to write them on their index cards. The purpose of this didactic exercise is also to assess the writing and general language skills of the individuals present in the workshop. If it becomes apparent that a youngster, or even an adult, is having major difficulty with the wording or understanding the rules, this should be noted. Once written, the rules are read back by different members of the participating audience. Where there are errors in recall, the facilitators should help with corrections.

At the conclusion of this exercise, a fifteen-minute break is given. After returning from the break, all members of the group are asked to participate in practicing good communication skills. The exercise requires that every child work with an adult. If there are significantly more adolescents than adults, then two or three of them can work with one or two adults. It is extremely important that participants, for this exercise, are not permitted to work with their blood relatives. The exercise involves small groups composed of one or two adults and two or three adolescents working on a hypothetical problem. The facilitators stress that this is a hypothetical problem, but the members of the work groups are encouraged to be themselves and not to spend time role playing. Once each group draws a card describing a problem situation from a hat or other container, it moves apart to work on solving its problem.

Each group is given up to thirty minutes for problem solving. The facilitators visit with different groups and encourage participants to make use of the rules of good communicating. The most common violations of those rules are that individuals, usually adolescents, want to make attributions to their parents or some other family member who is not a part of the problem-solving group. At the conclusion of the practice, each group is asked to report its experience to the larger group.

With few exceptions, all groups succeed at the task. In fact, it is very common for adolescents and adults alike to talk about how easy it was to work with their assigned partners. This report usually is met with chagrin and disbelief by the blood relatives of the speaker. This unique experience is deconstructed by helping the group think about why everyone was able to experience success in the group. What was different about working in this group from when they tried to do problem solving at home?

As this exercise draws to a close, one or another participant usually indicates that this experience is "all phony," not real-world problem solving, which just does not happen that easily. This is actually a desired response because it often moves the group into a task about solving a "real" problem. At the conclusion of this discussion of the staged problem solving, a facilitator announces that all present *can* follow the rules of good communicating, as evidenced by their recent behavior. The facilitator then recommends that the group work on real problems. This leads to the last activity of the day, utilizing communication skills in the real family context.

Utilizing Communication Skills in the Real Family Context

The final exercise is designed to give each family an opportunity to use all the communication skills participants have heard about during the course of the day. The exercise provides numerous opportunities for family members to reflect on their proclivity for making attributions of values based on behavior and their newfound understanding of their own dynamics in situations of problem solving. Families are reconstituted along blood lines, and each child and parent present is expected to participate in a family discussion of a real problem.

A forty-five-minute period is set aside for practicing skills in the real-family context. At the conclusion of this period, if any family members want to share what it felt like to do this level of problem solving, they are given an opportunity to do so. If no one is willing to share, the facilitator moves on to summarizing the events of the day. All participants are thanked for having invested a significant amount of time and energy in the interest of improving family dynamics. The sequence of follow-up events as determined by the agency or institution sponsoring the FIP is then explained in detail.

At the conclusion of the FIP, families are given clinical feedback by the facilitators. On the basis of the clinical impressions the families make on the workshop leaders, and in consultation with the probation department, a follow-up plan is devised. Typically, such plans encompass the following options: (a) refer the family for therapy if there is clinical evidence that the family has the capacity to benefit from therapy; (b) request additional diagnostic procedures such as drug screening; (c) seek additional psychological diagnostic information on the family; and (d) in extreme situations, request temporary out-of-home placement for adolescents and children deemed to be at risk for abuse by their parents.

Variations on the FIP

The family intervention project model is offered here as one of multiple-family work in a single setting. It requires a high level of clinical skills on the part of the facilitators and has some inherent professional liabilities associated with the work. For example, it is the responsibility of the facilitators at the end of this type of activity to be able to attest to the fact that no child or family member is in danger based on feelings or activities that may have been created as a result of participating in the FIP. This requires a close clinical assessment or check-in with all of the participants before they leave the site of the work. Such clinical assessments may extend beyond the skill level of many individuals who may be interested in adapting parts of the model for use in their setting. The following comments are offered as a variation on the FIP that can be used in a variety of settings.

1. In school settings, the idea of multiple individuals working collaboratively on issues of gangs and family conflicts is one that can be recreated. It is highly advantageous for children and adolescents to talk about things that bother them as a way to defuse their need to act on those things. I suggest that school counselors or teachers arrange small groups in which young people are encouraged to openly express their fears, concerns, and other feelings relative to violence in their communities. This should be an ongoing activity, under good circumstances, not simply a response when there is a crisis in a community.

2. The clinical work of the group in a school could come to be a part of a "social curriculum" in which students are asked to write essays or discuss current events related to violence and gangs. The intent of this openness of discussion, again, is to defuse any smoldering feelings and to eliminate the rumor mill.

3. From an ecological perspective (Garbarino, 1995), the socially toxic environment in which many children live and grow can be somewhat counteracted by looking at their worlds from a systems perspective. This suggests that talking about macrosystemic views about war and violence can help children understand that much of the violence that exists around them is part of a social milieu and not a response to them and their families.

4. The lessons that children learn from the FIP model can be related to the social studies and current events curriculum in a school setting. Children could be encouraged to talk about the impacts of wars in various parts of the world and to try to assume the perspective of the children who have to live through those wars. Other examples could be drawn from reading books that children have written about wars or narratives of children who have been captured and taken off into slavery or captivity.

5. Work can be done with parents around issues of violence and gangs in the school setting as well. It is important that in all variations of this work, individuals be considered as a part of an enclave and not made to feel alone in their struggles. Small group meetings of parents to talk about issues of violence in a nonreactionary fashion and to share information about resources available in the community is an activity that a school counselor or an assistant principal can conduct in an ongoing way.

6. Miniature variations of the FIP model can be staged in a school context. The focus could be on gangs and violence or it could be on children's initial adjustments to changes that take place in the school community. The intent is for multiple families to work jointly, learning from each other and even modeling for other families that are less developed in their ability to be introspective and self-sufficient.

Probation Department and Law Enforcement Efforts

Probation and law enforcement are areas that are often difficult for families of accused offenders to engage. This difficulty is understandable, since law enforcement and probation departments usually have very clear prescriptions about what to do with accused offenders regarding specific offenses. Despite that prewritten script, judges and other professionals feel that law enforcement officers can make a significant impact in redirecting families and troubled adolescents. I suggest that the FIP model may be an approach that law enforcement and juvenile court programs can use as a way to filter information to constituents in the community. The collective gathering in the FIP model prevents families from feeling that they are being targeted. It also provides an opportunity to reach a larger number of people all at once. I offer the following specific recommendations regarding the use of the FIP in a law enforcement or corrections setting:

1. In working with troubled families it is important to have a mental health consultant available. This is not to suggest that law enforcement officers may not be able to handle the difficulties that may arise but offers the opportunity for a neutral third party to also give feedback to both parents and law enforcement officers.

2. The FIP model can serve as a forum for the identification of larger issues that a community may want to pursue with the police department. This can be accomplished through allowing individuals to make formal presentations and inviting others to offer statements of support or disagreement with the positions of the presenters.

3. In law enforcement variations of the FIP, facilitators may want to consider sharing with families their understanding of the developmental course that adolescents follow in moving from small petty offenses to major violations of social codes. I believe that law enforcement officers are ideally suited to share this kind of information and to do so without being too evangelical.

4. A law enforcement variation on the FIP model may be designed to provide information for parents about getting help for troubled adolescents. Such an approach would require families to work on issues through the FIP

process but culminate with factual information relative to resources available in the community that could be shared with families attending the program.

It is suggested that the FIP model is one of several approaches to having families work conjointly with other families sharing similar difficulties. It is felt that such an approach helps to create a sense of connection and empowerment that many families struggling with out-of-control adolescents do not have.

11

Research and Evaluation

In many quarters, the word research is a bad word. Negative feelings about research are so intense that often it is difficult to conduct a rational and objective discussion about the topic. The reasons for these reactions are varied, but frequently they can be accounted for by a lack of understanding of the concept of research, bad experiences with research and researchers, an inability to distinguish between good and poor research, or an inability to see the practical utility of research. Because of these and related issues the metaphorical baby, in this case research, is thrown out with the bathwater—misgivings about the research process. In an effort to save the baby, here I examine some common misgivings about research and evaluation. I hope to give readers a new appreciation of the value of research after reading this chapter. In particular, I will show how the absence of clinical research is partly responsible for the lack of substantial progress in rehabilitating gang-affiliated adolescents and their families.

In this chapter, I show how research can be instrumental in evaluating the efficacy of clinical intervention programs designed to help gang adolescents. The absence of appropriate research paradigms for use in this area is a major problem. I critique current clinical paradigms and offer reasons why they are generally inadequate for use with gang adolescents and their families. Finally, I articulate the reasons for the near absence of a clinical outcome literature with this population. I cite the limited findings that exist.

Understanding Basic Research Concepts

Technically, research means to explore a topic and to make some level of comparison that aids in understanding the issue at hand. Typically, there have been two types of research, archival and empirical. *Archival research,* sometimes referred to as bibliographic, is concerned with reviewing existing information to illuminate an otherwise-unclear problem. Examples of archival research include looking for historical accounts of past events that might hold clues or critical pieces of information for dissecting a contemporary issue. Behavioral scientists make use of this type of research as a beginning point for empirical studies. In professional journals, archival research is often presented as literature reviews or background information. Such work can set the stage for launching an original study.

It is important to understand that archival research often becomes the basis for new knowledge that is flawed because the original findings or the methodology that led to them are flawed. It is generally accepted that juvenile delinquents are individuals who frequently live outside the boundaries of prevailing social mores. A researcher who looks back at historical sociological accounts of delinquents in urban settings in the United States in the 1920s and 1930s might come away with an impression that delinquents were overwhelmingly members of recently immigrated European families. That would be an accurate observation, but the findings themselves would not make any statements about why the groups were overrepresented in the findings or why people of color were not represented in the studies at all.

The real danger comes from, for example, repeatedly citing those findings as accurately and fully representative of life in another era in U.S. history and a solid foundation on which to build new archival research. The researcher should be careful not to take findings reported in older studies at face value. Many archival studies simply report findings as fact, depriving the researcher of the opportunity to reinterpret the author's findings. This is also a common problem with nonempirical archival studies. Empirical research may be guilty of the same shortcomings, but it does offer some opportunity for later researchers to decide how to interpret the data and decide if they accept the conclusions rendered by other researchers. In the current situation, the purpose of research would be to see if a clinical intervention is effective in facilitating the understanding of a gang-affiliated family or introducing change into a family system.

Empirical research refers to work that involves direct observations or measurements. This is the type of activity most individuals think about when they refer to research. The art of conducting empirical research dictates that the researcher collect data from subjects and then subject it to some type of systematic analysis. Inherent in the process is a belief that the measurements that are being analyzed are valid and reliable statements of the constructs that the researcher is interested in studying. Of course, these assumptions are not always met by researchers. In instances where there are violations of these very basic assumptions, researchers and the public can be misled badly. Precise standards for conducting research and establishing what is and what is not admissible evidence differ according to professional disciplines. I caution readers against accepting research findings as "fact" without investigating the standards by which the research was conducted and even the academic credentials of the investigator. Much misinformation is provided to the general public about a host of issues, adolescent gangs among them, by unqualified professionals masquerading as researchers.

To continue with a review of basic research concepts and how they might be of use to clinicians, the objective of a clinical intervention with a family is to make a difference in the lives of those who are subjected to it. The adjustment that is sought produces a change from the family members' old ways of behaving, collectively and individually. To determine the degree of change, and whether it was beneficial, a sampling of present and past behaviors needs to be measured, assessed, or reported in some objectively verifiable manner. Information on all members' behavior can be obtained from self-reports and preintervention assessment reports. In the case of gang adolescents, such reports come in the form of police reports, court judgments, and other documentation of their socially unacceptable behavior. These are evidence for a clinician to use in formulating an intervention plan. To create the possibility of being able to directly assess the impact of the intervention, it is necessary that the clinician complete a pretest, a statement of how the subjects behaved before the intervention. Again, the logic is that the intervention is eventually going to be introduced and may make a difference in the lives of the subjects. It is important that the pretest measure or procedures be relevant to the problem behaviors that will be addressed by the intervention. Not only should the pretest be relevant, it should also be known to be appropriate for use with the type of individuals constituting the family with whom the clinician is working.

Technical terms often used in assessing the pretest instrument include reliability and validity. They are not as ominous as they sound. *Reliability* refers to whether a measure consistently yields the same results when administered on several occasions. *Validity* refers to whether a measure really measures what it purports to measure. The level of reliability and validity that other researchers have found with a measure or procedure are usually reported in the instruction manual. For a detailed discussion of these two very important concepts, I refer readers to any standard psychological tests and measurement texts. Outstanding examples include Anastasi (1989) and Thorndike and Hagen (1986). The point here is that the clinician must have a clear assessment of how the clients are performing before intervening with them. There are a variety of ways in which this can be accomplished, some of them involving the clients directly and others that do not involve them. As noted earlier, often the preintervention assessment consists of reports from others about the family.

It is also important in situations in which others report about a family to determine whether the informant provided a fairly unbiased appraisal that could meet the tests of reliability and validity. In the absence of such confirmation, the clinician is likely to be operating on the basis of flawed information, much like the example of reading delinquency literature from other historical periods.

Another desirable attribute for an empirical investigation is *generalizability*. Generalizability is the level of confidence that researchers can make that their findings can be applied to other groups and settings. Before answering this question, however, it is necessary to ponder two closely related issues: How representative is the sample in the current study of the universal group to whom the findings might ultimately be applied? And to whom does the researcher wish to generalize the findings? If the answer to the latter question is a limited, small audience, then concerns about scientific rigor are greatly reduced. It is advisable that the researcher spend a fair amount of time pondering this issue before doing the clinical work and the ensuing research. Generalizabilty is a ground on which much clinical work is seriously challenged. In some situations, such questioning is not really necessary, since the researcher clearly articulated the limited audience to be addressed at the beginning of the investigation.

In the area of work with gang-affiliated families, generalizability across ethnic and cultural divisions is often problematic because of the different histories communities have had with gangs. The result is that different communities see the issues related to gangs very differently. Those differences can easily be observed in the levels and kinds of concerns parents express about the reality of gangs and the possibility that their child may be involved. This is not to say that the parents of any particular ethnic group are more likely to be accepting of the antisocial and destructive behaviors of gangs. I merely mean to show that different communities have idiosyncratically different strategies for confronting the reality of gangs.

Clearly, a host of questions need to be answered relative to the potential usefulness of an intervention. Perhaps most important is, Why do the intervention? Has it been shown to be useful with subjects like the family and adolescent in question? Is there archival evidence that suggests that such an intervention holds promise? Frequently the answer to all of the foregoing questions is no. That does not necessarily mean that the intervention should not be tried. It simply means that there will be nothing against which the outcomes can be compared, a necessary procedure for assessing the utility of a clinical intervention with any type of client.

The absence of a history of clinically oriented work with gang adolescents will make the issue of generalizability and having something against which results can be compared a problem for quite a while. Here, I assume that a clinician decides to proceed with a family-oriented intervention because information about the family's capacity to help a troubled adolescent is needed. The lack of archival research or even clinical anecdotal notes should not prevent the planning and execution of such an intervention that seems to make sense clinically. It does mean that the clinician may have to work harder in making sense of the results. The next step would be the choice of an intervention plan, a review of the assumptions that are inherent in that choice, and an understanding of how the intervention can be appraised (research and evaluation after it is completed).

The choice of an intervention plan should be made on the basis of what seems to make sense clinically and what fits with the clinician's skills and training. Trying out new techniques with high-risk, potentially volatile clients is a high-stakes proposition that should be undertaken only after carefully thinking through all of the possible ramifications.

Once the clinician has made a decision to intervene with a family, he or she should review what assumptions are inherently made about the intervention. The cardinal assumption is often that the intervention is appropriate. To test this assumption the clinician-researcher must be able to show that the intervention of choice has both validity and reliability. The absence of either or both means that the clinician must work harder to defend the decision to use the intervention. Sometimes, the only defense necessary for a new intervention is the observation that nothing has made a difference so far. Simply continuing on the tried, but untrue, path of stiff sentences in juvenile court coupled with monetary fines does not seem to significantly advance our understanding of, or ability to help, gang adolescents. There is value in both strategies, but they do not seem to be moving the field to a new level of insight about what drives gang adolescents psychologically.

What are the internal mechanisms that foster gang members' participation in random acts of violence? Do they have any sense of internal conflict about their new identity and how it brings them into conflict with their families, sometimes, and the larger society, often? What is the status of the mental functioning of a gang-affiliated youth? Is the family available as a psychological resource? These are all critical questions that can be answered, at least in part, through ongoing research into mental health–oriented interventions with gang adolescents.

A basic assumption of clinical work is that the answers to the hitherto unanswered questions can be discerned by engaging clients. It implicitly suggests that the tools of clinicians are adequate for penetrating the veneer under which families often find themselves. It further assumes that clinicians are competent. This constellation of assumptions needs to be examined very closely. Although mental health inquiries do reveal a lot about the inner life of individuals, many people are not receptive to such investigations. In addition, not everyone is ready to make use of them even when they are offered. Such resistances can be the result of conscious and deliberate effort or the by-product of unconscious processes. For example, families with members with major chemical dependencies have a difficult time engaging in mental health work. The chemical dependency and abuse behaviors unfortunately are sometimes not uncovered until the mental health work begins. Then, almost magically it becomes apparent why relationships and communication in the family have been so contorted for so long.

Resistance to mental health work can also manifest itself along racial and ethnic lines. Racial and ethnic isolation are often professed by families that find themselves in the dissonant position of having to work with a clinician from another racial or ethnic group. This is an awkward issue for many work dyads (family-clinician) to resolve because of the charged history of race and ethnicity in the United States. Both clinician and family are likely to have their own difficulties with the issues. This makes it even more difficult to talk about the issues. Despite that reality, the issues must be addressed. Otherwise, all parties involved lapse into the illusion of color blindness and the "Let's deny the obvious" syndrome. Allowing the denial to persist has implications for how truthful and probing family members may be in exploring the issues that brought them to the attention of the mental health professional. I do not suggest that the mental health hour should become the forum for the resolution of the clinician's or the family's issues about race and ethnicity as realities of life. Rather, the issues must be professionally addressed and the clinician should use information gathered from such a discussion in formulating diagnostic impressions of the family.

Another assumption underlying clinical interviews is that changes in the target behaviors can be measured in an objective manner. This is linked to the belief that the intervention will have an impact on the lives of the subjects. For this to be the case, the clinician must have a clear sense of what is to be accomplished with the family (i.e., therapeutic changes in members' thinking and behavior? a comprehensive diagnostic evaluation of the adolescent and the family?).

Other assumptions of clinical work include (a) data obtained from the family represent a true and accurate portrayal, (b) the development that occurs in the family during the work will manifest in the posttest, (c) clients have the capacity to be introspective enough to make good use of mental health services, and (d) findings can be reduced to a level of quantification that then can become the basis for interpretations and conclusions. Any or all of these assumptions may or may not be relevant to gang-affiliated families. It is the job of the clinician to devise ways of determining whether the assumptions are valid while reducing the likelihood of false positives or negatives.

After completing the clinical intervention, it is necessary to perform some type of posttest. A posttest, or after-the-fact evaluation, is a requirement of good research. The posttest is necessary to determine if the work done by a clinician, or the new conditions to which the subjects are exposed in the research, has had any significant and measurable impact. In this case, its purpose is to determine if the family looks different than it did at the time of the pretest now that the intervention has been administered. This pretest-posttest design is classic. It is, however, fraught with problems that seriously challenge the reliability and generalizability of findings. The most striking deficit of this type of research design derives from the frequent belief that all, or even most, of the change noted in the family between pretest and posttest can be attributed to the clinical intervention. Of the several other problems with the pretest-posttest design that compromise its utility for explaining changes in the functioning of clients, I discuss three here.

The first threat to the value of this design is *history*, referring to the events that the subjects experience as they participate in the study. Individuals continue to have life experiences even as they engage in psychological treatment and assessment. It is somewhat naive and self-aggrandizing for a clinician to assume that all of the change that occurs in the life of a client while he or she is under the clinician's care or supervision is directly attributable to the clinician's behavior. There is no easy way to eliminate the effects of ongoing history (i.e., life events) while a person is participating in an extended psychological evaluation.

A related concept that compromises the strength of the pretest-posttest design and its explanatory power is *maturation effect*. People continue to grow and to reassess their life situation with the passage of time. It may be that the changes noted by the clinician or researcher would have occurred even if there were no interventions. Perhaps, that is a bit of an overstatement. Maybe, the clients would have shown some changes as a result of the passage of time and would have reassessed their life situation even if they had not gone to a mental health professional and would have ultimately done things differently. It is hard to rule out the possibility that things may get better just by chance.

A third compromise of the pretest-posttest design arises from *dropout effects*. It is fairly well documented that many people leave therapy and psychological evaluations prematurely. Thus, at least part of the changes noted by researchers using this design may be the result of the most difficult and resistive clients having chosen to leave the intervention before it was completed. The outcome is that these who leave the research project early are not reflected in the final results. Readers interested in knowing more about threats to the reliability and validity of research designs as well as problems with this classic design are encouraged to read the excellent texts by Campbell and Stanley (1966) and Ray (1993).

After the intervention is completed and the data for appraising its effectiveness are collected, the researcher next should focus on analyzing the data. Because of widespread phobias about mathematics, statistics in particular, it is difficult to get many clinicians and other consumers of research to experience the richness and fun of data analysis. At the outset, the researcher needs to decide whether to take a qualitative or quantitative approach to the data. In fact, this decision must be made before the type of intervention and type of data to be collected. *Qualitative data* are concerned more with describing patterns and trends. They are not concerned with absolute scores or levels of functioning. These are areas of interest for *quantitative statistics*.

Any number of statistics can be reported to substantiate that there has been significant change in the subjects since the pretest, partially attributable to the clinical intervention. If quantitative statistics are used to measure the changes in clients, the big question becomes whether the results obtained were a chance phenomenon or likely to occur again at the same or higher level if the intervention is repeated with the clients. Reflecting on this question helps researchers determine if they have observed an outcome that is statistically significant, meaning that it is likely to repeat itself, or whether their findings were idiosyncratic to the clients with whom they worked. This issue of creating a set of outcomes that can be replicated by others employing the same techniques goes to the heart of research.

One special difficulty in completing clinical outcome research is in defining the variables to be measured. Clinical researchers tend to explore those variables that make sense to them personally and are easily identified and quantified. That means much interesting and significant clinical information is lost because researchers are not sure how to measure the constructs or they overlook concepts because of a lack of a personal interest in them.

The task of writing up the results of a clinical intervention is the next hurdle once the clinician has completed the work, reviewed the collected data, and made some type of statistical analysis. Several a priori decisions need to be made before beginning a write-up, including the most important question of anticipated audience. Having an answer for this question allows the clinician or researcher to decided how technical the write-up should be and what level of prior knowledge can be attributed to the readership. It also makes it easy to determine the direction and level of detail necessary. The same points can be made about level of interpretation as well. Writing for an audience of professional colleagues who have a basic knowledge about a subject is easier than writing for a group of outsiders who might need more basic information than the author is prepared to give.

Research as an Adjunct to Evaluating
Clinical Interventions

The foregoing discussion was intended as a review for clinicians considering some level of research to assess the efficacy of their own clinical work. In the next few pages, I focus on how research conducted by others can be a tool for clinicians to use in guiding their efforts in fruitful and productive directions. This use of research demands that the clinician is a knowledgeable consumer and can access archival and empirical research that has been completed by others. Much of the literature on gangs is found in sociological and criminal justice oriented publications that historically have included little psychologically oriented material. A recent review of journals devoted to adolescence and early adulthood contained no articles even remotely concerned with adolescent gangs (Branch & Rennick, 1995). The omission may represent a reluctance on the part of psychologists and other behavioral scientist to pursue knowledge in this area of high social relevance but high safety stakes.

In utilizing research as a vehicle for helping to improve the quality of clinical interventions with gang-affiliated youths and their families, it is necessary that the clinician make use of both archival and empirical writings. The former, much more plentiful in quantity, can be helpful in identifying issues for investigation. They also can assist the investigator in plotting a course for inquiry in this field, noting the overrepresented and the underrepresented topics. This type of interpretation qualifies as qualitative research and does not require manipulation of numerical data. That alone might cause some to feel more comfortable.

The frequency with which an issue has been investigated suggests where new work needs to be done. In the area of gangs and their families, such topics include girls and gangs, gangs in schools, and of course clinically oriented work with gang members. Once the researcher or clinician has become familiar with the literature by reading some of the descriptive and philosophical writings concerning gangs, venturing out to look for empirical studies becomes a less daunting task. For those unfamiliar with the behavioral science literature that has a psychological and psychiatric focus, there may be a problem of where and how to look for those nearly phantom empirical studies.

Archival-type articles that provide bibliographies are good places for the beginners to start a search. This can be a problem for clinicians, however, because available writings may not address the need for interventions or may express major misgivings about clinical work. Examples of the former might include a focus exclusively on the law enforcement or social deviance dimensions of gangs. Such writings are plentiful but do not further constructive discussions about the possibility of treatment for these adolescents. This lopsided focus also creates a situation in which new theory and ideas are thwarted because they do not fit the models of the canon. A classic example is the frequency and passion with which social control theory is invoked as an explanation for why gangs continue to grow. For many scholars, intervention simply means increasing the number of police on the streets and establishing tougher laws against crime. Both of these actions are necessary and admirable, but they fail to address the issues of the inner psychological lives of adolescents and the factors that help create a psychological niche that facilitates their joining a gang or engaging in self-destructive behaviors.

A careful reading of some of the nonempirical writings can provide valuable clues about the types of assumptions that are made, often without evidence to support them other than the fact that they have appeared in the literature with great frequency. It is almost as if these assumptions have come to be important simply because they are mentioned often. One "finding" that partly fits this description is the association between poverty and gang membership. This pattern was initially reported in the literature by Thrasher (1927) based on his work with gangs in Chicago. Because of that original grounding, it continues to be reified and as such is not open to questioning. Changes in social demographics and the greater frequency with which diverse populations are now represented in social science research are ample reasons for revisiting this poverty and gang membership axiom. Several new pieces of information raise questions about the assumed relationship between low socioeconomic status and risk for gang membership. In the early 1990s, the *New York Times* (Mydans 1990a, 1990b) and the *New York Daily News* (Dao, 1990; Siegel, 1990) ran articles that strongly suggested that gangs have penetrated the affluent suburbs of New York City. There was a hue and cry of disbelief from many readers. Was it denial and cognitive dissonance that prompted the intense way in which people said this just could not be true? Or was it that they simply found the evidence offered by the newspapers to be unconvincing?

A second piece of information that casts doubt on the time-honored belief that gangs and economic status are positively correlated relates to a recent tremendous increase in the rates of crime, violence, and gang membership in Fairfax County, Virginia, a solidly middle class and highly educated community. The problems there are so disruptive to the calm and demeanor of the community that special programs have been devised to counteract the growing pattern of youth violence.

A third and final piece of data that calls into question the poverty explanation for the proliferation of gangs has appeared in the literature with some empirical data to support it (Hagedorn & Macon, 1988). In their classic study of gangs in a midwestern town, Hagedorn and Macon assert that gangs do not seem to be directly attributable to the economic condition of the host city. Even when the economic picture looks promising, the gangs continued to thrive.

It has been suggested that part of the New York pattern of gangs surfacing in affluent suburban communities may have to do with White adolescents and young adults romanticizing what they have come to perceive as the gangster life, which in their stereotypic thinking is endemic to people of color and urban lifestyles. Brief excursions into the assumed lifestyle of urban dwellers become the source of temporary psychological gratification for them. It provides a thrill for a little while, and after the thrill is gone they return to their normal routine.

Another possible explanation is that the suburban gangs represent a connection to gang affiliations that extend back to "the old country." Recently, a suburban New York police department arrested a group of young men who call themselves the YACS (Yugoslavian, Albanian, Croatian, Serbs). That are suspected of being members of a gang of criminals responsible for several burglaries of significant proportion in the tristate area (New York, New Jersey, Connecticut). Could there be other politically associated extremist activist groups with ties to other countries operating in the suburbs detailed in the *New York Times* series by Mydans (1990a, 1990b)?

The changing demographics of U.S. society have also made it plausible that the poverty and gangs connection is not as clear as much of the archival research suggests. Colleagues in Fairfax County (Gotie, 1996) report that incidents of youth violence there involve diverse groups of young people, a finding that runs counter to the empirically documented finding that gangs and crews (groups organized exclusively for the purpose of engaging in criminal activity) tend to be homogeneous on the basis of race and ethnicity.

Research Findings About Gang Youths

What do we know about the efficacy of clinical interventions with gang-affiliated adolescents and their families? Unfortunately, the answer is, not very much. There are a couple of reasons for this circumstance that should be explored here. Until very recently, adolescent gang members were seen almost exclusively as a part of the juvenile justice system. Interventions with them were mostly concerned with meeting the conditions of court sentences. Family counseling historically has not been strongly advocated by the courts. In cases where families are referred for counseling, the assumption is often made that a narrowly defined problem such as the one that brought them to the attention of the court can be dealt with swiftly and by conventional treatment methods. These are assumptions that sound good but lack empirical validation. There is a virtual absence of research on clinical interventions with gang adolescents. This is due, in part, to a pervasive belief among many therapists and researchers that gang adolescents will not be responsive to psychotherapy.

It is well known that more severe psychiatric diagnostic labels tend to be assigned to people of color and poorer clients. That pattern of attribution also categorizes individuals who participate in violent acts and probably appropriately qualify for diagnostic labels of antisocial personality types as being good candidates for psychotherapy or comprehensive mental health evaluations. There is also a small body of research on conduct-disordered boys, but researchers have not made the connection that these youths are necessarily affiliated with gangs. In addition, a tendency to provide psychotherapy to gang adolescents in conjunction with substance abuse problems is starting to be noted by program administrators who are familiar with the area of working with troubled adolescents. This represents a step forward, but it still does not establish gang involvement as warranting services except as an extension of a substance abuse syndrome. Note in this regard that Johnson (1994) suggests that the pattern of drug use among gang bangers is a recent phenomenon, replacing the more familiar pattern of them being vendors of drugs, not consumers. He thinks the change arises from self-medicating in the wake of losing friends to drive-by shootings and other acts of violence associated with gang activity.

Finally, a few intervention programs have targeted gang-affiliated adolescents and their families. The FIP is an example of one approach that has been employed to expedite the clinical evaluation of gang members, their family members, and the family system. Vargas (in press) and some of her colleagues at the University of New Mexico Medical School are exploring the use of culturally focused group psychotherapy as a mechanism for redirecting the lives of gang members who express a desire to change. Both of these models show signs of promise, but the evaluation literature on each is very sparse.

There is much evidence in the archival literature attesting to the virtues of one program or another, but there are rarely accompanying descriptions of procedure, thereby compromising attempts at replication or objective outcome evaluations.

Textbooks and edited volumes offer one alternative to empirical outcome studies. A recent book, *Gangs, My Town, and the Nation* (Randolph, 1996), includes an excellent chapter in which the authors delineate in considerable detail approaches that seem not to work in counteracting the negative impacts of gangs on communities. They specifically note the following approaches as being ineffective in isolation: law enforcement, the threat of increased jail sentences, communities ignoring vulnerability, preaching "just say no," disorganized communities attempting to combat the problem, useless program evaluations, polarization among community leaders and agencies, and denial.

The Gang Intervention Handbook (Goldstein & Huff, 1993) has been a powerful catalyst in moving the field forward through introducing the evaluation of programs along dimensions that meet prevailing professional standards. The text covers a wide range of types of interventions, but it devotes only three of eighteen chapters to clinically oriented interventions. That criticism aside, there is much rich information contained in those chapters. Hollin's (1993) chapter on cognitive behavioral interventions ends with a meta-analysis of work on juvenile offenders who have participated in residential treatment programs. He concludes, "Programs with specific clinical aims tend to produce beneficial outcomes in terms of clinical, personal change. However, a major contribution of the meta-analytic studies is that they begin to allow some firm statements to be made about what works in lowering recidivism" (p. 73). Hollin's focus is on recidivism, however, a concrete and measurable dimension that can easily be assessed. There is no specific documentation to confirm that the subjects being discussed in the meta-analysis are indeed gang members. This distinction is important because it raises implications of providing treatment interventions on an individual versus group level. It also speaks to whether the offenders are isolates or have found reinforcement for their behaviors through cohorts. Hollin also raises the question of extrapolating from offenders as a generic category to gang members. Are they perhaps functionally two distinct groups, with gang members being subsumed by the more global group of offenders? Among his many conclusions, Hollin notes, "The more structured and focused approaches, including behavioral, skill-oriented, and multimodal treatments, appear to be more effective than less structured and focused approaches, such as counseling" (p. 74).

Also contained in Goldstein and Huff's (1993) handbook is Goldstein's (1993) extensive discussion of interpersonal skills training as an intervention of choice in working with youthful offenders. Goldstein's analysis of the empirical research in the area of social skills training with aggressive adolescents is tempered by his belief that "skill acquisition is a reliable outcome, but the social validity of this consistent result is tempered substantially by the frequent failure, or at least indeterminacy, of transfer and maintenance"(p. 93). This observation seems to be of critical significance in dealing with gang members. In addition to the usual difficulty of transferring training outside of the clinical training setting, the researcher now has to contend with the pervasive and seemingly unrelenting impact of the gang. Goldstein indirectly acknowledges the same thing as he notes that the models outlined in his chapter have been successfully employed with chronically aggressive, at-risk youths and individual gang members. He notes that knowledge about the effectiveness of the interventions with intact gangs is still in the embryonic stages. The premise of the interpersonal training proposed by Goldstein is that adolescents can be taught responses that extend beyond the aggressive and inappropriate responses they have used in the past. He notes that the setting in which the training takes place has the potential of adding to the credibility of the clinician.

The context in which training takes place is important because some adolescents perceive mental health services—and providers—as things not to be taken seriously. Much of that thinking appears to be traceable to the high frequency of role playing in some therapeutic modalities, causing the adolescents to develop an inability to distinguish the real from the unreal in the treatment setting and in the outside world. A particular strength of Goldstein's (1993) chapter is that it offers a detailed accounting of how to conduct the social skills training. He also focuses on training in group settings, a configuration that closely approximates functioning in a gang. Goldstein suggests that perhaps more substantial research on the efficacy of this approach with "active gang members" needs to take place before the model can be adequately assessed.

Moral cognitive interventions are discussed in Goldstein and Huff's (1993) handbook as another option for clinically based interventions with violent antisocial adolescents (Gibbs, 1993). The approach itself does not really qualify as clinical intervention in the mental health sense of the word, but it does highlight the immense need to resocialize many of the adolescents who find their way into violent collectives. Gibbs's chapter is based heavily on Kohlberg and Higgins's (1987) work. Most of the ideas in the chapter are predicated on clients having a reasonable level of insight into their behavior before significant changes can be realized in therapy. Moral-cognitive interventions are problematic, however, in that proponents have shown no direct link between the work being described and its potential effectiveness with organized gangs—that is, no evidence shows that providing moral education to gang members makes an appreciable impact on their subsequent behavior.

Does the Family Intervention Project Work with Gang Youths?

There is some evidence that the FIP model makes a significant difference in the level of understanding that a clinician is able to reach in a short period of time. This evidence has been gathered from the clinical experiences of the facilitators, not from the perspective of the families being served. It is hard to know the appropriate standard against which the FIP should be critiqued. Following are four benefits to the approach that have been verbalized by agencies using the model:

1. The first comment comes from an agency outreach officer who is responsible for providing services to victims of violence and psychological abuse. He reports, "The FIP is a different way of working with individuals who are perpetrators. In a lot of ways I guess we are quick to forget that gang bangers have families too. With all of the media hype about gang adolescents we are often guilty of assuming that their families are necessarily disturbed and uninterested in their children." His agency makes use of the FIP as an early diagnostic procedure to try to determine which families have the capacity and motivation to utilize traditional mental health services. He

specifically is impressed with the fact that the program is time- and cost-effective. "We get to see several families all at once and don't have to invest several therapy hours in order to do so."

2. Another professional uses the FIP as a preliminary screening procedure and is responsible for out-of-home placements for abused children. Her observations about the potential benefits of the program focus on how one is able to observe families in a "semi-naturalistic" setting. The presence of other families makes the work seem less artificial, she thinks. "Having other families present also creates a therapeutic quality to the gathering that would not exist in a clinician's office." On several occasions she has been responsible for gang adolescents. Having gang members and their family participate in something that almost approximates "multiple-family therapy" helps her gain critical answers for critical questions even before they are asked.

3. "The FIP approach is an economical procedure that reduces the likelihood that someone is going to miss every other appointment and thereby sabotage the work of the family. In most traditional family therapy work relationships, the clients see the therapist for perhaps one hour every week. One absence by a family member can have a very disruptive impact." These observations made by a case manager/intake officer led her to conclude that the FIP is "a good alternative to linear thinking about families, gangs, and the worlds in which many of our clients live."

4. A probation officer who has worked with the FIP as a facilitator thinks it is a "powerful ally to have when you're trying to make decisions about people's lives. In addition to its many other virtues, it provides a forum for troubled families to once again try to be a family. . . . Not only that, they also get to work with other families who may be having similar difficulties. It helps people understand that they are not alone in their struggles."

These testimonials provide some insight into how the FIP model is perceived. Corroborating parametric statistical data are now needed. Some limited data concerning compliance with conditions of probation among alumni of the program are available, but as is the case with most empirical outcome studies, they fail to tell the whole story. Perhaps the real testament to the effectiveness of the FIP, as for other projects like it, will be the qualitative changes that occur in the lives of gang adolescents who seek to find themselves, only to discover that their true self really resides where they had their beginnings, with their families.

Appendix A

The Case of Ramon

Many gang adolescents do not fit the stereotype of being conduct disordered, drug dealers, and habitually out of control. Indeed, some find themselves living between two worlds, the larger community in which their family lives and the underworld of the gang. They are often in conflict about the choices they are forced to make between these two reference points. The case of Ramon is a good example of such conflict, made even more intense by his status as a recent immigrant to the United States.

Ramon is a sixteen-year-old Latino male who was referred to me for psychotherapy after he had been removed from his home by the local social services department. Ramon had participated in school and church activities with a high level of success up until six months before he was taken out of the home. He was an active member of a local gang at the time of his referral. Ramon indicated that his activities in the gang included participating in drive-by shootings, although he absolutely insisted that he never shot anyone. In addition, he gave several indications that he had actively been involved in selling drugs and participating in random car thefts throughout the community.

At the time of the initial evaluation, Ramon presented himself as a neat, well-groomed, friendly, and cooperative young man. He expressed a high level of enthusiasm, even fascination, about the possibility of having his own psychotherapist. Ramon was most eager to share information concerning his gang involvement but did express some concerns that he might become the target of retaliation by the gang if they suspected that he had been discussing their "private business" with an outsider.

Ramon immigrated to the United States with his mother and three younger sisters approximately nine or ten months before he was referred to me. According to him, and records corroborated by his social services worker, he was an outstanding student in school, earning primarily As and excelling at track and field. Ramon's involvement in psychotherapy was requested by his department of social services case manager to "help him straighten out his life." He was not exactly sure what the referral concerns were but was willing to be engaged in the process to see if it indeed did make things go better for him.

Developmental History

Information about Ramon's early years was not available to me. Several factors account for this situation. Ramon and his family immigrated to the United States recently, sponsored by a local church organization. He informed me that there were some questions about his father's identity. Back in the old country, Costa Rica, his father was a member of an upper-middle-class family. His mother, by contrast, came from a poor family and was strictly forbidden to have any contact with Ramon's father after Ramon was born. There is some information to suggest that early prenatal care was provided for by the father's family, but something happened in the relationship between the mother and the father that caused the termination of this arrangement. The result was that Ramon was born in a poor village with very little neonatal care. He indicated that the first few years of his life were spent in the home of his maternal grandparents. That fact was confirmed indirectly by the social services worker. Efforts to get Ramon's mother involved in providing developmental history and other background information proved to be fruitless. It was felt by the department of social services that the less she had to do with the psychotherapy and out-of-home placement, the easier it would be to effect long-term changes.

The first few months that Ramon and his family were in the United States went extremely well for them. They were greeted by the members of their church community and immediately established in a residence in an urban setting. He noted that the neighbors seemed to be especially welcoming of him, his mother, and his three younger sisters. It is not clear what events precipitated a change, but approximately one month after the family arrived, he recalled that his mother started to spend more and more time away from the children. He and his oldest sister assumed this was because the mother had a romantic interest who did not like children. After approximately three or four weeks of the mother being on long stays away from the home, the children were placed in the custody of the department of social services. An investigation ensued and for a variety of reasons the children were returned to the mother. Ramon was very resentful of all of these events and immediately started to act out his rage and disappointment. This took the form of staying out late at night and periodically coming home under the influence of alcohol. Not knowing what else to do, his mother reported him to the department of social services as being an incorrigible adolescent. The department intervened with some attempts at short-term family therapy. The results were not positive. Ramon's recalcitrant and defiant behavior increased in intensity and frequency. Approximately six months later, he was removed from the home and placed in foster care. According to the social worker supervising the case, the rift between him and his mother had reached a point of being irreparable.

Relationship with Family

Ramon is the oldest of four children. He has three younger sisters aged twelve, ten, and eight. His mother divorced when he was an infant. Ramon reports that the man whom his mother divorced was not in reality his biological father but was the only father who ever claimed him. The next five or six years of Ramon's life were spent in the home of his maternal grandparents. Shortly after he entered school, his mother married a man who was quite abusive to Ramon. That marriage ended in divorce when Ramon was approximately eleven or twelve years of age.

Ramon describes his relationships with his sisters and mother as being quite close and protective. This information conflicts with the reports provided by the social worker supervising his case. She indicates that his relationship with his mother has been quite volatile for an extended period of time. His mother's decision to come to the United States to live produced a major rupture in her relationship with Ramon. He had grown to be quite attached to his maternal grandparents and was fearful that coming to the United States would mean that he would never see them alive again.

In addition to these family conflicts, there was also a conflict of religious values, as Ramon and his mother differed dramatically in their interpretations of the religious doctrines of their community. He insisted that according to the religion parents are to set a good example for their children. According to Ramon, a failure on the part of parents to provide a good role model for their children in some practical ways terminated their parental rights. He also thought that a termination of parental rights gives the children the authority to act as their own judges about behavior and compliance with directives from parents. The conflict over *religious doctrine* between Ramon and his mother led them to seek counsel from some of the elders of the church. When neither had their position reinforced by the elders, they decided that pastoral counseling was "useless."

Relationship with the Gang

Ramon was quite proud of his affiliation with a local gang. He indicated that he joined the gang of his own free will. When asked what function the gang serves in his life, Ramon said, "They are like my family. . . . Those people I used to live with aren't my family anymore. . . . The gang is everything to me." Ramon was quite eager to share details of his involvement in gang activity, with little or no regard for confidentiality. On several occasions, he named individuals by first and last name. After I urged him to not divulge the identity of individuals, he was able to restrain himself, but continued to paint very graphic and detailed pictures of the activities of the gang. According to Ramon, he earned his way into the gang by being in a car from which a drive-by shooting occurred. He was quick to point out, however, that he did not pull the trigger but was assigned the duty of functioning as a "look-out person."

Ramon did not answer questions about the hierarchical structure of the gang. It is not clear whether this means he is not aware of the information or if he was selectively monitoring how much detail he would provide me.

It was very striking that he evidenced no remorse about the many antisocial acts that he attributed to the gang. At one point, he seemed to smile and to be very proud of the fact that his gang was responsible for the disruption of a local cultural festival. Ramon indicated that within the ranks of the gang, there are all types of members, but they are not tolerant of members who are drug abusers. Related to the issue of drugs, Ramon indicated that he has frequently worked as a seller for the gang. His assignment has been to sell drugs to other students during the lunch hour at school. Ramon sees nothing dissonant about such behavior. He insists that the gang sells drugs as a way to earn money to help its members, many of whom are economically deprived.

When I asked Ramon what he gained as a result of being in the gang, he noted that he was able to "assert myself." Ramon thought that participation in gang activity was a desirable, freely chosen activity that most males would prefer if given the option. He also indicated that the gang provided him with an opportunity to define himself. In his home country, he said, gang activity was part of the right of passage to manhood. His understanding of gangs in the local community was that gangs are a way in which an individual, particularly an adolescent of color, could "make a name for himself." Ramon was particularly fascinated by African American culture and saw his affiliation with a gang that was primarily African American as a way to earn a reputation that would win him acceptance in the larger community. He also noted that being a part of the gang increased the likelihood that he would have girlfriends and would earn a level of respect that was not likely to be forthcoming to him as a member of the local church community.

In the early stages of treatment, Ramon evidenced a high level of idealizing the gang and what he perceived to be its image in the larger community. It became increasingly clear that much of his image of the gang was only from the perspective of the gang. He was surprised to learn that much of the gang activity ran counter to the folkways and mores of the community in which he lived. Late in the therapy process, he shared with me that he thought the images portrayed of African Americans on television back in his home country were indeed accurate portrayals. The dissonance that arose when he discovered that many of the portrayals of pimps, drug dealers, and otherwise antisocial characters were indeed caricatures was not sufficient to cause him to consider leaving the gang. Several episodes in which he had gone to parties and was confronted by rival gang members (and once shot) did prompt him to consider the possibility of terminating his involvement with the gang. Ramon indicated that he really did not want to do that but was feeling some pressure from his social worker as well as teachers at school that he should "straighten out his life." He was uncertain what they meant since what he was doing with his life was exactly what he thought he wanted to do.

Relationship with the Clinician

The work relationship Ramon had with me could best be characterized as overly compliant and somewhat naive. Despite his above-average intelligence, his understanding of social issues, particularly issues of racial and ethnic discrimination in U.S. society, was quite low. He eventually reached a state of confusion and dissonance when in his dealings with me his stereotypic characterizations of Black males were not born out. Ramon was able to verbalize his surprise that I did not become enraged whenever he behaved in a way that seemed to create more problems. Finally, Ramon indicated that he came to have a high level of regard for me, because he thought psychologists "control other people's lives. That's what I want to do, be in charge of other people." After a few sessions, Ramon observed that if he continued to "gang bang," he might not have the opportunity of fulfilling his newfound ambition of being a psychologist.

Ramon continued to excel in track and field throughout his six months of psychotherapy. He came to the conclusion that perhaps he could find some way to distinguish himself that did not involve as many risks as being a member of a gang. That this insight, however, was short-lived was evidenced by the fact that Ramon continued his gang associations even in the final stages of his work with me.

The relationship between Ramon and me was one of cooperation and a high level of respect on both sides. In some ways, his respect bordered on being too intense and resulting in overly compliant behavior. Ramon expressed a great deal of interest in the clinician's work outside of the clinic and on one occasion appeared with me on a local radio talk show devoted to issues of adolescent gangs. Much of his compliance toward me seemed to be an attempt to win approval from someone whom he perceived to be powerful and worthy of his respect. These are traits that he did not attribute to his mother or the other adults in his life, especially the social worker from the local department of social services. Ramon was able to express his anger that the local minister had not "supported him" when he had been in a rather entrenched disagreement with his mother. I respected the frankness and candor with which he expressed his views, even antisocial attitudes.

Analysis of Ramon

Several features about the clinical work with Ramon are interesting and merit highlighting. His case represents a classic example of exclusion of the family working to the detriment of the clinician. (I stress that the mother was excluded from the clinical work on the very strong recommendation from the department of social services. It is not entirely clear to me why the department opted to exclude her from any clinical work. Without department approval, I made two attempts to contact her. Both efforts were unsuccessful.) Here, I discuss Ramon's case with regard to three sets of issues: issues with family, issues with the gang, and issues with the clinician.

Issues with Family. Ramon was trying desperately to individuate and separate from his family. The move from his family's native country of Costa Rica intensified his attempt to distance himself from the family in a way that was not to his liking, and it also generated another set of problems. Ramon indicated that he and his mother were not in agreement about some very fundamental things in their lives, such as religious practices and theology. It appears that this argument about philosophy and religious doctrine was really a smoke screen hiding the larger issue of him feeling a sense of growing detachment and displeasure with the type of life his mother could provide for him. In the early days of the family immigrating the United States, Ramon became resentful of his mother spending long periods of time in the evening away from the family. He suspected that she had a romantic interest. It was never confirmed why she was out of the home so often or for what reasons. It should be noted, however, that Ramon's automatic assumption of romantic interests probably is a projection of his own heightened sexuality and interest in dating. In some ways, he was unable to own these as his own issues but found it easier to project them onto his mother. In so doing, he reacted with rage and anger because he felt she was neglecting him and his younger siblings.

The cultural imperatives regarding mother-son relationships are quite evident in the material that Ramon discussed in his individual sessions. His confusion seemed to intensify around wanting to live the old cultural script of his homeland and his desire to acculturate and become "an all-American type." Ramon never fully resolved this dilemma. He overidentified with the African American gang members and teenagers in his community as part of his attempt to become acculturated very quickly.

Ramon's sense of loss at leaving his grandparents was never fully resolved. He was resentful of the family's decision to move to the United States but was never able to resolve in his mind that perhaps he would see his grandparents again. Instead, he internalized those feelings, which periodically got acted out in the form of antisocial behavior.

Ramon's paternalistic attitudes toward his younger sisters provided another source of conflict between him and his mother. He reported that his mother wanted him to baby-sit, but he took the role much more seriously and extended his control over his sisters to providing ongoing parenting even from a distance at his foster home placement.

Issues with the Gang. Ramon's approach to involvement in the antisocial acts of his gang was somewhat naive. He did not evidence any moral conflict or any cognitive dissonance associated with the antisocial acts he helped commit. When asked about how he saw his role in the gang, he simply indicated that it was a way to become popular in the community and "find yourself and a place." His freedom from criminal charges perhaps made it easy for him to continue on this path.

Ramon's apparent lack of resolution of racial and ethnic identity issues found expression through his gang involvement. He indicated early on a rather stereotypic image of African American males as being "gangsters" and expressed a high level of positive regard for that identity. Ramon indicated that he saw himself moving in the direction of affiliating with that social image. It seemed clear that Ramon was using the gang as a forum to resolve the perennial question of "Who am I?"

Issues with the Clinician. Ramon's behavior throughout the six months of psychotherapeutic work was highly compliant and cooperative. He made an extraordinary effort to arrive at appointments on time, and he even asked for additional meeting time during a particularly difficult time at his foster home placement. It appears that the overly compliant Ramon is a stark contrast to the recalcitrant, uncooperative Ramon who existed within the family. On some levels, it is tempting to interpret this as his wanting to please me as a way of replacing the father that he never really knew. On the other hand, one could simply interpret this as his realizing the potential power that I had as his therapist over keeping him out of juvenile hall or some other place in the penal system. It is clear also that Ramon spent a lot of time struggling to avoid conflicts with me. Whenever points of disagreement arose, Ramon very quickly abandoned his position and said what he thought I wanted to hear.

Overall Summary. The case of Ramon illustrates a good example of an adolescent who is detached and has no sustained relationships that expand across settings. His level of nonmembership in the community has produced a drive to affiliate even at the expense of being considered a juvenile delinquent. Ramon's behavior in the community is very much in contrast with his exemplary behavior at school. This suggests a dual kind of identity that is problematic for many adolescents.

Appendix B

Case Examples from the FIP

The following clinical vignettes of families who have participated in the FIP are offered here as examples of the benefits that can be derived from participating in such a program. The presentations are not full clinical case studies but rather brief overviews of the types of problems that gang-affiliated families may experience. I hope the vignettes will stimulate clinicians to think of creative ways of reaching families who might be very isolated and entrenched in their internal dynamics, the end results of which are often that people lapse into hopelessness and despair and become unable to provide a structured and meaningful socialization experience for their children.

Case 1: The Problem Is the Police

Ms. W, a thirty-eight-year-old African American female, was the head of a family of five adolescent boys. Three of the boys are known to the juvenile justice system, having recently been adjudicated as being involved in gang activity. Ms. W and two of her sons came to the FIP in response to a directive from the juvenile court judge. Once she and her sons arrived at the program, they had a very difficult time buying into the rationale and procedures of the program. In the initial stages of the "Why Are We Here?" exercise, Ms. W indicated that she was not convinced that her sons were a problem. Instead, she was absolutely convinced that the local police department was the problem. She noted that her sons had been targeted by the police because of their racial identity. Ms. W indicated also that she is aware of other neighbors who share her sentiment. She was so adamant in her position that she became quite agitated, often interrupting the facilitators and other parents who were attempting to be compliant with the directions given to them. Ms. W went on several tirades about inherent racism in the local police department and its manifestations in the local Black community. No amount of defusing of Ms. W and her evangelical presentation was successful. Finally, after approximately thirty minutes of her interrupting others and being extremely judgmental when other families did not share her views, another female head of household was assertive enough to attempt to place some limits on Ms. W. As all of this was happening, her sons appeared to be quite embarrassed by their mother's behavior and distanced themselves from her by sitting in another part of the room. Ms. W was not able to tolerate the eight hours of the program and excused herself at the lunch break.

Clinical Interpretation

The type of presentation exhibited by Ms. W is quite common in families in states of anxiety and despair. Ms. W appeared to have obsessive thoughts about the police and their racist behaviors toward the African American community. It is striking that this sort of fixed thinking, in the absence of someone to confront it directly, results in high states of agitation and noncompliance. The temptation to say that Ms. W is obsessed with the police extends significantly beyond the data that were available at the FIP. Her participation in the process of the FIP provided her and others with some opportunity to be introspective about their behavior and thinking. Ms. W, unfortunately, was not able to be very introspective and opted to disengage from the process. I believe, however, that her unwillingness to look at her own behavior, together with her adamant and unrelenting position, provided a major therapeutic contribution to the process of the FIP. Others benefited from her presentation and were able to engage briefly in reflecting on the issues of race and ethnicity in their thinking about treatment that they receive from the police as well as other public agencies. The conclusions that others reached concerning Ms. W were that she was not ready at this point to make a major investment in working on her contributions to her difficulties. It was also concluded that providing a forum such as a multiple-family workshop was not a wise decision. Ms. W needs additional work and it was thought, because of her high level of volatility, that this might most appropriately occur in an individual session.

Case 2: Is That a BMW in the Driveway?

Another household consists of Ms. X, a single African American mother, and her sixteen-year-old son. The family attended the FIP in response to a directive given to them by the probation officer for the son. Ms. X came to the program but indicated that she did not have a high level of investment in it, nor did she believe that it would make a significant difference in her life. During the course of the small group work and over lunch, Ms. X shared with several individuals an experience that she had had a few weeks before coming to the FIP. Her son, who is known to be involved in local gang activity, had driven a BMW to their home and parked it in the driveway. During the first few days that the car was there, Ms. X obviously saw the car but never asked her son to whom the car belonged or when he was going to return the car to its owner. Instead, Ms. X continued in her typical relationship with her son, one in which he provided large sums of money to help meet household expenses. After the car had been in their driveway for approximately a week or ten days, Ms. X's neighbor engaged her in conversation about the new car. It was at that point that Ms. X professed to have been oblivious to the fact that the car was there and expressed some surprise on seeing it. When she was later asked about this episode by the probation officer, she indicated that she really saw the car but did not place much importance on the fact that it was there. She had not seen her son for several days following the car being parked in their driveway. Instead of reacting with alarm, she assumed that he had gone to visit his grandmother. Ms. X held on to this belief for several days, despite the fact that she and her son's grandmother, her own mother, spoke on the telephone at least a couple of times a day. During the course of their conversations over the week or ten days the car was in the driveway, the grandmother never remarked that the grandson was at her home.

Clinical Interpretation

Ms. X's case represents an extreme example of denial and the dual systems in which many economically poor, gang-affiliated families find themselves functioning. On the one hand, Ms. X was appreciative and grateful for the financial assistance that her son provided. On the other hand, she learned not to inquire about how and where he acquired the money that he shared with her. This, for some of the parents whom she shared her experiences with, raised a major moral dilemma. Some of them indicated that they would not have accepted the money knowing that it had come from tainted sources. Others indicated that their daily survival is far more important to them than moralizing about how their children acquire economic stability. These issues are also significant for clinicians attempting to work with gang-affiliated families with respect to maintaining confidentiality when there is no evidence to fully substantiate suspected illegal activity.

Case 3: At Least I Know Where My Children Are

This vignette involves a Latino family that consists of both parents, Mr. and Ms. Y, and three teenage sons. Because the father works outside of the town in which the family resides, he is gone most of the week, returning to the home on the weekends. During the father's absence, the mother is overwhelmed by the psychological and physical demands of her very large teenage sons. As part of her attempt to reduce the dissonance and conflict that occur between her and her sons, she has acquiesced in the demands of some of their gang-affiliated friends who identify the family home as a "hangout." It is interesting to note that they only utilize this hangout when Mr. Y is out of town. Thus, the gang resides in the home of Mr. and Ms. Y approximately four days a week. When it becomes clear that Mr. Y is returning home, the gangsters do not visit the home and the sons dramatically readjust their level of cooperation with and respect toward their mother. It should also be noted that Ms. Y is a cooperating party in this routine and experiences little if any dissonance about gang members using her basement as a place to congregate and apparently engage in smoking marijuana and planning illegal activities. When engaged in a conversation about this with one son's probation officer, she indicated that this arrangement did not produce any dissonance for her at all. Rather, she was proud of the fact that she knew where her children were and that she could provide a protective environment for them even as the larger community was reacting toward them in very negative and hostile ways.

Clinical Interpretation

The participation of Mr. and Ms. Y in the FIP provided them with an opportunity to hear other parents who are struggling with some of the same issues and the approaches they have taken to counteracting the problems that they and their gang-affiliated adolescents experience.

Case 4: This Is All a New Experience to Us

Mr. and Ms. Z, a White middle-class couple, were referred to the FIP because their seventeen-year-old son was arrested for being involved in gang-related selling of drugs. The family was somewhat reluctant to come to the FIP, partly because they did not live in the community in which the program was being held. In addition, they had expressed a preference for "taking care" of the problem privately, meaning to hire an attorney and if necessary secure the services of a mental health professional to help them and their son renegotiate their relationships. The probation department handling their son's case disagreed with that approach and suggested that they should attend the FIP.

Mr. and Ms. Z repeatedly said, during the course of the day, that to hear about the struggles and stories of other families that were in a position similar to their own was a very powerful experience for them. In particular, they commented on the feelings of isolation and disenfranchisement that many families verbalized. Mr. and Ms. Z noted that being White and very much in the minority caused them to feel an exaggerated sense of discomfort while participating in the FIP. Despite that, they persevered and completed the eight-hour exercise. At the end of the day, they noted that this experience had given them some firsthand experience at what it is like to be different and, even more, it had provided them with a level of association with individuals whom they would not interact with on a daily basis that produced a meaningful experience for them. Race and ethnicity were issues that were discussed frequently during the course of the day, and Mr. and Ms. Z were often the objects of projections during that discussion.

Clinical Interpretation

The presence of Mr. and Ms. Z at the FIP sent a very clear message that gang affiliation is not an issue that is limited to poor people or to people of color. The ambivalence that many other members of the workshop experienced because of the presence of Mr. and Ms. Z provided some interesting dynamics over the course of the day. Mr. and Ms. Z indicated that they left the workshop feeling that many of the experiences they had heard about during the course of the day were not matters that they had a high level of acquaintance with, nor did they want to have to continue to experience them on a frequent basis.

Appendix C

An FIP Family Case Study

Composition: The A family consists of Mr. and Ms. A and their three teenage sons, James (thirteen), Ronald (fifteen), and Tyrone (eighteen). Tyrone is attending college on a football scholarship at an East Coast university.

Description of Family: The A family is an interracial family that lives in a working-class neighborhood in a California town. Mr. and Ms. A both attended college, but neither earned a degree. He stopped in his senior year to support her and their first child. She quit in her junior year because she was pregnant. The family has lived in several different cities because of Mr. A's military service. He was recently discharged from the military. During the last four years of his duty, the family stayed in the United States while he completed assignments overseas. It was during this period that Ms. A reports that she seems to have lost control of her sons. No amount of limit setting seemed to make a difference. Finally, in a state of desperation, she sent the two youngest sons to live with their paternal grandparents. That arrangement worked well for a while, until it was time for Mr. A to return to the States. At that point the relationship between his wife and the grandparents deteriorated dramatically. The grandparents refused to send to the boys back to their parents until their father arrived.

Both Mr. and Ms. A are employed in professional jobs, he as a personnel manager at a local corporation and she as an administrative assistant at a publishing company. The marital discord between the two of them has escalated recently, and he has moved out of the family home.

Referral Background: Both James and Ronald are known to the local juvenile court department. They have extensive records of violent behavior in school and around the community. Their behavior problems in school date back to when they were in elementary school.

Mr. and Ms. A are considering a divorce but have made no decision. They have sought marital counseling, but things have not improved significantly. Each blames the other for the lack of control over their sons. Ms. A notes with a great deal of pride that she has always had the oldest son with her and that the good outcomes that he is showing are a direct testament to her parenting skills.

Referred by: Probation department of the local juvenile court.

Referral Question(s):   Several questions have been raised concerning this family. The probation officer is most eager to know if the parents are able to put aside their personal differences long enough to provide closer and more consistent supervision for their sons. Other related questions include:

1. Should an out-of-home placement be considered?
2. Is there an underlying mental disorder evident in the behavior and thinking of either or both adolescents?
3. How much of the sons' acting-out behavior can be attributed to the parental conflicts?

Report to Be Sent to: Probation department social worker.

Due Date: Two weeks after completion of FIP.

FIP Participation Summary

Referral Letter Sent by: Probation department social worker.

Date: February 1, 1995

Initial Response, if Any, to Letter of Invitation: None reported.

Attendance at FIP (date):   March 4, 1995.

PARTICIPATION NOTES

Orientation

Ms. A attended with her sons Ronald and James. Mr. A did not attend. He spoke with the court social worker a couple of days before the scheduled session and indicated that he was not sure how much good this type of group work would do. He and his wife had "already attended couples groups, spent a lot of money, and have very little to show for it." He restated his interest in doing whatever he could to help his sons that did not require him to "air the family dirty laundry" in the presence of other people. He even indicated that he would be willing to meet privately with the family and a social worker or a therapist, but he was not willing to work in the presence of perfect strangers.

"Why Are We Here?" Exercise

(Note that in this exercise each family member is observed carefully by one of the facilitators. At the conclusion of the day the facilitators share notes and impressions of the client whom they observed directly.) Ms. A was an active participant in the activity. She shared feelings early in the process and helped others reframe their thoughts.

At one point, Ms. A emerged as the equivalent of a junior staff member, to the annoyance of her sons. She kept repeating that in addition to being present to satisfy a demand made of her by a social worker she was there to "gain some new insight" into her own behavior. Ms. A showed an impressive ability to move beyond the superficialities of the exercise.

Ronald was not very invested in the exercise. He sat across the room from his mother and brother. During the first hour he spent a lot of time watching the clock and getting coffee. Periodically, he made one-line jokes about comments that his mother had just uttered. He grimaced when the group was reminded that this was an eight-hour activity.

James sat with his mother but spent a significant amount of time conversing with other teenagers near him. When he introduced himself to the group he stressed the fact that he really did not want to be there but thought he would "give it a try." He asked appropriate questions of other teenagers as they shared their stories.

"Black Delinquent Gang Youth Values" Exercise

Individual Responses: Ms. A's responses to the exercise were similar to those offered by the members of her group. She seemed to get stuck on the idea of behaviors *not* thinking.

James completed the exercise but was reluctant to share any of his responses in the group. It appeared that he had some difficulty reading several of the items.

Ronald completed the form before most of the other teenagers. He kept asking how others had responded even before the group response activity.

Responses in Group: Ms. A was eager to hear how others had responded. She shared stories of her own struggle with trying to understand what was important to her sons. She noted that it appears that there are some things important to them but "the list keeps changing . . . so quickly." There was much sharing in the group about how parental values seemed to be consistent across all of the parents present. They wanted the best for their children and they wanted their children to be happy. The consensus of the group was that it is often difficult to convey those messages.

James did not respond in the group. He simply gave someone else his list to read. He kept mumbling something about this all being "so stupid . . . it's a joke."

Ronald emerged as a leader in his group. He volunteered to be the resource person for the group. He seemed to enjoy being in charge. He was able to argue for his answers without being overbearing with the others. The discussion of the difference between values and behaviors caused him to become very animated.

Communication Exercises

Again, Ms. A was open to hearing the positions of the facilitators. She noted that often communication is blocked because of "bad blood" from previous attempts at communication. Immediately following that comment, she and James engaged in a three- to five-minute dialogue about when they have have not been able to get beyond the effects of their history together. Both parties appealed to Ronald to act as the referee. He refused, repeatedly saying that he didn't remember back that far.

Family Group Work

The members of the A family all worked with other families during the supervised structured activity. James was successful in the role play because his partners refused to allow him to not respond. Ms. A was surprised that they could get him to work.

Clinical Impressions

Ms. A is overwhelmed. She seems to suffer from a lack of assertiveness. Her sons often interrupt her. When she says something that they do not want to hear, they simply stop talking. When that happens Ms. A also stops talking. Just as quickly as the conversation stopped, it starts up again, usually with James initiating a new subject. Ms. A joins in as if nothing has happened.

James presents clinical symptomatology that resembles depression. This needs to be evaluated. Also, his sudden mood swings and his general lethargic mannerisms hint at substance abuse. Several features of his delayed mentation, echolalia, and difficulty tracking the conversations were other clinical indicators of problems. James seemed to be having problems reading the rather simple statements of the "Black Delinquent Gang Youth Values" exercise. Dyslexia?

Ronald has an impressive array of social engagement skills. His capacity for delay of gratification in the context of the group was impressive. While others were racing to share their answers, he kept calming the group. There is some evidence of a high capacity for introspection. He denied involvement with a gang, a statement that runs counter to the information available to the court social worker. Good candidate for insight-oriented psychotherapy!

Psychosocial Stressor Index

Identified Client:

Family: Impending divorce.

Recommendation(s)

1. Closer diagnostic evaluation of James, possibly a neuropsychological battery. Does the family have insurance that will cover this?
2. An out-of-home placement might be premature at this time. More information is needed. Ideally an extended inpatient evaluation will answer this question. The neuropsychological testing could be part of that evaluation.
3. Can we get a drug screen on James?
4. Ronald appears to be ready to work in psychotherapy.
5. Ms. A looks as if she has spent all of her time taking care of others, even ungrateful others. What can we create to help her become more assertive and fulfilled, soon?
6. Do we want to arrange a private family session with Mr. A present or is that giving in to his long-standing pattern of dominating and controlling? Perhaps

we should talk with Ms. A, James, and Ronald to see how they would feel about such a meeting. If it does happen Tyrone should be included also.

Contributors to Assessment

_____ (signature) _____ (date)
_____ (signature) _____ (date)
_____ (signature) _____ (date)
_____ (signature) _____ (date)

References

Adams, G., Gullotta, T., & Markstrom-Adams, C. (1994). *Adolescent life experiences.* Pacific Grove, CA: Brooks/Cole.

Ainsworth, M. (1979). Infant-mother attachment. *American Psychologist, 34,* 932–937.

American Psychiatric Association (1994). *Diagnostic and statistical manual of mental disorders* (4th ed.). Washington, DC: Author.

Anastasi, A. (1989). *Psychological testing* (5th ed.). New York: Macmillan.

Archer, S., & Waterman, A. (1983). Identity in early adolescence: A developmental perspective. *Journal of Early Adolescence, 3,* 203–214.

Archer, S., & Waterman, A. (1990). Varieties of identity diffusions and foreclosures: An exploration of subcategories of the identity statuses. *Journal of Adolescent Research, 5,* 96–111.

Asbury, H. (1927). *The gangs of New York.* Garden City, NY: Garden City Publishing.

Atwood, E. (1996). *Adolescence* (4th ed.). Upper Saddle River, NJ: Prentice Hall.

Baker, B. (1988). Gang rule: Living in the battle zone. *Los Angeles Times.*

Balk, D. (1995). *Adolescent development—Early through late adolescence.* Pacific Grove, CA: Brooks/Cole.

Bernard, W. (1949). *Jailbait.* New York: Greenberg.

Berndt, T., & Perry, T. B. (1990). Distinctive features and effects of early adolescent friendships. In R. Montemayor (Ed.), *Advances in adolescent research.* Greenwich, CT: JAI.

Bing, L. (1991). *Do or die.* New York: HarperCollins.

Bloch, H. A., & Niederhoffer, A. (1958). *The gang: A study of adolescent behavior.* New York: Philosophical Library.

Blos, P. (1962). *On adolescence.* New York: Free Press.

Blos, P. (1979). *The adolescent passage.* New York: International Universities Press.

Bobrowski, L. J. (1988). *Collecting, organizing, and reporting street gang crime.* [Mimeo]. Chicago: Chicago Police Department, Special Functions Group.

Bowlby, J. (1969). *Attachment and loss. Vol. 1: Attachment.* London: Hogarth.

Boyd-Franklin, N. (1986). *Black families in therapy: A multisystems approach.* New York: Guilford.

Boys and Girls Club of America. (1993). *Targeted outreach to youth at risk of gang involvement: A prevention approach.* New York: Author.

Branch, C. (1995, August). *Adolescent gangs—Internal and external images.* Paper presented at the annual meeting of the American Psychological Association, New York.

Branch, C. (1996). *Clinical assessment of gang adolescents.* Unpublished manuscript.

Branch, C. (Ed.). (in press). *Adolescent gangs: Old issues, new approaches.* Washington, DC: Taylor-Francis.

Branch, C., & Rennick, M. (1996). *The gang goes to school.* Unpublished manuscript.

Bronfenbrenner, U. (1979). *The ecology of human development: Experiments by nature and design*. Cambridge, MA: Harvard University Press.

Brooks-Gunn, J. (1987). Pubertal processes: Their relevance for developmental research. In V. B. Hasselt & M. Hersen (Eds.), *Handbook of adolescent psychology*. New York: Pergamon.

Buhrmester, D., & Furman, W. (1990). Perception of sibling relationships during middle childhood and adolescence. *Child Development, 61,* 1387–1398.

Buros, O. (1972). *Mental measurements yearbook*. Lincoln: University of Nebraska Press.

Callender, C., Henkel, C. (Producers), & Anders, A. (Director). (1993). *Mi Vida Loca*. Los Angeles: Four Films International. Film.

Campbell, A. (1984). *Girls in the gang*. London: Blackwell.

Campbell, A. (1987). Self report fighting by females. *British Journal of Criminology, 26,* 28–48.

Campbell, D., & Stanley, J. (1966). *Experimental and quasi-experimental designs for research*. Boston: Houghton Mifflin.

Capp, B. (1977). English youth groups and the Pinder of Wakefield. *Past and Present, 76,* 127–133.

Carter, R. (1995). *The influence of race and racial identity in psychotherapy*. New York: John Wiley.

Covey, H. C., Menard, S., & Franzese, R. J. (1992). *Juvenile gangs*. Springfield, IL: Charles C. Thomas.

Curry, G. D., & Spergel, I. A. (1988, August). Gang homicide, delinquency and community. *Criminology, 26*(3), 381–406.

Dao, James (1990, April 29). Masters of mayhem. *New York Daily News,* pp. 14, 36, 37.

Doucette-Gates, A. (in press). Hope sustaining a vision of the future. In C. Branch (Ed.), *Adolescent gangs: Old issues, new approaches*. Washington, DC: Taylor & Francis.

Douvan, E., & Adelson, J.(1966). *The adolescent experience*. New York: John Wiley.

Duck, S. (1975). Personality similarity and friendship choices by adolescents. *European Journal of Social Psychology, 5,* 351–365.

Dumpson, J. R. (1949). An approach to antisocial street gangs. *Federal Probation, 13,* 22–29.

Duster, T. (1987). Crime, youth unemployment, and the underclass. *Crime and Delinquency, 33,* 22–29.

Erikson, E. (1959). Identity and the life cycle. *Psychological Issues, 1,* 1–171.

Erikson, E. (1968). *Identity: Youth and crisis*. New York: Norton.

Fagan, J. (1989). The social organization of drug use and drug dealing among urban gangs. *Criminology, 24,* 439–471.

Fagan, J. (1996, June). *Gangs, school and social change*. Lecture given at Teachers College, Columbia University, New York.

Fender, D., & Block, J. (1989). The role of ego-control, ego-resiliency, and IQ in delay of gratification in adolescence. *Journal of Personality and Social Psychology, 57*(6), 1041–1050.

Fletcher, J. (1988). Neuropsychological assessment of brain injured children. In *Behavioral assessment of childhood disorders*, L. Terdal and E. Marsh (Eds.). New York: Guilford Press.

Fox, M. (1985). Mission impossible? Social work practice with black urban youth gangs. *Social Work, 30,* 25–31.

Fyvel, T. R. (1963). *The insecure offenders*. Harmondsworth, UK: Penguin.

Garbarino, J. (1985). *Adolescent development—An ecological perspective.* Columbus, OH: Merrill.

Garbarino, J. (1995). *Raising children in socially toxic environments.* San Francisco: Jossey-Bass.

Gibbs, J. (1993). Moral cognitive interventions. In A. P. Goldstein & C. Huff (Eds.), *The gang intervention handbook.* Champaign, IL: Research Press.

Golden, C., Hammeke, T., & Purisch, A. (1978). Diagnostic validity of a standardized neuropsychological battery derived from Luria's neuropsychological tests. *Journal of Consulting and Clinical Psychology, 46,* 1258.

Goldstein, A. P. (1991). *Delinquent gangs: A psychological perspective.* Champaign, Il: Research Press.

Goldstein, A. P. (1993). Gang intervention: A historical review. In A. P. Goldstein & C. Huff (Eds.), *The gang intervention handbook.* Champaign, IL: Research Press.

Goldstein, A. P., & Huff, C. R. (Eds.). (1993). *The gang intervention handbook.* Champaign, IL: Research Press.

Gonzalez, R. (in press). Welcome home boyz. In C. Branch (Ed.), *Adolescent gangs: Old issues, new approaches.* Washington, DC: Taylor & Francis.

Griffith, M. (1977). *Effects of race and sex of client and therapist on the duration of outpatient psychotherapy.* Doctoral dissertation, University of Colorado–Boulder, Department of Psychology.

Grotevant, H., & Cooper, C. (1985). Patterns of interaction in family relationships and the development of identity exploration in adolescence. *Child Development, 56,* 415–428.

Hagedorn, J. M., & Macon, P. (1988). *People and folks: Gangs, crime and the underclass in a rustbelt city.* Chicago: Lakeview.

Hamm, J. (1993). *Skinheads: Shaved and ready for battle.* New York: Baswell.

Harris, M. G. (1988). *Cholas: Latino girls and gangs.* New York: AMS.

Harter, S. (1989). *Self-perception Profile for Children.* Denver: University of Denver, Department of Psychology.

Harter, S. (1990). Processes underlying adolescent self-concept formation. In R. Montemayor, G. R. Adams, & T. P. Gullotta (Eds.), *From childhood to adolescence: A transitional period.* Newbury Park, CA: Sage.

Hartup, W. W., & Overhauser, S. (1991). Friendships. In R. M. Lerner, A. C. Pertson, & J. Brooks-Gunn (Eds.), *Encyclopedia of adolescence* (Vol. 1). New York: Garland.

Hill, J., & Holmbeck, G. (1986). Attachment and autonomy during adolescence. In G. Whitehurst (Ed.), *Annals of child development.* Greenwich, CT: JAI.

Hill, J., & Palmquist, W. (1978). Social cognition and social relations in early adolescence. *International Journal of Behavioral Development, 1,* 1–36.

Hollin, C. (1993). Cognitive behavioral interventions. In A. P. Goldstein & C. Huff (Eds.), *The gang intervention handbook.* Champaign, IL: Research Press.

Horowitz, R. (1982). Adult delinquent gangs in a Chicano community: Masked intimacy and marginality. *Urban Life, 11,* 3–26.

Horowitz, R. (1987). Community tolerance of gang violence. *Social Problems, 34,* 437–450.

Horowitz, R. (1990). Sociological perspectives on gangs: Conflicting definitions and concepts. In C. Huff (Ed.), *Gangs in America.* Newbury Park, CA: Sage.

Horowitz, R., & Schartz, G. (1974). Honor, normative ambiguity, and gang violence. *American Sociological Review, 39,* 238–251.

Huff, C. R. (1989). Youth gangs and public policy. *Crime and Delinquency, 35,* 524–537.

Huff, C. R. (1990). *Gangs in America*. Newbury Park, CA: Sage.

Huff, C. (1993). Gangs in the United States. In A. P. Goldstein & C. Huff (Eds.), *The gang intervention handbook*. Champaign, IL: Research Press.

Incardi, J. (1978). *Reflections on crime: An introducation to criminology and criminal justice*. New York: Holt, Rinehart & Winston.

Jankowski, M. (1991). *Islands in the street: Gangs and American urban society*. Berkeley: University of California Press.

Johnson, D. (1993). *This thing called gangs*. Topeka, KS: Lone Tree.

Kandel, D., & Lesser, G. (1969). Parental and peer influences on educational plans of adolescents. *American Sociological Review, 34,* 213–223.

Kaplan, H., & Sadock, B. (Eds.). (1989). *Comprehensive textbook of psychiatry*. Baltimore: Williams & Wilkins.

Knox, G. W. (1991). Perceived closure and respect for the law among delinquent and non-delinquent youths. *Youth and Society, 9,* 385–406.

Kohlberg, L. (1969). Stage and sequence: The cognitive developmental approach to socialization. In D. A. Gaslin (Ed.), *Handbook of socialization theory and research*. Chicago: Rand-McNally.

Kohlberg, L., & Higgins, A. (1987). School democracy and social interaction. In W. M. Kurtines Wiley–Interscience.

Kyle, C. (1984). *Los preciosos*. Doctoral dissertation, Northwestern University, Department of Sociology, Evanston, IL.

Leon, R., Bowden, C., & Faber, R. (1989). The psychiatric interview, history, and mental status examination. In H. Kaplan & B. Sadock (Eds.), *Comprehensive textbook of psychiatry*. Baltimore: Williams & Wilkins.

Maccoby, E. (1991). [Discussant, symposium on the development of gender and relationships.] Symposium presented at Society for Research in Child Development, Seattle, April.

Mahler, M., Pine, F., & Bergman, A. (1975). *The psychological birth of the human infant*. New York: Basic Books.

Mallory, M. (1989). Q-sort definition of ego identity status. *Journal of Youth and Adolescence, 18,* 399–412.

Marcia, J. (1966). Development and validation of ego-identity status. *Journal of Personality and Social Psychology, 3,* 551–558.

Markstrom-Adams, C. (1994). The Ego-Virtue of Fidelity: A case for the study of religion and identity formation in adolescence. *Journal of Youth and Adolescence, 23*(4), 453–469.

Maslow, A. (1954). *Personality and motivation*. New York: John Wiley.

Mathis, R., & Yingling, L. (1990). Divorcing intact families on the circumplex model: An exploration of the dimensions of cohesion and adaptability. *Family Therapy, 17*(3), 261–272.

McCall, N. (1994). *Make me wanna holler: A young black man in America*. New York: Random House.

McWhirter, J., McWhirter, B., McWhirter, A., & McWhirter, E. (1994). High and low-risk characteristics of youth: The five C's of competency. *Elementary School Guidance and Counseling, 28*(3), 188–196.

Miller, W. (1981). American youth gangs: Past and present. In A. S. Blumberg (Ed.), *Current perspectives on criminal behavior*. New York: Knopf.

Miller, W. B. (1989). [Review of the book *People and folks: Gangs, crime, and the underclass in a rustbelt city*.] *American Journal of Sociology, 94,* 784–787.

Mischel, W., & Baker, N. (1975). Cognitive appraisal and transformations in delay behavior. *Journal of Personality and Social Psychology, 31*(2), 254–261.

Mitchell, J. V. (1983). *Tests in print III*. Lincoln: University of Nebraska Press, Buros Institute of Mental Measurement.

Mitsutomi, T. (1994). The problems of research in the delay of gratification: From the point of view of the types of failure to wait. *Japanese Psychological Review*, *37*(2), 204–219.

Monti, D. (1994). *Wannabe: Gangs in suburbs and schools*. Cambridge, MA: Blackwell.

Moore, B., Mischel, W., & Zeiss, A. (1976). Comparative effects of the reward stimulus and its cognitive representation in voluntary delay. *Journal of Personality and Social Psychology, 34*(3), 419–424.

Moore, J. (1978). *Homeboys, gangs, drugs, and prisons in the barrios of Los Angeles*, Philadelphia: Temple University Press.

Moore, J. (1993). Residence and territoriality in Chicano gangs. *Social Problems, 31,* 182–194.

Morales, A. (1981). *Treatment of Hispanic gang members*. Los Angeles: University of California, Neuropsychiatric Insitute.

Mydans, S. (1990a, January 29). Life in a girls' gang: Colors and bloody. *New York Times,* pp. 1, 12.

Mydans, S. (1990b, April 10). Not just the inner city: Well-to-do join gangs. *New York Times National Magazine*, pp. A–F.

Newman, J., Kosson, P., & Patterson, C. (1992). Delay of gratification in psychopathic and non-psychopathic offenders. *Journal of Abnormal Psychology, 101*(4), 630–636.

Offer, D. (1969). *The psychological world of the teenager: A study of normal adolescent boys*. New York: Basic Books.

Olson, D. H., Lavee, Y., & Portner, J. (1985). *Family adaptability and cohesion evaluation scales III*. Unpublished manuscript, University of Minnesota, Department of Family Social Science, St. Paul.

Peterson, A. C., Schulenberg, J. E., Abramowitz, R., Offer, D., & Jarcho, D. (1984). A self-image questionnaire for young adolescents: Reliability and validity studies. *Journal of Youth and Adolescence, 13,* 93–111.

Phinney, J.(1989). Stages of ethnic identity development in minority group adolescents. *Journal of Early Adolescence, 9,* 34–49.

Phinney, J. (1991). Ethnic identity and self-esteem: A review and integration. *Hispanic Journal of Behavioral Sciences, 13,* 193–208.

Phinney, J. (1992). Multigroup ethnic identity measure: A new scale for use with diverse groups. *Journal of Research in Adolescence, 7,* 156–176.

Phinney, J., & Allipura, L. (1990). Ethnic identity in college students from four ethnic groups. *Journal of Adolescence, 13,* 171–183.

Phinney, J., & Tarver, S. (1988). Ethnic identity search and commitment in black and white eighth graders. *Journal of Early Adolescence, 3,* 265–277.

Piaget, J. (1965). *Moral judgment of the child* (M. Gabain, Trans.). New York: Free Press. (Original work published 1932)

Piers, E., & Harris, D.(1964). *Manual of the Piers-Harris Self-concept Scale*. Knoxville: University of Tennessee Press.

Randolph, N. (1996). *Gangs, my town, and the nation*. Holmes Beach, FL: Learning Publications.

Ray, W. (1993). *Methods toward a science of behavior and experience* (4th ed.). Pacific Grove, CA: Brooks/Cole.

Robison, S., Cohen, N., & Sachs, M. (1946). Autonomous groups: An unsolved problem in group loyalties and conflicts. *Journal of Educational Sociology, 20,* 154–162.

Rosenberg, M. (1986). Self-concept from middle childhood through adolescence. In J. Suis & A. G. Greenwald (Eds.), *Psychological perspectives on the self* (Vol. 3). Hillsdale, NJ: Lawrence Erlbaum.

Rotenberg, K., & Mayer, E. (1990). Delay of gratification in Native and White children: A cross-cultural comparison. *International Journal of Behavioral Development, 13*(1), 23–30.

Rourke, B., Fisk, J., & Strang, J. (1986). *Neuropsychological assessment of children: A treatment-oriented approach.* New York: Guilford Press.

Sanders, W. B. (1970). *Juvenile delinquency: Causes, patterns, and reactions.* New York: Holt, Rinehart & Winston.

Santrock, J. (1993). *Adolescence* (4th ed.). Dubuque, IA: William C. Brown.

Schweitzer, J., & Sulzer-Azaroff, B. (1995). Self control in boys with attention deficit hyperactivity disorder: Effects of added stimulation and time. *Journal of Child Psychology and Psychiatry and Allied Disciplines, 36*(4), 671–686.

Selman, R. L. (1980). *The growth of interpersonal understanding: Developmental and clinical analyses.* New York: Academic Press.

Sessa, F., & Steinberg, L. (1991). Family structure and the development of autonomy during adolescence. *Journal of Early Adolescence, 11,* 38–55.

Shaffer, D. (1994). *Social and personality development* (3rd ed.). Pacific Grove, CA: Brooks/Cole.

Sherif, M., & Sherif, C. (1947). Intergroup conflict and cooperation: The robber's cave experiment. Norman: University. of Oklahoma Press.

Shoda, Y., Mischel, W., & Peake, P. (1990). Predicting adolescent cognitive and self regulatory competencies from preschool delay of gratification: Identifying diagnostic conditions. *Developmental Psychology, 26*(6), 978–986.

Short, J. F., Jr., & Strodbeck, F. L. (1965). *Group process and gang delinquency.* Chicago: University of Chicago Press.

Shorter, E. (1977). *The making of the modern family.* New York: Basic Books.

Siegel, J. (1990, June 3). Teens of prey. *New York Daily News,* pp. 12–13.

Spergel, I. (1967). *Street gang work: Theory and practice.* Garden City, NY: Anchor.

Spergel, I. A. (1984). Violent gangs in Chicago: In search of social policy. *Social Service Review, 58,* 199–226.

Spergel, I. A. (1990). Youth gangs: Continuity and change. In N. Morris (Ed.), *Crime and delinquency: An annual review of research* (Vol. 12). Chicago: University of Chicago Press.

Spitz, R. (1945). Hospitalism: An inquiry into the genesis of psychiatric conditions in early childhood. In A. Freud (Ed.), *The psychoanalytic study of the child* (Vol. 1). New York: International Universities Press.

Steinberg, L. (1985). *Adolescence* (2nd ed.). New York: McGraw-Hill.

Steinberg, L., & Silverburg, S. (1986). The vicissitudes of autonomy in early adolescence. *Child Development, 57,* 841–851.

Tajfel, H. (1981). *Human groups and social categories.* New York: Cambridge University Press.

Taylor, C. (1990). *Dangerous society.* East Lansing: Michigan State University Press.

Thorndike, R., & Hagen, E. (1986). *Measurement and evaluation in psychology and education.* New York: John Wiley.

Thrasher, F. M. (1927). *The gang.* Chicago: University of Chicago Press.

Vargas, A. (in press). Group psychotherapy with Latino gang members. In C. Branch (Ed.), *Adolescent gangs: Old issues, new approaches.* Washington, DC: Taylor & Francis.

Vigil, J. D. (1983). Chicano gangs: One response to Mexican urban adaptation in the Los Angeles area. *Urban Anthropology, 12,* 45–75.

Vigil, J. D. (1988). *Barrio gangs: Street life and identity in southern California.* Austin: University of Texas Press.

Vigil, J. D. (1990). Cho-Los and gangs: Culture change and street youth in Los Angeles. In C. R. Huff (Ed.), *Gangs in America.* Newbury Park, CA: Sage.

Vontress, C. (1969). Cultural barriers in the counseling relationship. *Personnel and Guidance Journal, 48,* 11–17.

Wang, A. (1994). Pride and prejudice in high school gang members. *Adolescence, 29*(114), 279–291.

Wasserman, T. (1987). The effects of cognitive coping statements and cognitive development on delay of gratification behavior of emotionally disturbed children. *Southern Psychologist, 3*(1), 41–44.

Wattenberg, W., & Balistrieri, J. (1950). Gang membership and juvenile misconduct. *American Sociological Review, 15,* 744–752.

Weiss, R. (1974). The provision of social relationships. In Z. Rubin (Ed.), *Doing unto others.* Englewood Cliffs, NJ: Prentice-Hall.

Whitfield, R. G. (1982). American gangs and British subcultures: A commentary. *International Journal of Offender Therapy and Comparative Criminology, 26,* 90–92.

Wilson, W. J. (1987). *The truly disadvantaged: The inner city, the underclass, and public policy.* Chicago: University of Chicago Press.

Witt, A. (1990a). Delay of gratification and locus of control as predictors of organizational satisfaction and commitment: Sex differences. *Journal of General Psychology, 117*(4), 437–446.

Witt, A. (1990b). Person-situation effects and gender differences in the prediction of social responsibility. *Journal of Social Psychology, 130*(4), 543–553.

Wylie, R. (1989). *Measures of self-concept.* Lincoln: University of Nebraska Press.

Yardley, K. (1987). What do you mean, "Who am I?" Exploring the implications of self-concept measurement with subjects. In K. Yardley & T. Honeiss (Eds.), *Self and identity psychosocial perspectives.* New York: John Wiley.

About the Book and Author

This volume is bold and revolutionary, a clinically oriented primer for clinicians and others interested in the mental health functioning of gang youth and their families. Providing a well-integrated mixture of theory, clinical axioms, and practical ideas, the book offers invaluable information to clinicians, researchers, and program planners working with gang-affiliated adolescents. Standard psychotherapeutic and assessment procedures are discussed in terms of their specific use with gang members. The oft-made assumption that a gang member's life is one continuous state of antisocial and violent behavior is abandoned in favor of a developmental orientation that considers pregang functioning as well as the transformation that occurs as a result of joining the gang.

Discussing gangs from historical and ethnic cultural perspectives, the author takes a developmental orientation toward the evolution and psychological dimensions of gangs. Branch discusses the Family Intervention Project, a specific multiple-family assessment model, at length. He concludes with a review of the research literature on clinical interventions with gang members and practical suggestions for judging the efficacy of treatment approaches.

Those working with adolescents who are in at-risk environments or who are already involved in gang activities will find this a useful and welcome tool. This book will also appeal to advanced students in departments of clinical and developmental psychology, education, counseling, and social services.

Curtis W. Branch is assistant professor of psychology in the Department of Clinical and Counseling Psychology, Teachers College, Columbia University. He is also codirector of the Center for Urban Youth in New York City and a partner in a clinical consulting practice in Denver.

Index